# THE ETERNAL AVATAR

## DISCOVERING WHO & WHAT YOU REALLY ARE BEYOND THE MATERIAL REALM

## PHILIP KINSELLA
### WITH CHRIS JOHN MAYES
#### BRILLIANT FOREWORD BY JOSHUA CUTCHIN

**"EMPOWERING & AMPLIFYING THE VOICES & VISIONS OF RIDICULOUSLY ORIGINAL AUTHORS AND CREATORS."**

Where there are insights to relay, observations to be noted, stories to be told and creation at its most ungovernable, Ridiginal Publishing is there. In the heart of the free and open minded. The inspirations of the critical thinker, the spirt of the artist in harmony with flow, the face of a child holding their first book. We gratefully empower and harmoniously amplify the voices and visions of the ridiculously original found scattered throughout the land. Weary seekers find sanctuary in a garden rich with authenticity and purpose. A safe place for ideas to grow. We thank you for your participation in the expansion of this most important of missions.

Take to the interweb to connect and find out more about Ridiginal Publishing and it's expansive catalogue.

RidiginalPublishing@gmail.com      TicTok@RidiginalPublishing.      Instagram@RidiginalPublishing
YouTube@Ridiginalpublishing         Rumble/RidiginalPublishing       Patreon/RidiginalPublishing

This is a work of nonfiction. No names have been changed, no characters invented, no events fabricated. The views expressed in this collection are solely those of the author. Ridiginal Publishing is grateful to participate with the support and logistics needed to amplify this author's message and does so with love and without prejudice.

The opinions expressed in our published works are those of the author(s) and do not reflect the opinions of Ridiginal Publishing (referred to as RP) or its Editors.

Information contained in our published works have been obtained by Ridiginal Publishing from sources believed to be reliable. However, neither Ridiginal Publishing nor its authors guarantees the accuracy or completeness of any information published herein and neither Ridiginal Publishing nor its authors shall be responsible for any errors, omissions, or claims for damages, including exemplary damages, arising out of use, inability to use, or with regard to the accuracy or sufficiency of the information contained in RP publications.

Neither the editor, authors, publisher, or any other party associated with the production of RP published works accept responsibility for any accident or injury resulting from the use of materials contained herein.

All rights reserved. This book or any portion thereof may not be reproduced or used in any manner whatsoever without the express written permission of the publisher, except for the use of brief quotations in a book review or other flattering manner.

Copyright © 2025 by Philip Kinsella
Cover Illustration Copyright © 2025 by Kurt Sopel
Cover design by Kurt Sopel - www.ksopel.com
Book design, formatting and production by Brandon Thomas - Ridiginal Publishing Editing by Mary Margaret
Chapter opening illustrations © 2025 Kurt Sopel

ISBN: Hardback - 979-8-9919712-4-9

ISBN: Paperback - 979-8-9919712-5-6

ISBN: Ebook - 979-8-9919712-6-3

Ridiginal Publishing

Millsap, Texas

# 'The Eternal Avatar'

## Discovering Who & What You Really Are Beyond the Material Realm

### Philip Kinsella with Chris John Mayes

## DEDICATION

**Philip Kinsella's Dedication**

I dedicate this book to a special soul, Chris John Mayes, artist, author, healer and clairvoyant who helped me in the development of this project. You don't know how grateful I am for your assistance, amazing friendship and connection. Like an Angel, your arrival was nothing less than a miracle. From the depths of my heart and soul, 'thank you!' I send much love and gratitude your way, and I'm humbled to be walking life's path with you. Those deepest secrets we seek beyond the veil of life only serve to enrich our knowledge, friendship, and unity of spirit within the great beyond!

For my identical twin, Ronald, for sharing this journey with me, and for his incredible talents.

To my mother, Sandy, with love, and to my maternal grandparents, who are now on the other side and helping me cope with everything on Earth. I love and miss you with all my heart. Although I have cried many tears since you left this world, I know we will meet again.

For Neil Geddes Ward, author, artist, and overall great guy. Also, to the legendary Steve Mera and Barry Fitzgerald for their invaluable expertise within the subject of the astral planes, and beyond. To author and researcher, Paul Sinclair who's an incredible friend.

To Wendy Lynn Alamouti, who has been gracious, kind and supportive of my efforts, and who is, herself, a spiritual Avatar.

To Brandon Thomas of Ridiginal Publishing for being a true Avatar and always being there when things got tough. You and your family are legends.

To Western author and literary mentor, 'Aunty' Eileen M. Pickering (1940-2024), whose novels under the pseudonym Mark Falcon greatly inspired us. Now among the stars, both my twin, Ronald, and I love and thank you for all you did for us through the many years of knowing you. I hope you're on your horse with '*Lightning*,' guns blazing and having so many incredible adventures on the other side in your Western worlds, along with the amazing characters you created. 'Go get 'em, Cowgirl!'

Thank you, Colin Skevington, writer, producer, and director of '*The Lossen.*' Your friendship and circle of actor friends make life rich in every way.

Lastly, to all those who yearn to discover your true brilliance and what you ultimately represent on a universal level beyond the material, you are all true Avatars.

### **Chris John Mayes' Dedication**

I believe all our paths are crisscrossing at specific times, just when we need them to be and for reasons bigger than we could imagine, not just for our own benefit but for everyone. Even when we find certain people who challenge our sensibilities they can still provide us with a chance to reflect and change, or even solidify our beliefs as a catalyst for self-development, and just when we need them to be.

We all have certain people in our lives we can give thanks to, whether they are hugely instrumental in our life or just a helping hand when we need it.

Sometimes moments like these come along that give an opportunity to show appreciation for those very people. This book would simply not have happened without my good friend, Philip Kinsella. For someone I have only known in a comparatively short time, surprisingly already feels like I have known him for lifetimes. His friendship, talents, and kindness are boundless. His timely humour, insights, and inspirations always reach me just when I need them, and I am incredibly grateful to share this spiritual adventure together with him. A true friend with whom I give much love and thanks, and like all good friends, was meant to be!

My loving parents, Carol and John, and my brothers, Darren and Steve, have all been so supportive. Looking back, we have been a great family unit. I remember many happy memories as a child. We were taught to appreciate everything we had and never spoilt. As parents, they were always happy if they knew we were doing our best, and I am eternally grateful for their love, and showing the value in everything that came our way, and for providing all they could.

My partner Jon Zulueta, thank you for being by my side throughout and sharing this experience together, and making this journey so special. With more family and friends who know me, I wish to pass on my love to you, too. Life is full of distractions and busy schedules, but the times together are always special to me. Thank you.

## 'The Eternal Avatar'

'See our lives anew and bound no more,

to shed the path of times before,

our fate to go beyond our dreams,

and rise aloft from Earthly means.

My soul relinquishes the chains of time,

and revel where my heart's divine.

Show us the light to travel far,

And wonder in the ways of the eternal Avatar.'

Chris John Mayes

# 'The Eternal Avatar'

## Discovering Who You Really Are Beyond the Material Realm

### Philip Kinsella with Chris John Mayes

### Chapter Summary

Foreword by Joshua Cutchin

Preface by Chris John Mayes

Introduction

Chapter One: A Meeting & Revelation Surrounding Death

Chapter Two: Genesis

Chapter Three: The Soul

Chapter Four: Incarnation

Chapter Five: Reincarnation

Chapter Six: The Incredible Etheric & Astral Body

Chapter Seven: Clairvoyance & Healing

Chapter Eight: The Astral Planes

Chapter Nine: Higher & Lower Spheres

Chapter Ten: Bringing Your Light into a Dark World

Chapter Eleven: Those Evil Forces, the Archons, The Holographic Simulation & the Trap

Chapter Twelve: The Eternal Avatar

Chapter Thirteen: God & Our Gateway Back to Source

Chapter Fourteen: Hope

Channelled Message

# Foreword

## By Joshua Cutchin

I want to talk about shapes and textures.

Imagine yourself as a child, sitting down to a page plucked from a simple coloring book. Nothing too ornate—just simple geometric patterns. Inside each one a void, begging to be filled by your crayons.

As someone who always had trouble staying within the lines, I had difficulty admitting the fact that I couldn't change the shape of what was on the page. Now, with the benefit of age, I see the benefit that restriction places upon art. It is only by first defining parameters that we can begin to express ourselves. Restriction breeds creativity, as the adage goes.

I've learned a lot since those days. Not just the value of staying within the lines, but also how some lessons can be applied to other areas of life, even those seemingly wholly unrelated. The older I get, the more comfortable I feel applying lessons from art to spirituality.

But where to begin? Does the page in front of you have any shapes for you to color? Just as they dispense pages from coloring books, parents sometimes give us the shape of our spirituality. Some of us fill these shapes in dutifully. Others crumple up the whole page. Still others start, only to abandon the endeavor halfway. They want a new page. New shapes.

They find no shortage. An endless variety, frankly, of new shapes on new pages to choose from. Those of us rifling through the stack of pages long enough are likely to find one that is completely blank.

I think that this blank page can be a lot of things. I'd probably call it the New Age Page—the New Page. Most of the time, it is indeed blank. Oh, sure, there are faint outlines here and there… but, by and large, you can draw whatever you want. Within these bespoke shapes, you are free to color and texture however you like.

The idea of a blank page never really appealed to me. Don't misunderstand me. I may be a Christian, but I color outside the lines of those shapes *plenty*. That is still a whole separate affair compared to an empty space. The New Page is completely blank, and that never held much allure for me. Because, as already stated, restriction breeds creativity.

But now you, as a reader, find yourself holding a whole book of pages, one that I have already held. Like you, I didn't know what to expect. More blank pages? Or something more substantial?

I am pleased to say that Philip Kinsella and Chris John Mayes are offering something different. They are *not* offering more blank pages. There are *tons* of shapes in here. Shapes that I strongly feel are neither platitudinous nor arbitrary, but for the most part *accurate*. These are *good* shapes. *Defined* shapes. Shapes drawn through personal experience, eyewitness testimony, myth, and vanguard science—which, as I'm sure you are aware, grows stranger by the day.

*The Eternal Avatar* is remarkable. It is a book full of *both/and* thinking, rather than our usual reductive binaries. By refusing to shy away from such contradictions, Philip makes sense of the tangled contradiction of spirituality within each of us, providing form to the formless mass that most of us face when approaching such concepts.

I say all this to emphasize the *quality* of shapes on offer. *The Eternal Avatar* contains some of the strongest, most logically presented interpretations of a realm that many of us have long found confusing. Although that's part of the point: it shouldn't *be* confusing. These are all things that we know, within the deepest parts of ourselves. This Earth is not our home. It is part of a journey. *The Eternal Avatar* offers a sense of why we all seem afflicted by a profound sense of homelessness and longing, even when our needs are met.

Now for the tricky part, not just of navigating your way through what Philip and Chris propose, but of *filling in the shapes* they provide. The expressive act of adding *color and texture.*

Like anyone, Philip and Chris have their own box of crayons with which they are working. As they should. We *all* have our own palettes and preferences, and you could hardly write a book like this without adding your own textures—especially when so much of this book is informed by personal experience. I am not one to judge that.

To that end, you might not agree with the *texture* Philip and Chris provide. I, for one, don't agree with every word in this book. (For starters, I dislike crayons. I prefer colored pencils.) Mine is a different path. Sometimes, those dissimilar choices are a simple matter of disagreement. Other times, my choices are informed by my own brushes with that ultimate arbiter, personal experience.

None of this takes away from the *shapes* of *The Eternal Avatar*, the *shape* of the spirituality proposed. As I said, these are among the best shapes ever to emerge on the New Page. And to my mind, the shape of spirituality is its most important aspect. Textures? Those are more interchangeable. Use the shape. Then forge your own path.

In a sense, that approach feels entirely appropriate. This book is all about the shifting boundaries of existence, of learning lessons, of passing through and emerging on the other side *better*.

Among the many revelations to be found within, Philip shares personal tales of transcendence, hinting at the fact that we are all so much *more* than we have been led to believe. He proposes solutions that reconcile contradictory models of reincarnation. He suspects—as I do—that *all* mysteries are tied to the *ultimate* mystery, and that such a mystery orbits around nothing so less important as the human soul, the very thing that makes us *us*. To that end, he discards the *whats* of near-death experiences—rightly so, we *know* the damned things happen—in favor of the infinitely more interesting questions: *Why? How?*

All of this, bolstered by Chris's own confronting testimony, as well as his poetry. Not just any poetry, but poetry channeled, remembered, and written from that place beyond ourselves, where all true art originates. It guides and conveys like an adjuvant to spiritual truth. Because—as I've already stated—we can apply lessons from art to spirituality to great effect.

The timing couldn't be better. We have long required better soul craft in the modern era. Now, more than ever, we desperately need an awareness of this part of ourselves. To that end, *The Eternal Avatar* is more than just a book. It is a manual for navigating troubled times. As the façade of our world seems to crumble around us, Philip and Chris call us to turn inward. We can't fix what is happening around us until we fix ourselves. Only there can we facilitate *actual* improvement. Despite what everyday existence and society would have us believe, the amount of change we can effectuate on the physical world pales in comparison to what we can accomplish on higher levels of reality.

So many of us involved in tracking down the strange and unusual get too wrapped up in the chase. I suspect that—should any of us succeed in our pursuit of ghosts, monsters, and UFOs—we all might feel a bit like the dog that caught the car.

What then? What will it mean? Most of us won't have a clue.

Not Philip. He'll know what to do in that situation. He will know *exactly* how to integrate it into his own worldview.

After reading this, you will, too.

# Preface By

## By Chris John Mayes

From a child to an adult, we search for our next meaningful relationship with objects and loved ones. It is an elevation of our lifelong search to find a god-like connection that is ultimately about making our inner world feel complete. Are we merely vacuous beings searching for an external entity to make us happy and purposeful, or have we been misdirected and missing the point of life? Have we lost our knowledge and ability to unify our connection with the universal source with each breath and step we take? I believe that we have been given living proof by certain individuals that we can indeed be more than just this.

We each have work to do, to steer away from our increasing need and availability for what is falsely promised to make us happier in our lives. This is not an anti-materialistic view by any means, but the point of it is understanding our focus is sadly trained outwards from birth - when everything that is magical and powerful is within us. Any psychic or medium, for example, will tell you that we can gain access to incredible information beyond the use of our normal five senses and even beyond the constraints of time. From our early years, the world within us is educated to be shut away. When did you last take a gentle walk and notice how different parts of your journey gave rise to inexplicable variations of your thoughts and feelings? Or when you have heard wind through the trees and felt that it was telling you that an important part of your life was about to change? There is energy all around us, a quantum field that connects us all and is always available. As abstract as it might seem, we do not use our ability to see the world in this way and listen anymore to the deep inner connection we all have. Experiencing the world in this way expands our internal awareness to an interconnectedness that is not limited to space and time. Encouraging these thoughts and feelings that emerge from your personal unseen world are keys to strengthening your soul into an existence that brings you fully into the present, while bridging the gap between the physical world and something far richer and multidimensional.

There are daily tools and techniques to train our brain and behaviours to begin tapping into a fulfilling and more spiritual existence. Our path within to rediscover our true nature and connection is calcified with years of neglect. We first must trust and believe that when we take our first small steps to search inside ourselves, it is there. It will be a spark, a small ember at first, but once we recognise and start using our thoughts and emotions in this way, a whole new world within you will emerge that will eventually make sense and be just as real and, ultimately, make it more magical than this one. The portion of time we spend thinking during our day is probably about 90 percent based on what is happening externally. We are reacting too much, too often, to everything. If we want to reawaken and connect with our true source, we must admit and observe this within ourselves and change it. How can the inner world within us have any positive impact if we largely ignore it and do not give it any space within our daily thoughts for it to emerge and grow? It's a simple truth, but one that we casually accept or ignore because we are too busy, but most commonly we are so little self-aware of Who and What we truly are and what we can become.

Artists and creative minds alike, to some degree, have a more receptive capacity and can view this world differently due to their work, and will have traits that align themselves with an inner source of inspiration that connects and aligns them with it. This is purely because they spend more time in their day visualizing, feeling, and listening inwardly. It's one thing to listen to an inner voice or idea, but it's another thing entirely to know where they might all be coming from! I do believe that this internal, invisible world is very much our home, our source. It wants to inspire us so our lives can be a physical expression of whatever we can dream to be.

# 'The Eternal Avatar'

## Introduction

*Avatar meaning (Hinduism) Ava-tar – an incarnation of a deity or released soul in bodily form on Earth, an incarnated divine teacher.*

The tragedy of life is the certainty of death! How many times have we privately wept when considering this fact? The seeming mechanical nature and functioning of the human body, along with its progressive waltz towards the grave, can leave us in total shock, and which, oftentimes, can be too hard to contemplate mentally. Many cover their eyes and narrow their minds when such issues are addressed, because to question the seemingly inevitable idea of no longer existing and being a part of life can hurl the very essence of our purpose of being right out the window. This is a book both Chris and I have written to demonstrate that you're more than the flesh and bone you currently occupy, and that beyond the material, you are an Avatar with extraordinary powers, most of which you are unaware of.

Do you feel trapped on this planet? Have you had feelings that you don't belong here? And, more importantly, do you have a hunch there's more to life than mere existence before we give up the ghost, so to speak? Many people often wonder why they're born into a world that gives little in the way of answers surrounding these fascinating questions. We are told that life was brought about by the whim of chaos, and that everything we see and experience is nothing less than a fleeting moment caught in time before death ensues, and then it's lights-out! The end. Those experiences that many people have encountered surrounding life after death clearly define a more fantastic version of events (other than the Official Narrative) and tell a completely different story, but one which is censored or hidden, along with being ridiculed. It appears that Man has created His own version of how it all happened, as opposed to at least examining the raw data, which tells us otherwise. Much of the public has been fooled by the lies from an Establishment that is at pains to keep secrets, and cares not for their fellow Man's spiritual advancement in this spectacular dance of life. Why are those in governance so adamant in blinding the public to these areas, which would categorically inform us we are part of something much larger than ourselves in the physical sense, and that we are not alone in this infinite expanse of space either? Such restricted, dogmatic views only subjugate human intellect, but that's the very reason why the powers-that-be are intent through centralised control in dumbing us all down.

*The Eternal Avatar* brings such revelations to the table, along with personal accounts from the authors themselves. In a chaotic and troubled world, there is hope, and I, along with Chris, willingly reach out to you with our hearts and souls in an effort to demonstrate how amazing you really are. You, as an evolving bundle of consciousness, fixed within a temporary biological body-suit, are more than the sum total of all the stars which grace space. Your inherent right to explore gifts hidden in plain sight from a 'System' which cares not for you, or your spiritual advancement matters not! You have the power and ability in truly transforming the very nature of your being through 'thought' alone. This, primarily, is the basis and very nature of your sovereignty.

# 'The Eternal Avatar'

## Chapter One

## A Meeting & Revelation Surrounding Death

*'Let me hear the voices in your breeze,*

*As birds fly high like messengers with ease,*

*To tell me in your myriads of ways,*

*Like sunlight through leaves with dappled rays,*

*I walk each step to discover more,*

*To know thyself and never ignore,*

*That each day brings a chance and place,*

*To trust my soul in life's embrace.'*

*Chris John Mayes*

The way I see it, we come into this world being the pupil and go out as the teacher. Whether you're a believer in life after death, reincarnation, or the process of soul development matters not. Even for those devout atheists who are themselves convinced life beyond the material is impossible, there is one thing for sure: we come into this world with a blank canvas of memory which is filled by a rich tapestry of experience before our physical embodiment ceases to exist upon the act of death. There is no escaping this fact. Yet are we to believe that such memories are erased forever, and the personality of that individual snuffed out like a candle's flame?

As a child, I used to have night sweats just thinking about death; that when I died (which is inescapable to us all), I would be no more. The end! My whole self would be extinguished – completely. The church my identical twin brother, Ronald, and I joined when we had been around the age of eight gave little comfort, other than the teachings relayed within the Bible, which appeared to give us some hope, but that was about it. I used to attend choir regularly, but didn't get involved with too much of the doctrines addressed by the priest during his sermons. Both my twin and I had excellent singing voices, and we'd been followed home from school by a small, bespectacled man who wanted to speak to our mum about getting us to sing in the church choir. He'd seen us singing during a school event, and being involved with the church himself, felt we'd make an excellent addition to their house of worship. Being donned in a long, red robe along with frills made me feel uncomfortable, but gave the audience a perspective of who you were. That got me thinking. Who was I, really? Listening to God being addressed during the intervals of singing made me ponder this thought, even way back then. I recall both my brother and I having to sing in Soprano on a high balcony where, from below, we viewed the huge congregation. It had been a terrifying experience making sure we didn't muck any of the verses up, as well as staying in tune with one another. We got through such incidents unscathed. The night sweats and fear, however, continued, and the thought of dying only increased.

It was upon the passing in 1982 of my paternal step-grandfather, James Patrick Kinsella, which brought the full force of this fear of death forward. I'd been aged thirteen when the news was announced, and I recall running up to my room and lying on my bed where I wept uncontrollably. My grandfather had passed suddenly from a heart attack. The total shock and feelings I'd had surrounding the extinguishing of consciousness resurfaced. James had been the kindest of men to me and my brother, and so generous too. I had been numb with devastation, even more so during the funeral. It was when I saw his coffin being lowered into the ground during the burial that started the tears again. This wonderful, kind, and charming man was no more. It all seemed so final. Horror welled up inside of me when I heard the vicar, who was perched at the head of the open grave looking down upon the coffin, saying '…. ashes to ashes…. dust to dust….' I would never forget those lines.

Afterwards, it was business as usual. No one in the family really spoke anymore about grandad. It was as if he'd disappeared off the face of the earth! However, things would take an unexpected turn, and something which would give me hope in the sense that death (so I had been led to believe) was not the end as many considered, but a continuation of what is known as the soul beyond the confines of our material world, and which appeared very much in evidence. This had been revealed by a lady known to us as Nan, who was a widow herself but looked after grandad for many long years. They lived in separate flats adjacent to one another, and Nan was very much a part of our family, even though she wasn't related. Nan was a beautiful lady. Ronnie and I had many talks and adventures with this charming and sweet soul. She knew even when we'd been aged ten that we wanted to be famous writers, and she used to buy us a whole bunch of second-hand science fiction books from the local charity shop to help fuel our ambition. Thinking back, I am so blessed that Nan treated us like her own, as we did with her.

It turned out that on the day grandad died, he'd been sitting in his living room with Nan. He heard the doorbell ring and asked her to go and see who it was. Nan could not hear any bell going off and told Jim so. He wasn't having any of it and almost demanded that she answer the door. So, Nan ably took herself out of the living room and into the hall, checking to see who it was. There was no one, and when Nan came back to tell Jim this and take her seat, he immediately absconded her and informed her that she could not sit in her usual chair, because his long-deceased wife, Catherine, was now seated there! Nan was shocked. Catherine had died when both Ronnie and I had been very young. She'd had a severe stroke, which rendered her immobile and unable to walk or talk for thirteen years before she died. However, Nan decided to play along with Jim's strange request. He then informed her that he had to go to the bathroom. When he'd finished, it was then, and only when upon opening the door to the toilet that he collapsed after suffering a fatal heart attack. The medical profession said he'd died before hitting the floor!

When Nan told my brother and me about this, I recalled being shocked. It was evident that she'd kept this from the adults, as though they'd, perhaps, consider her crazy! Nan was anything but, and we respected her wishes in keeping it to ourselves for many long years. The incident gave me comfort, but in an altogether different light, and so removed from the varied religious interpretation of what *they* believe happens to the soul after death. It was apparent that Grandad had been visited by his late wife as a forewarning of his earthly departure. A decade later, I would find myself in the presence of this most generous and wonderful of men from the other side.

When I was in my twenties and our family had moved to the village of Marston Mortaine just outside Bedford, I had an incredible experience, and one which categorically proved that my grandfather was watching over me. It happened on a Sunday morning. I recall seeing the sunlight coming through the curtains and wondering what a fine morning lay ahead. It was at that moment when I felt myself being lifted through the roof and high up into the sky. The sensation had been so fast, there had been no time to contemplate what was transpiring. I knew enough to assume that the astral part of me had separated from its biological form while now floating within what I can only describe as a space between the spaces. I hovered for a time over a strange city now below me. The skyline was a hazy red and blue colour, and when I observed the metropolis, I could see tall, structured, modern buildings with hundreds, maybe thousands, of lights emanating from within these formations. I could see no people at all, and there came a beautiful silence. I wondered where this place was, and what reason there was in my observing it. For a while, I just hung there, until I felt myself moving upward yet again before arriving in a land which literally astounded me.

I stood within a vast landscape, and as far as my eye could see, there lay fields of poppies. Looking above, I observed a clear, blue sky, but there was no sun. I wondered where I was and what force had summoned me here. Had I died? That thought never occurred to me. The scenery in which I stood took my breath away, casting aside any other considerations which preceded my arrival. There was, however, one single structure within this carpet of red poppies which was a sight to behold. A large, imposing, white windmill was the only indication that any person inhabited this incredible and rich world, the sails of which remained motionless. I was puzzled as to who would live in such a place, and no sooner had this thought entered my mind when I found myself now standing at its door. I knocked and it opened instantly. I was shocked to see my deceased grandfather now standing in the entrance, his face beaming, and eyes filled with love. What was incredible was the fact that he looked so well. In his later years, he used a cane and was finding it difficult to get about. As he stood before me, arms now open, ready for a warm embrace, there was nothing to indicate he was ill. In fact, he looked strangely younger, yet I recognised him immediately. We embraced, and he gestured his right arm outward as an invitation for me to enter what I assumed was his home, but why a windmill still puzzled me. As far as I knew, grandad never had any interest in them, but the penny would drop much later, and something he'd cleverly orchestrated from his side of life.

The interior displayed a cosy environment. On the walls hung paintings of horses depicted in dramatic scenes with them running against a backdrop of lightning and dark, moody clouds. I remember he had these renderings in his flat. As an Irishman, he loved his horses, wrestling programs, and whisky, attributes which made me love him even more. He'd been the most generous of men to me and my brother, and on each visit, he would ask us to open his magic cupboard where a gift would lie in wait. He would dramatize the moment by making silly sounds as one of us slowly drew back the door to reveal the hidden treasures inside.

I noticed a lady sitting behind the table, drinking what I assumed was tea. I didn't recognise her at all, but she smiled at me warmly, indicating that she too was pleased to see me, just as much as my grandfather. I was ushered in, and grandad told me that he loved me, that he would always be here for me, and if there was anything I wanted, I just had to ask. I think I was more in shock at seeing him so well than taking notice of what he was saying, but eventually I understood. He hugged me one more time before seeing me to the door, and I found myself once again within the field of poppies.

The serenity and peace overwhelmed me. I felt joyous that my grandad was not dead as I had thought, but very much alive. The image of his coffin being lowered into the ground seemed less painful as I contemplated this otherworldly meeting. But there was more to come, much more!

I immediately found myself floating once again above the metropolis I had seen before my encounter with the world of poppies, and could discern no recollection of just how I journeyed there. To my mind, both places appeared instantly, with only the sensation of movement as one would come to expect when travelling, although it felt as though I was being pulled rather than shifting myself to these strange places. Even to this day, I have never understood the relevance of the beautiful city, but I have come to understand the meeting place my grandfather had seemingly stage-managed, and for reasons I will explain.

I felt myself gradually descending until I awoke to the sun coming through the curtains. For the rest of the week, I pondered over this incredible reunion. I assumed that the only way to meet a loved one on the other side was when you *yourself* died, but I found this was a clear misconception. Consciousness, as we shall explore, is multi-faceted and not always restricted to this dimension of reality.

The windmill puzzled me, along with the lady seated behind the table. My paternal step-grandmother, as explained, had a massive stroke, which severely incapacitated her. Basically, she'd been a vegetable, and the only memory I have is of her lying in a hospital bed, her eyes staring into mine, conveying love but also a need to escape her bodily imprisonment. Her hair had been cut into a simple bowl, and I remembered seeing her clawed hands by her side. Grandma had been wasting away, literally! To my mind, it seemed a cruel lot that she existed this way for so many long years. For her, death would have been a happy release. Her stroke occurred when she'd been doing the ironing, and a call came through from her daughter, who lived in Australia. As soon as Grandma had finished speaking to Aunty Maureen, she collapsed on the floor. The stroke had struck her down there and then.

My parents had long since separated, but Ronnie and I had gone over to my stepfather's house to view some silent movie footage on an old projector which he'd had boxed up for years in his loft. He assembled the 'Cinema Projector' and directed its lens upon the blank wall, with my brother and me not knowing quite what to expect. The reel of film started to slowly reveal the past, and we were instantly met with the soundless animation of family, many of whom had long since gone. I saw Ronnie and myself at Bignell cottage as young boys, and upon the grounds of Bignell House. I was moved when I saw the outdoor swimming pool, complete with a huge stone wolf, the head of which came to the water's edge and which we'd used as a diving board, and my brother and I in our swimming trunks, ready to take a dive. There came other scenes of family at a party, and I saw my late grandfather dancing with a lady I recognised in the windmill. I asked my stepfather who the woman in the film was, and he looked at me incredulously and said that she had been my grandmother. I was floored! Her features and hair were so very different from the lady I remember seeing lying on the hospital bed when she'd been ill.

I knew for a fact that I'd seen my grandmother in excellent health within this beautiful world, which I had been summoned to. It was incredible also to think how my grandfather had orchestrated just such a rendezvous in a way which would get me to sit up and take notice, although I had the impression this was not Heaven, but, rather, a contrived mental plane created, perhaps, for the sole purpose of just such a meeting. I later discovered the significance of the poppies and, of course, the windmill.

Although the red poppy is usually linked to recognizing fallen soldiers (most notably those in World War II), it also symbolizes the eternal peace that comes after death and is a remembrance of our demise as well as the eternity that follows. The realisation of this fact helped me in my struggle dealing with our apparent mortality, along with the nonsensical approach to life, where many assume this is their lot. This made no sense to me whatsoever, no matter what I was told by those who professed to have everything in life worked out. There had to be more!

It was some time later when the penny dropped regarding the windmill. As kids, and while living in the cottage within the grounds of Bignell House, our stepfather, Jim, had built a good-sized, electronic windmill, complete with turning sail and small lights that lit both the inside and exterior of his magnificent accomplishment. My stepfather had been a dab hand at both carpentry and putting electronic things together, and both my brother and I marvelled at seeing this wonder. I imagined back then what it would be like to shrink and be able to live inside this beautiful construction. Jim's dad (our grandfather) came up to the cottage one weekend and viewed his son's work, knowing of his grandson's delight at seeing its sail slowly moving around, along with it being lit like a Christmas tree. I personally feel that he'd used this event and constructed it into a real-life scenario where a communion on a spiritual level could be achieved.

There is the belief by many that death is the only way for you to be able to see your loved ones who have crossed over to the other side. Taking into consideration night-time visitations, and where mourners would perceive their dearly departed standing at the foot of their bed, or dreams which appear as real to the experiencer as if they were in the waking state. We know enough about astral projection, whereby consciousness can temporarily affix itself within any point of time and space while still attached to its biological form, or the controversial nature of what is called '*remote viewing*,' and something connected to secret, military experiments back in the day. So, you see, we do not have to expire to have such other-worldly meetings. Consciousness can, on occasions, temporarily remove itself from its locale and enter multiple worlds which are hidden from us. This is merely because of our limited perception of what we call reality here on earth, and which our current senses are not always attuned to. However, visitations from the deceased can work in one of two ways. The first being that we on this side of life can, on occasions, '*will*' the experience through conscious intent to make just such a connection, or the other, which is orchestrated by those who have died, and whereby we *seemingly* have no control over such manifestations and are brought into *their* reality. Either way, this categorically proves that what we consider ' death' is merely a fallacy, and what has happened is that the souls of those who die have merely moved to a higher expression of life.

The problem within the multi-complexed opinions surrounding death is due to varied restricted belief systems imposed within certain religious ideologies. To my mind, there is nothing wrong with having a belief, but one which can develop at one's own pace, and without the indoctrination of others. There is every reason to consider that such opposition, where conviction is concerned, restricts consciousness to a narrow viewpoint and leaves no room for expanded enlightenment. After all, does not '*thought*' shape reality? This much is true, but the enforcement of one person's belief onto another's can seriously hinder the growth and ability for the indoctrinated to think. Fear is also another factor that overpowers human cognizance. We have seen this within certain faiths, which has caused the corruption of the brainwashed person whose mental state of mind has been seriously infected through the enforcement of certain devout beliefs. Both fear and control have brought about their own narrative surrounding death, and one which is extremely unhealthy, to say the least!

We are born into this world innocent, and no centralised programming has been initiated from our emergence within the womb. It is only when we develop around the age of six to seven that our minds begin to imprint the viewpoint of the biosphere in which we have arrived, and imposed, no less, by others, namely our parents, along with schooling, and so forth. The initial period before this age heralds a connection to what we call the other side. This is why, and in many cases, a young child will have invisible friends, or themselves are able to clearly recollect the environment in which they came from before their arrival on earth took hold, and, on some occasions, also able to recount past lives in specific detail, along with seeing and describing family members accurately who have long since gone. What does this tell us? It informs us that there is a life before this one, and that a process of incarnation (along with reincarnation) has seemingly taken place. Such memories have not been influenced by anyone else. These recollections have surfaced directly from the mind of the child with *no* form of indoctrination whatsoever. There is no religion, cult, or any other organisation to be had here. None! Such recalls are pure and completely innocent.

There are those within academia who will tell you that such astounding claims of past lives, memories within what we call the 'Spirit World,' invisible friends, or the appearance of long-dead relatives are all explainable. The workings of the human brain are still very much a mystery, along with how consciousness operates, but, nevertheless, others have it all worked out! Something termed *'Genetic Memory'* is an area that best describes the apparent explanation for these remarkable events. Within psychology, genetic memory is a theorised phenomenon whereby certain kinds of recollections could be inherited from birth, in the absence of any associated sensory experience, and such reminiscences could be incorporated into the genome over long periods of time. Surely, and through genealogy, the accumulation of millions (perhaps billions) of 'recalls' would literally override the individual's mental processing! How on earth can anyone operate consciously with these hereditary imprints attached to the new arrival? I'm not doubting that certain genetic traits on a *physical* level influence the foetus when in its developing stages (hair, skin, eyes, etc), but for memory to be influenced by past generations is a little too much to believe. Such individual retentions from past lives and so on would be unique to the individual within what is known as the auric-energy field, which surrounds the etheric body. This is something we will describe in more detail later, but much like your mobile phone which has the record of every text, picture, along with just about everything else - if your phone was to suddenly expire, all information is stored within a cloud, and which can be retrieved when buying a new phone. Isn't that amazing! People ask, 'Well, when you die, where do you go?' I give them the mobile phone analogy as a simple example, and they get it, if you know what I mean. We are talking about pure, blessed consciousness which operates on a completely different level from its biological housing, but which complements one another while affixed within this matrix, if only temporarily. There will come a point in time when the brain dies, but consciousness remains. That's the difference! It appears to me that science wants you to accept their side of the coin, but not the other, which denotes any form of continuation beyond this material existence.

There evidently is a process of incarnation, whereby the soul (the real essence of what we embody beyond the flesh and bone) enters this dense plane of reality. But the question begs, where is the soul coming from? And, most importantly, how is the process of incarnation achieved? It is clear from accounts across the world that our dearly departed survive on their return trip to heaven, and occasionally make contact on our side of life to allay any fears that their personality has been extinguished forever. They themselves would have incarnated long before our arrival here, which proves beyond any shadow of doubt that a process of soul selection would have occurred. No one would randomly put on a space suit and go off into space, any more than someone jumping in a deep-sea diving suit to explore the depths of the ocean. There is normally an intent from the individual to do any number of these things, and mostly by their choosing, and not others. Therefore, it stands to reason that a choice is made to enter the Earth system, and for reasons which might well surprise us.

However, before we examine the soul's sojourn, we shall investigate the genesis and our incredible emergence upon this planet. Life appears not to be random in nature as many consider, but a carefully orchestrated construct, and one seemingly planned by a higher intelligence other than a singular God. We will discover that, as Avatars ourselves, there is so much more to us than we have currently been led to believe, and something kept secret through indoctrination, fear, and control by those who govern within the earth pyramid of power.

# 'The Eternal Avatar'

## Chapter Two

## Genesis

*'Let my soul reach out for this world to see,*

*A mystery within a tapestry,*

*Of stars unborn and galaxies,*

*Beyond the unknown that is a whole of me.'*

Chris John Mayes


How did humanity evolve? Many of the greatest philosophers have pondered this question. The significance of our existence has varied angles, and none of which truly connect those dots when searching for the penultimate answer to one of the greatest mysteries of our time. As human beings, we are extremely complex within our thinking, and diverse within our actions, many of whom are at loggerheads with their varied beliefs and opinions. Much of our history is buried in controversy and hearsay that it's nigh impossible to form any coherent picture when tackling issues surrounding our overall creation, along with purpose. Are we merely a fluke of nature, brought on by some Big Bang that made everything possible, that we are part of some cosmic fluke that *just* happened? Something cannot derive from nothing. If we are to accept the hypothesis that our creation was all brought about by some universal explosion, what then caused that eruption in the first instance? And, more importantly, what was there before the Big Bang? It's rather like the 'Chicken and the Egg' conundrum, whereby we find ourselves going round in circles with no clear indication of an answer in sight. Many believe we derived from chaos, while others see our emergence as preordained. Varied religious establishments across the world have their own version of how it all happened (if only loosely), but most of these are tied up in very humanised dogma; it's hard to sieve the wheat from the chaff. We are aware that large portions of wording within sacred books had been changed in accordance with those that governed from each passing epoch throughout human history and used more as a doctrine that promoted faith, fear, and, above all else, control. However, there is an agreement by many who walk varied sacred paths that we each possess a soul. This has never been disputed.

The '*immortal*' soul was first promulgated in ancient Egypt and Babylon, but can be dated much earlier, and reaches as far back as 200,000 years ago, where there had been some interesting and highly speculative occurrences which saw to a radical change within the development of the human.

What then is the soul? No one is exactly sure, but there are some leads within our past which may give us a few clues, if only vague in their symmetry. The classic definition of a soul is described as *'The immaterial aspect or essence of a human being, which confers individuality and humanity. It is often considered to be separate from the body and able to survive physical death in some religions and philosophical traditions; the soul is also that part of the individual which partakes of divinity. The soul is often considered synonymous with the mind or self.'*

Although arguments rage within academia surrounding the 'Cradle of Life,' there can be no doubt about the evidence as it stands. Our genus can be traced back as early as Homo Habilis (circa 2 million years ago) leading up to Homo Erectus (circa 1.9 million years ago) and then to Homo Sapien Neanderthalensis (circa 400,000/30,000 years ago) and finally to Homo Sapien Sapiens (circa 160,000/90,000 years ago) the latter of which became modern human beings within the region of central African in the Gauteng province. However, within this period, and during the emergence of the Homo Sapien Sapiens was a female who geneticists have named '*Mitochondrial Eve,*' (mtDNA) and it is *she* who is the common female ancestor of every one of us in the world, and of which we have all inherited the genetic remnant known as '*Mitochondrial DNA.*' Naturally, we inherit genes from both parents, which reside within the nucleus of our cells. Within every cell is a compartment that encloses and maintains the DNA, which regulates access to all information therein. There is also another area that also contains DNA, and which is known as the Mitochondrial respectably. This produces the energy that each cell needs to function, and how it is that we can become animated and think. At the same time, there was a man who was titled 'Y-chromosomal Adam,' who is the most recent common male ancestor of every man alive during this same period.

This sudden physical and genomic remodification of what we would ultimately represent as the human through varied levels of development clearly indicates that '*design*' and '*intent*' had been initiated by *something*. That *something* is considered as '*Gods*' to those who prefer to look beyond the cold and rational scientific and religious explanation of how we suddenly sprang onto the stage of life within such a relatively short period of time, where evolution is concerned. Let's consider also that science cannot enlighten us as to what had occurred which caused the human to suddenly migrate 65,000 years ago beyond the borders of Angola and Namibia, a region they had occupied for 135,000 years, and sometime after receiving the capacity for universal, syntactical language and communication which no other species (not even our distant ancestors) had developed. This newly advanced model of the human began to create, think, and above everything else, bury their dead, complete with all the honours which we would normally bestow upon the deceased. The animalistic functioning of what we had previously mutated from had been overridden by some unseen force through '*intent*' rather than a miraculous biological rewiring of the brain, giving rise to an understanding that death is not the end, and something considered by our early ancestors. Thus, through the female 'Mitochondrial' and 'Y-Chromosomal Adam' was born Adam and Eve, although very different from the religious interpretations which has fuelled the imagination of millions worldwide. With any real event, the rawness of life has always been smoothed over to portray a romanticised version and less crude than its original counterpart. Of course, as creative beings ourselves, and all thanks to our predecessors, along with a little help from that '*something*,' these are exactly the qualities we have attained within our fast progression from beast to human, and assets, nevertheless, which gave rise to a deeper understanding of the soul. Ostensibly, a switch had been thrown within our mental processing to bring about such a radical shift in the way we developed.

The Bible takes on an altogether different version, preferring that both Adam and Eve had been in their prime (as we appear today in terms of our physical appearance) during their creation, before being banished from the Garden of Eden by their creator through a betrayal of trust. The holy scripts across the world all portray a rather more elegant stance to the unfolding events of Man's ultimate emergence, but this may be forgiven since some form of narrative had to be established to get the main point across. Many of the facts have been handed down like Chinese whispers, muddying the water where any reasonable transparency could be established. Although countless holy books within varied cultures have been heavily sanitised to control thought rather than enlighten it, the reality paints an even more incredible picture, and one in which devout believers will undoubtedly reject outwardly. Certainly, much of the documentation recorded on ancient cuneiforms (most notably those of Sumerian, Babylonian, Akkadian, along with Egyptian hieroglyphs, to name but a few) reveals a pantheon of varied Gods and deities that presided over the development of our species. The question of a main entity known as God taking on human form seems not to have occurred (regardless of the supernatural qualities some of these beings described in cuneiforms exhibited), but that emissaries from this ultimate power of the God-force itself infiltrated the earth system to better guide the evolving genus of the human. Although too numerous to mention here, incredible knowledge regarding agriculture, the arts, astronomy, science, incarnation, and reincarnation, death, rebirth, along with mention of the soul appears to have been handed down to us by these elevated beings which materialised through certain epochs to enlighten and move, it would seem, the human away from our primordial past and awaken us to this fact.

As with all things, there are always two sides, and those devoted to the theory of Charles Darwin (*English naturalist, geologist, and biologist, 1809-1882*) and his famous philosophy on 'Natural Selection' which was published in his controversial book '*On the Origin of Species*' in 1859 certainly upset many within the religious factions. Darwin's work is the foundation of evolutionary biology, and he is correct within his assumptions that organisms evolve over generations through the inheritance of physical or behavioural traits, although many of his ideas have been brought up to date throughout the decades. To his mind, the human is nothing more than a descendant of our cousin, the ape, but many have argued that his hypothesis cannot explain why we still have primates today if this were evidence of our radical development. At the time, the churches vehemently opposed Darwin's concept, for lack of a God, and this division is still met within the halls of '*Darwinism*' in our present times. However, Darwin may well be right, and as previously discussed, '*something*' initiated such a radical change within the genetic material of the future human model which Darwin himself would, I am sure, openly reject. For all intents and purposes, and within the continual disagreements between science and religion on how the human evolved, in my opinion, a happy medium can be met within this hypothesis if we merge both together. The deliberate DNA upgrade of the Homo Sapien Sapiens gave rise in not only a break-away species which we have evolved into, but also an awareness of self – in other words, a soul! That '*something*' considered the anthropomorphic organism to be a prime suitor in developing far beyond any other creature on this planet in terms of consciousness and its ability to create. It's interesting to speculate that such sacred knowledge transcribed on tablets has no room within science in our not-so-distant past to postulate theories regarding our overall genesis, other than the official narrative, which eradicates any notion of there being a soul, or even a God! Those within religious sectors only touch upon the subject, with no pursuit of the absolute truth, which may well be staring us all in the face, other than mere faith that '....*it all happened this way! No need to question – just accept!*'

The Sumerians from ancient Sumer, which began in 5300 BC and ended around 1940 BC, were the first known civilisation within the historical region of southern Mesopotamia (now south-central Iraq) to have practiced a polytheistic religion, with anthropomorphic deities. Two out of twenty-five Gods worshipped within this period have created much speculation as to the birthing of humanity. In essence, we are talking about space Gods, and not the one, true God, which, I believe, is omnipresent and has never taken on physical form in this regard. We are all, to an extent, Gods in the making (and certainly does not cancel out a creator in this regard), carrying elements of energy which permeate beyond the fabric of our biological bodies we temporarily inhabit. It must be said, however, that before discussing our next point, the reason why we are not able to make any sense of our true genus is simple because everything has been decompartmentalised into varied boxes, and which, I might add, have certain labels attached to them, ostensibly baring no relevance from one to the other, or so it is believed. For example, there are many who see spiritualism as an entirely different phenomenon than, say, UFOs. Yet are not all things connected – however bizarre. It seriously puzzles me as to why there are those who are so opposed to the idea of an afterlife. The same applies to intelligences which, I am certain, interacted with us in the past, and are still making frequent visits to Earth today. Yet, as with all things, there are divides in every corner, and many refuse to open their minds to the fact that certain documentation which has firm bases for legitimacy cannot be soiled (mainly ancient cuneiforms which, in the majority of cases, are hidden away from public scrutiny) by a 'System' which promotes its own narrative in making us believe that everything has a rational explanation, but which also reveals a very different story entirely. Scholars of comparative so-called mythology have noticed remarkable similarities between the stories recorded in Sumer and those found in the Hebrew bible. This proves that a watered-down version of such incredible historical events within varied religious cultures around the world has deliberately altered the original narrative to fit *their* preferred one!

The two influential Gods who it is theorised had presided over the creation of Man within the Sumerian period were Enlil and Enki, although Enki had been foremost in embryonic procedures in developing a new genus which would benefit his people considerably, seeing as he was chief scientist, geneticist, and overall keeper of secrets. In light of the bible's interpretation of how it all occurred in the beginning does not take into account a vast proportion of missing information, as well as misinformation which has radically altered through time, although this could be forgiven in some cases due to scribes within the passing epochs not having access to the primary cuneiforms as they were communicated. The original events and names of each pantheon of Gods can be found in the Babylonian epic of creation, *'Enuma Elish.'* Within Genesis 1:26, it is stated: *'Let us make man in our image, in our likeness.'* If God had been the only intelligent being around to make such a statement, it seems totally bizarre that He is referring to other Gods, and not just Himself as the overall creator.

The descending sky-gods are thought to have arrived from their planet of Nibiru 432,000 years ago, also known as 'Planet X' beyond Neptune, which has a 3,600-year-long elliptical orbit around our Sun. Prominent and respected author of '*The Earth Chronicles*' and researcher into the Sumerian and Babylonian culture, Zecharia Sitchin, concluded within his findings encompassing ancient civilisations that Man had been created by these Gods, better known as the Anunnaki, as a workforce to mine gold. According to his study and deciphering of the Sumerian cuneiforms, Enki had been wholly responsible for the development of our species, nurturing an intelligent being that could be utilised as a slave within the province of Africa when the supplies of gold extraction had dried up in the Iraq-Iran district. The Anunnaki had set up a base themselves to work within the Persian Gulf, but a rebellion of the Anunnaki led to the decision that the earth's hominid could be re-developed as a labour force and used to carry on with the exertion which the Anunnaki found too gruelling. The gold was needed to restore a collapsed atmosphere on their home world of Nibiru, and one wonders even to this day why this precious element is so sought after by our own people, as though the inherent memory of gold has left an indelible mark upon human consciousness. By applying his knowledge in advanced genetics, Enki saw about the creation of varied mutations of the earth hominid which failed over a prolonged period, until the 'Adam' paved the way forward in a being that had intelligence, but also deliberately flawed within the configuration of the DNA programming in terms of the human's overall longevity, unlike the Anunnaki whose lifespan was considerably much longer, spanning an incredible 331,000 years. This had been decided because the Gods did not want their new creation to become overly smart, although it is clear that some of their creations had been afforded an extended life cycle, while the majority were not. Originally, the Anunnaki forbade their new genus to reproduce (preferring instead to have an infertile species), but the introduction of Eve changed all that. This had infuriated some members of the Gods within the Sumerian pantheon, but Enki looked upon his creation with love and affection after going against the ruling from his peers in allowing procreation among the humans to take effect.

The presiding God, Enlil, who rose to prominence during the twenty-fourth century, had also become enraged by the fact that his very own people were mating with human females (since the Anunnaki members on Earth's expedition had mostly consisted of males). Both he and Enki had opposing views, which led to varied clashes between the two overlords throughout their separate leadership, and something prevalent within the reign of the Anunnaki, oftentimes leading to wars between certain factions within their command. In the bible, Genesis, Chapter 6, Verse 4, it states that: *'The sons of God came in unto the daughters of men.'* This, in turn, created a crossbreed between the Anunnaki and hominids, which we recognise within the biblical text as the Nephilim. Even the scientist and geneticist, Enki, had mated with an Earth woman whose son would be Ziusudra (better known in the bible as Noah), and something Enki kept secret from Enlil until after the Great Flood.

The Anunnaki's home planet of Nibiru, during its elliptical orbit in our solar system, was drawing dangerously close to Earth, which would cause a massive gravitational shift within the polar regions of our planet. Aware of this impending calamity, the Anunnaki had remained steadfast in not informing their human creation, along with the half-breeds, the Nephilim, which they had come to reject as monstrous. Instead, they would take their crafts within the perimeter of Earth's orbit and observe as the cataclysm took hold. Before this, however, Enki approached his son, Ziusudra (Noah) and enlightened him on how to construct an Ark capable of safeguarding himself and family, along with a genetic bank of every species which graced mother earth, seeing as no human or half-breed would be permitted to escape the impending doom. Enki knew that Enlil forbade this information from ever reaching the ears of their offspring, but felt that a large proportion of their work could be saved after the destruction of the planet.

Noah would have been aged 600 when the deluge occurred. The flood transpired approximately 1,656 years after the creation of Adam, which would place the incident around 4004 BC and occurs in chapters 6-9 in the book of Genesis, wiping out almost everything in terms of life, and lasting 40 days and nights. Noah's Ark came to rest on the peaks of Mount Ararat in Eastern Turkey, safeguarding himself and his family, along with the precious cargo secured onboard. As the waters subsided, Noah erected an altar in honour of the

Gods, offering an animal as a sacrifice, which he burnt, the smoke of which had been detected by Enlil's ship. Enlil had taken a dim view that Enki had secretly stirred Noah away, but Enki appeased the situation when explaining that Noah was his son, and that they (the Gods) could create better settlements and direct their creation in a new way of life. This tale of Ziusudra is known from a single fragmentary tablet written in Sumerian, and datable by its writing to the 17th century B.C. '*Old Babylonian Empire*' and covered by the author, Arno Poebel, in 1914.

The most plausible explanation for the emergence of our species lies, I believe, surrounding these facts, and as they stand within the ancient cuneiforms. The system in which we serve does not, in any way, want their carefully constructed model to be questioned, as this will invariably change the way we as a species think, and something we shall explore in more detail later. The issue of natural selection within our genus also appears to oppose the very laws of time. As humans, we had gone through a radical shift in what we had been and what we became through varied genetic enhancements. This is incredible in terms of both natural selection and the theory of chaos. It is important for us to at least contemplate an issue that we humans of today have such a challenging time accepting. To my mind, it is far easier to believe in something that cannot be proven, and, as such, forever remains a tantalising mystery within the human psyche. It's safer and not as hard to deal with on a psychological level. We must also come to accept that such elevated Gods had, themselves, been created by an ultimate force which we call God – a supreme deity which is so far removed from this physical matrix we currently inhabit, but which we are all connected to in terms of our current perception of self and consciousness as a whole. I very much doubt carrying that spark of God within us makes us in His image and His likeness – far from it! We had evolved from part animal, which is indigenous to this physical system, and the other part Anunnaki, who were, themselves, connected to the stars; therefore, we would be in '*their*' image and '*their*' likeness, and not Gods as such. We are, it appears, literally an amalgamation of the stars (heaven) and earth.

The revelation that so-called 'Sky-Gods' had been the original Overlords within the creation of Man continually falls into the category of so-called 'conspiracy theory,' yet large portions of the Sumerian cuneiforms indicate this to be the case. After all, this was the period of our development as a species. And not only this, but those precise recorded events have been altered in fashioning an altogether warped version of how it all occurred, and one which, to this day, leaves us just as baffled in terms of transparency. Lest we not forget the importance of heaven and earth. We are composites of the two, temporarily merged into the one, and this is just the start of it! There is much more which will be examined later, and an area which may indicate a warring faction against the Anunnaki (also known as the Archons) and the very spirit of Man through the ultimate God-source. The intriguing notion of there being a soul, however, gives rise to even further wonderment, and one which far exceeds the biological bodysuits we occupy whilst existing on terra firma. As we shall discover, the Avatar is far more than human, and one that exists beyond our concept of both time and space.

# 'The Eternal Avatar'

## Chapter Three

## The Soul

*'Our skin and bones remind us that the flesh is all we own,*

*Our thoughts will tell us daily of what we have learnt and known,*

*But something true within us should always lift our hearts,*

*That we are everything we cannot see and are connected to a greater force beyond the stars.'*

*Chris John Mayes.*

What exactly is the soul? Varied religions and cultures across the world have their own interpretation of what they believe the soul is, and, moreover, what becomes of it once physical death has ensued. Although each creed differs within their vigorous and oftentimes alarming conclusions concerning the fate of the individual when our last breath is taken from this life and subsequent journey into the next, our understanding of what is termed '*soul*' is the very essence of what animates our biological form, and allows us to have an awareness of self, along with our ability to think and progress. As we have briefly discussed earlier in the book, we are the only species on this planet afforded the right to a consciousness that permits the creation of thought. All of nature is so far removed from the '*human*' in this respect, acting primarily upon an instinct to survive, but not advance consciously. After all, you don't see a dog playing a game of cards with its human master now, do you? Through our genesis, a re-wiring within the DNA and neurological functioning has led to a subsequent allowance of what we term '*consciousness*' to operate within its temporary biological housing. This in no way signifies that all life within its varied levels of development beyond the human does not have a soul. The human is graced with acknowledging a God-like presence, along with understanding a far deeper connection with all of creation. The trouble with this notion is that many see the soul as a different component from that of the mind. Is consciousness and the soul one of the same? Or are they unconnected entities altogether?

The Egyptian dynasty had been one of the major influencers who acknowledged there being a soul known as 'Ka/ba,' and of its subsequent journey through the Underworld called 'Duat.' Interestingly, the Egyptian settlement at Giza appears far older than Egyptologists suggest, and the construction of these incredible edifices at the Giza plateau could not have been achieved through mere human labour, which many within their field of so-called expertise maintain. The Egyptians harboured extraordinary knowledge, and something which takes us back to the time of Sumer before the deluge. Such wisdom appears not to have been lost but carried forward by the Sumerian Gods in the reconstruction of our race after the Earth's deluge, but under different leadership throughout the epochs. Of course, there will be those following that all-too familiar official narrative who will vehemently deny this, but the evidence once again points directly to an extremely advanced culture, the likes of which put most of our architecture in present times to shame. The consensus is that we have always progressed as a species, but I'm convinced that through varied catastrophes like the great flood and the sinking of Atlantis, which occurred sometime in 9600 BC within the region of the Atlantic Ocean saw us going backward, and not forward within our evolution.

The Egyptians were aware of the soul and its transmutation beyond this sphere of matter, and it would also have to traverse the Underworld, where it would be judged. They also assumed the soul was made up of eight parts, which consisted of the physical, spiritual, name, personality, vital essence, heart, shadow, along with its form. To them, the world had been created by the God 'Atum' who brought order where there had once been chaos, and inherently believed that the soul, along with all life, was brought about by magic. This magic, the Egyptians understood, took the form of the soul and the varied parts which encompass it, an eternal force that resides in every one of us. The concept of the soul having many parts was derived from the '*Old Kingdom*' (third dynasty to the sixth, circa 2686-2181 BC) through to the new one, and occasionally changing from one dynasty to the next. Their rigorous funerary procedures via mummification indicated that the physical body, along with all the departed's worthy goods, would accompany them into the afterlife where their heart would be weighed by the jackal-headed God, Anubis, within '*The Halls of Two Truths.*' The God Osiris (lord of the Underworld) would be present to decide the fate of the newly arrived soul. It was believed the heart recorded all deeds within the soul's physical life, and if the heart weighed too heavy upon the scales of justice (against the feather of Maat) the soul would be damned to the monster 'Ammut' where it would be devoured, resulting in eternal death. If, however, the heart weighed favourably, then the soul would be granted eternal peace in the afterlife. This is interesting, considering cases of NDE (*Near-death Experience*) whereby a person dies and goes through varied spiritual experiences into a plane of reality far different from anything they've ever encountered before. Here, the individual soul reports having a type of panoramic life-review, and whereby the entire contents of the NDEers life-recording are dramatically seen and felt by the newly arrived soul, but not as a form of retribution (unlike the Egyptian's beliefs) but as a procedure of balancing, so that the experiencer realises how their actions affected others on earth, along with their own. This life-review brings greater clarity to the soul and a period where they can contemplate the larger picture of life, and one which was not always recognised in terms of how their actions touched or hindered others while in their biological bodies. Usually, elevated masters or spirit guides are present during this evaluation process. Many who go through an NDE normally have very uplifting encounters, often to the point where their lives (and upon their return to earth) have been completely transformed for the better, and where their fear of death has been rescinded. There are some, however, who experience quite the opposite, and upon their homecoming, change their entire life around in the hope that they will never face those negative forces they'd encountered whilst passing from this world into the next.

The soul would appear to be the eternal life-force we associate with God, and whereby we are all part of; that omnipresent intelligence which has varied names and faces, but has, I believe, never incarnated upon this planet, other than certain elevated masters such as Christ, Mohammad, Krishna, among others, to bring spiritual knowledge from their side to ours in guiding and teaching us that we do not die, and are themselves a fragment of a much larger entity in God as divine messengers, and of which they had been identified as such within the holy books. Such individuals had come to earth to offer hope in a somewhat continuous collapsed society we appear to adopt throughout the prevailing epochs. What does this tell us? I feel that our understanding of just why we are here on this planet in the first place, and with no memory (in many cases) of our former existence beyond the flesh, if we bring reincarnation into the equation, and which poses a multitude of questions, along with problems, must be addressed. To many, we simply live and die within a single incarnation, and certainly within the Christian teachings, they believe that we are born once within the womb and, upon death, remain in some type of spiritual limbo and are only awoken by the heralding of Christ's resurrection. One wonders where these souls are hanging out, if they are in a queue, ready to be judged before they can enter the kingdom of heaven! Who knows? Maybe they're right, but this also creates more issues when examining those cases of NDE which seemingly contradicts the whole cycle of just why the soul has incarnated here in the first instance if all it means is that we are given a right dressing down by a man with a white beard, along with the fact of remaining in sleep-mode until Christ's return! I mean, let's face it, we are born on earth with no instruction manual with which to guide us (only the Bible which Christian's maintain is the one, true book which has everything worked out for us) only to realise that, and in the majority of cases, not only have you to go through a lot of bad experience while on earth, but there's little hope for you in the next! It's as if the Christians have an exclusive pass to heaven and everyone else – well, you've had it!

There are three main areas of contemplation from varied sectors within the religious and New Age fraternity surrounding the soul. The first is '*Creation Theory,*' whereby the human body is transferred from parents, but the soul comes directly from God during the moment of conception, or not long thereafter. Within Creation Theory, it is thought that God creates a new soul with each pregnancy, and whereby that soul, and upon completing its physical incarnation on earth, returns to the Godhead with no reincarnation to be had, rather like a warehouse of souls all pending before their release and subsequent incarnation into a human body. The second theory by what is known as '*Traducianism*', believes that the soul comes directly from the parents. In the beginning, Adam was the only true soul created by God, and the rest of us, it is thought within Traducianism, are merely an echo of that main connection to Adam. Within traditional New Age thinking and a few other religious sectors (most notably Indian), the third idea involves reincarnation, and something which is an accepted process, whereby the soul will have innumerable incarnations upon the earth until it has completed its mission. However, all these pose incredible issues for many to accept when considering our purpose within the grand scheme of life. Apart from the belief in a soul, there are many who do not think that we possess one; that we are mere biological mechanisms which, upon death, snuff out like a candle's flame, and that's your lot!

Creation Theory

Creation Theory stipulates that the universe, along with all life, was brought about by God through divine intervention (supernatural means). This idea is literally based on the interpretation of the bible's Genesis narrative. Those who believe in the Creation hypothesis do not accept the modern evolutionary theory. Indeed, elements of reincarnation are all but rejected by the Christian community, considering that there is no need for the soul to continually go through a wheel of reincarnation, and that one life is had by all. They have a firm belief in a heaven, but that to enter this kingdom can only happen through a devotion to Jesus from within the heart, along with following the bible's interpretation of how things are. It must be said that not all Christians accept this and consider that the process of the soul going through multiple incarnations is indeed possible. However, that said, most Christians consider that reincarnation would only create more sin and thus lead the soul further away from God. To them, the soul goes into a deep sleep during the state of death and is awakened upon judgment day.

Traducianism

Traducianism believes that Adam, from within the bible (the first model of Man created by God), is the only being to have a soul, and that his primary essence is merely an immaterial aspect which is transmitted via natural lineage through the act of procreation to his descendants. Eve was purely a byproduct of Adam, in the sense that his physical and non-physical substance was used to generate reproduction henceforth. The act of original sin in the '*Garden of Eden*' by Adam spawned a kind of devolution of the soul, whereby all humans from that point onwards are a mere shadow of Adam's original template, ostensibly falling from grace. This may indicate that our creators in the physical sense had not foreseen drastic alterations within the spirit, soul, and body.

New Age Thinking

Prominent esoteric thinkers such as Helena Blavatsky and Carl Jung, who spearheaded what we know today as '*New Age Thinking*', had varied beliefs surrounding the soul, most notably in Western society, where a multitude of philosophies embrace the soul and its survival beyond its physical incarnation. Such spiritual and religious doctrines have spread across the world, and an area that is more widely accepted than most of the rigid views held within varied orthodox places of worship. New Agers see the soul as multidimensional in nature and have the ability to exist within other worlds, whether spiritual or material. They see the soul as a by-product of an ultimate God-force that we are all connected to, and which transcends both time and space upon physical death. This period, which grew, most notably within the 1970s, promoted clairvoyance, psychic phenomena, along with a plethora of other subjects once considered sacrilege by the churches from ages past.

If we take the hypothesis that we had been created by ancient astronauts which our ancestors saw as Gods as mentioned in chapter two (and which appears the most plausible explanation other than the mere supernatural quality which does not consider the evolutionary course) then it would make sense to presume we carry that inherent divinity from our creators, as they do in turn with theirs, and so on. Although areas surrounding the soul's ultimate whereabouts is nigh impossible to prove (other than our acceptance of their being a primary source which generates itself called God in the first place) a '*belief*' clearly defines something inherent in each of us; a spark of awareness that gives us the ability to think and progress, as well as create. And although we are still a relatively new species when taking into consideration just how old our universe is, our understanding of our place within this cosmos literally boggles the mind. Earth is insignificant within the solar system, which shares a tiny fraction, in terms of space, in the Milky Way, which spans an incredible 120,000 light years across. When we take a step back and consider this, it's enough to blow your mind away!

Although most scientific establishments rigidly condemn there being any form of a soul throughout the epochs, let alone an afterlife, there are some within the systematic community who have (and still are) looking into this area of research to find out just what we as the human ultimately represent beyond our biological workings. Consciousness is another major area of interest which appears to be independent of the brain, although there are some who have argued for consciousness being nothing more than a byproduct of cerebral functioning, and which is stimulated by the firing of neurons in a purely organic manner. However, there is mounting evidence to suggest that consciousness is indeed separate from the brain, and the big question must be asked: are the soul and consciousness one of the same, or separate in nature, respectively? Perhaps we have found evidence of the soul within consciousness itself.

In varied religious groups, there is the suggestion that the soul is an entirely separate entity from the mind. Much of the Christian faith, for instance, considers that cognizance dictates thought, perception, and memory, while the soul is a more abstract concept, connected to spirituality, ethics, and our individual essence. One wonders how our unique spirit can be split into two ways once the body perishes. We can take a simple example here when describing your mobile phone, which requires energy and a signal. The mechanism has three parts to make it work efficiently. The hardware of your mobile phone itself can be likened in a simplified fashion to that of the human brain, whereby consciousness permeates this temporary organic unit, along with nourishment, which enables it to function. As humans, we have energy (food and water) that sustains its organic counterpart. The phone transmits, records, and receives information via its unique signalling system, and if your phone should die, all information is stored within a cloud. Energy (your phone's information) cannot be destroyed. And yet, are these not two, separate components within themselves once the physical body is discarded, and only one of which (the information) survives when it has given up the ghost, so to speak? It *is* the signal, which is the phone, not the other way round. Only one part of this three-way process of shared components within this matrix survives when its energy and apparatus are no longer required. Such signals permeate all around us, even though our senses cannot detect them. Obviously, there is a reason regarding the infusion of mass (biology and sustenance) along with consciousness (signals) which heralds our place within this universe. The soul is energy, and it connects to the source of all that is – the God-force.

Many international scientists from around the world have announced that proof for the existence of a soul can be measured by quantum physics, suggesting that the soul has a quantum state just as real as wave-particle dualism. Quantum mechanics is a fundamental theory in physics that tries to predict the behaviour of all living organisms at the scale of the atom. Strangely, a negatively charged subatomic particle such as the electron (which can be bound or not bound 'free' from an atom) operates as a wave and acts like a wave when it is travelling through space. The three primary elements that make up an atom are electrons, protons, and neutrons. Together, they form the nucleus of the atom, and the protons have a positive charge that counters the electron's negative charge. When the atom has equal amounts of protons and electrons, it remains in a neutral state. Incredibly, the smallest part within subatomic research reveals nothing more than space known as the 'quantum field.' Subatomic particles behave paradoxically within that space, and only behave according to the known laws of nature when such particles combine into larger elements. This, it is surmised, is where the creation of consciousness exists within a state of possibilities. Isn't that amazing? It's totally incredible to know that a once-hidden science is now being explored within quantum research. While many are looking outward in their search for answers in assessing what the soul and, indeed, consciousness are, we may be surprised to find our answers deep within the once unobservable world, and one in which creation appears more wondrous than we currently imagine. The true nature of the particle only becomes apparent when the electron is observed and measured. Such elements remain in a state of pure potential until the act of observation brings them into our reality. This makes for fascinating speculation in terms of both awareness and creation itself. It is considered that consciousness can affect its environment through our 'thoughts' alone. Everything in our world, both organic and inorganic, is arranged and created from the atom. But the question begs, where is this consciousness emanating from? Arguments rage within New Age and religious circles, just as those associated in science. Indeed, the quantum world is still a puzzle in trying to establish the origins of the soul and consciousness itself.

British physicist and Nobel laureate, Sir Roger Penrose, along with American anesthesiologist, Stuart Hameroff, developed a theory between them in their search for such answers, centred around consciousness called 'Orchestrated Objective Reduction' (Orch OR), and known as the Penrose-Hameroff Theory. Their incredible hypothesis asserts that during an episode of a NDE, the individual's quantum substances constituting the soul (which they believe is located within what is called *Microtubules*) leave the nervous system and reintroduce themselves back into the universe. The researchers consider that perception is a direct result of quantum gravitation, which predicts the relationship between quantum mechanics and general relativity. Penrose and Hameroff consider that consciousness originates at the quantum level inside neurons and is held there by a process called 'Objective Reduction' orchestrated by the cellular structures, Microtubules. Although complexed within its scientific terminology, both men consider that upon the death of the brain, which holds consciousness within this field of reality is dispersed back into its original, universal state. This makes for interesting speculation, and not the first time where the idea of consciousness appears to be emanating from the very structure of what we call space. Waves and particles play an important role within the world of quantum physics, and very little is still understood about it within academia. Theory normally paves the way towards a greater understanding of all things least understood, but knowing that our awareness may actually create reality is a fundamental theory generally accepted within many sections of the scientific community.

If we look at the universe, we are left with a paradox. Is it eternal? Or does our cosmos come to an end? The same question surrounds not only the controversy of our human genesis, which has been briefly explored, but also the evolution of the soul and the subsequent rise in conscious awareness itself. Is consciousness, then, operating as a wave throughout space, (that the whole of the cosmos is some kind of sentient organism) which attaches to those lifeforms ready and able to receive the coherence necessary for development, ostensibly giving us a soul? Perhaps there are systems of development initiated by the main source of all-that-is (a force we call God) which construct in an effort to expand upon the creation process. Giving an example again to the mobile phone analogy and its signalling system, such waves are all the same, but impressed with separate, unique information being developed by its user (conduit), which is connected to the hub. We could perhaps see this hub as something akin to God, whereby all information is fed directly back into the core unit itself, and not as a 'think-tank,' but 'experience-tank.'

Although many theories have tried to tackle this complex subject, it is something that leads us deeper into the knowledge that there are matters we will never truly grasp. Perhaps we are all an aspect of the mind of God, each facilitating a unique experience within the dance of life which the 'One' works through in each of us to better understand '*Itself.*' This now leads us to the process of 'Incarnation,' and our subsequent journey from the other side into the womb. There is a necessity, it would seem, for a soul to emerge into this physical corporeality and forget what they have known while existing in the world of the '*spiritual quantum reality.*' While many on earth have no memory whatsoever of a former life beyond the flesh, there are some Avatars who do indeed recall the journey from source to the womb.

# 'The Eternal Avatar'

## Chapter Four

## Incarnation

*'I always whisper from beyond the veil,*

*To let you know that all is well.*

*You believe our worlds are far apart,*

*But revealed to me is what's in your heart.*

*Your soul is like a pealing bell,*

*Reaching far beyond what you can tell.*

*So, listen close to what I'm about to say,*

*I am just a gentle thought away.'*

*Chris John Mayes*

Is there a process beyond the womb that heralds the arrival of a soul? How is this achieved? Is the method of incarnation a choice we make? Or are we at the mercy of mere chance, rather than order? Such questions have been debated within varied circles across the world, and those willing to at least accept the hypothesis that souls appear to gravitate from an altogether different dimension of reality, and far diverse from the earth sphere where our development heralds a form of amnesia, and whereby we cannot always recall any previous life from the one we have separated from. As a professional working medium, these questions have haunted me for obvious reasons. We live in a world where such penultimate enquiries appear non-existent and reside within the halls of continual debate. Varied departments of science contradict many areas of research, which suggests an individual having any recall of either life in what we call '*spirit*,' or '*past lives*' from those regressionists who are dedicated to discovering the holy grail of our sojourn beyond this physical matrix, and no less through the mind. Many books have been written on the topic, and I can attest to the fact that there *is* truth in not only past lives, but also memories of those in what is termed the '*quantum spiritual dimension,*' because I have total recall of some of these myself, but not the memory of incarnation. This is rare for anyone to recollect coming into the womb, and without any form of regression being implemented. My understanding concerning the process of incarnation, which heralds our emergence into this dimension of reality, is that a choice is made from any soul wishing to go through an experience here. The amnesia would take effect for obvious reasons. If the soul were to have total recall of its former life in spirit while taking on a temporary biological bodysuit here on earth, all manner of problems could occur. Let's just say you have the memory of your existence beyond the womb, and let's also suppose that you've grown tired of this cumbersome process of dealing with the physical, emotional, mental, and spiritual glitches that appear prominent on this planet. What's to say you decide to end your life? Taking away most of the religious fear-mongering as to what occurs to the soul within those cases of suicide, you'd naturally want to return to your former existence on the other side. I'm not saying that I in any way agree with suicides at all, but their former selves still pierce through the veil when clairvoyance is implemented. For example, I am still able to connect with a mother's deceased son who had passed in such sad circumstances without any problem whatsoever, and no different than someone who has died through natural means. They come through on a slightly lower field of vibrational energy, which tells me this is the way they perished. I don't see them burning in flames, or their consciousness being snuffed out by some vengeful God! The way I see it is that we are all part of the whole, and therefore cannot be separated whatsoever. This does not take out of the equation lower dimensions of reality, which will be explored later, but there is always hope and redemption for any corrupted soul that has walked off the beaten track, so to speak. I agree that the delicate and somewhat complex path that a soul which has chosen to take its own life would, to some degree, upset the delicate balance with regards to any earth future which they would naturally have imprinted within their soul-chart, and, perhaps, change many factions of others whose lives they themselves would have affected had they decided not to terminate their physical existence, but this does not herald the expiry of their entire being. Quite the contrary. Elevated prodigies, however, who had walked this world to remind us of our inherent greatness throughout varied epochs, along with immortality, recall their former continuation and journey beyond the womb. One of these adepts, such as the Egyptian deity Thoth, knew of the salvation of the soul and a world which far exceeds the one in which we currently reside. His encrypted hieroglyphs within the '*Emerald Tablets*' have fascinated scholars across the world, whereby Thoth was able to detail his spiritual emergence from spirit into matter. In this way, such Avatars brought incredible knowledge from their primary side of life into this one, simply because their consciousness was not inhibited by the natural process of amnesia, which billions upon this planet experience when the full process of incarnation takes hold. This indicates that there *must* be a reason we are afflicted by this oblivion of conscious recollections prior to our biological materialisation.

'*The Emerald Tablets of Thoth*,' also known as '*Tabula Smaragdina*,' is an ancient artifact that contains cryptic inscriptions, leading many scholars to speculate that such writings embody the secrets of the universe, along with creation. Discovered in 1925 within the Great Pyramid of Giza, it is thought that Thoth himself had authored such documents throughout his varied incarnations upon this planet, amounting to over 36,525 manuscripts. Thoth was known within Egyptian mythology as the god, priest, and king who lived for thousands of years and was allegedly responsible for the building of the Great Pyramid of Giza after his rule in Atlantis ended during its sinking around 9,600 B.C. According to interpretations of the Emerald Tablets, Thoth escaped the sinking of Atlantis via a ship (UFO) which later landed in Khem (Egypt) where he attained governance for 16,000 years. His physical description is engraved within a relief in the Temple of Seti (Abydos), where the image of him is seen giving the Ankh to Seti I, who was the second pharaoh of the Nineteenth

Dynasty of Egypt during the New Kingdom period. Thoth is usually portrayed as having the body of a man, but the head of an Ibis (a sacred bird of Africa). He was the god of the moon, wisdom, science, magic, knowledge, hieroglyphs, and judgment. Author and founder of the Brotherhood of the White Temple, Maurice Doreal (1898-1963) was said to have attained and deciphered much of the tablets he acquired in 1925 during his visit to the Great Pyramid of Giza, and of which was later published in his book *'The Emerald Tablets of Thoth the Atlantean.'* It is clear, regardless of what many scholars within Egyptian antiquity believe, that there is much more to this incredible civilisation than we have been led to believe. We still cannot fathom how the pyramids of Cheops (along with many other temples around the world) were built, due to the incredible size and weight of each stone used within their construction. Giving an example, the Great Pyramid of Cheops has a sum total of 2300 million blocks, weighing around 2.5 tons to 15 tons. In the funerary chamber, the limestone weighs up to 51 tons! So, how did the Egyptians pull off such overwhelming feats? Scholars will tell you their version of how they considered these metropolises had been constructed but attempts in our modern times to replicate such accomplishments using current technology has failed and merely cast aside in preference that, if we can't explain how it was done, we walk away and carry on promoting a narrative which does not hold well in terms of explanation. Indeed, most of antiquity is forced into a box which many are not willing to challenge, despite the huge discrepancies which are blatantly obvious, along with using the word 'mythology' in an attempt to brush such levels of enquiry under the carpet. It's far safer to have a belief, conviction, or faith in something that hangs in the balance of half-truths, and something which cannot be proven as fact. This also applies in areas of afterlife research, along with topics encompassing the UFO/UAP phenomenon. Wash away any apparent considerations that make sense, and which are not to be considered within human evolution, and you have millions believing this is the only way things occurred.

The Egyptian dynasty was wrought in esoterica, along with an understanding of the afterlife. In fact, this appeared to be an essential part of their way of life, and long since disappeared within our modern times. We know that within religious ideology, much of the ancient texts have been altered in an attempt to control and subjugate the way the masses think. The human mind is far more powerful than we have been led to believe, and this is what has led to the spiritual devolution of our race through an alteration of such knowledge throughout time.

The Great Pyramid is known as a temple for the dead, but there are those who theorise that this incredible metropolis was actually an initiation chamber, and where elevated Avatars such as Jesus, Solomon, Apollonius, among other masters who walked the earth had received their enlightenment and vast spiritual knowledge through the teachings of Thoth and varied other deities. It was also discovered that the Great Pyramid within the Giza plateau is in direct alignment with the stars, and an area which most scholars who follow the old school of thought vehemently deny. However, the work of authors Robert Bauval and Adrian Gilbert has uncovered an incredible discovery. In their book, '*The Orion Mystery: Unlocking the Secrets of the Pyramids,*' published by Crown Publishing in 1994, consider the pyramids to be more than just tombs, and that such monuments were nothing less than a replica of heaven and earth. Such astronomical precision served as a gateway to the stars for the pharaohs. Several hidden chambers within the Cheops pyramid clearly show shafts which the researchers/writers discovered, and which are also in direct alignment with Orion's belt of the constellation Orion. The stars of Orion were associated with Osiris, the god of rebirth and the afterlife, by the ancient Egyptians. By definition, this would indicate that the soul (being the real essence of what we as humans represent beyond the biological form we currently inhabit) is able to journey across both time and space, as well as within the ether, once it is freed from its biological counterpart. This brings into the equation elements of reincarnation. The incarnation process is even more interesting, especially when we are debating just how this method occurs, and whether the experience itself is entirely random in nature, or whether there is purpose, design, and intent behind the soul's sojourn upon earth.

During Thoth's reign, and whose worship began in lower Egypt around the pre-dynastic period (c. 6000-3150 B.C.E.) carrying on through to the Ptolemaic period (c. 323-30 B.C.E.) marking Thoth's veneration as one of the longest of the Egyptian gods from any other civilisation, great knowledge had been imparted to his adepts from across the stars to the lower form of Man. In this sense, Thoth was able to recall his emergence from spirit and thereby attain information not inhibited through the process of incarnation, which we go through. This may indicate that our processing of data within the brain is restrained within its flow of conscious awareness, and only within one life period. Such gods were exempt from this; in the sense that our retention of memory as humans in former lives, and those in what we term '*spirit*' cannot be retrieved fully while within a material body, and which is limited within a certain timeframe (although such retrieval can be explored by a professional regressionist, and which has proven to be quite fascinating when investigating past lives, and those lived within what is commonly referred to as the spiritual quantum realm). Such deities had instant access to wisdom way beyond our comprehension, without any form of regression either! Although on rare occasions, there are those of us on earth who have had moments of enlightenment which cannot be explained in the conventional sense, indicating that certain gods were neurologically wired differently from us. Back in my younger years, the first computer I ever had was a Sinclair ZX-81, which was upgraded to a 16K, thus allowing it more space to save data. Previous to this, it only had 1K of memory, giving hardly any room to store anything within its memory bank. It is conceivable to assume that Thoth, along with a whole array of other Avatars, had much more in terms of retention, which could be bypassed instantly when needed, allowing for their incredible ability to lift Mankind beyond its primordial emergence as part spirit and part animal. This begs the question as to where our former memories are held while traipsing across this world with little or no idea why we are here in the first place. It would be wonderful if we could recall our former selves beyond the known stars, but something that would also create enormous psychological issues. Such attributes appear to be afforded only to those gods who were able to create balance and order within the processing of such vast knowledge within each of their incarnations on earth and beyond. Those other memories are stored within what is called the etheric body.

Let's take a brief look at another great Avatar before continuing with Thoth: that of Jesus of Nazareth. Christ's arrival within a stable was overseen by the Star of Bethlehem, and one wonders whether there was more to this apparent setting than considered within the conventional sense, and an area that many Christians will openly reject. The subject of UFO/UAPs tells us there is more to us and the universe in which we reside than currently thought, whatever method such intelligences are using to get here, through the varied arguments between researchers. The fact of the matter is that non-human entities, along with their crafts, *are* here, and always have been, even though the media cartel has done everything in its power to subjugate this fact, which is becoming more accepted due to the mass sightings and capturing of these objects on film. Both religion and UFOs have always been separated into their own categories, but there could well be connections to be made here. After all, many now consider that Thoth was some form of extraterrestrial. Furthermore, those who preach the holy books do not consider that such miracles from the past can be repeated in our current times!

Could the Star of Bethlehem have been one of these such objects that was overseeing the parturition of Christ? There are some scholars who believe this is mere fiction, and that the Star represents a great conjunction which occurred between Venus and Jupiter on the 17th of June, 2 B.C. The two stars would have come so close, they would have appeared as one. It is thought that Christ was conceived around 4 to 6 B.C. Most biblical scholars and ancient historians have no real record of the correct date during this epoch, but have settled on the aforementioned as being roughly accurate through analysis of the bible. There have been two main approaches which were used in determining the year of the birth of Christ; those accounts within the Gospels with reference to King Herod's sovereignty (also known as King Herod the Great) and the other by subtracting his age, thought to have been 30 years when Christ began advocating his beliefs and preaching. Herod wanted Christ killed (illogically on his part for fearing that Jesus would eventually take over his throne), forcing Mary and Joseph to flee to Egypt when an angel had come to Joseph in a dream soon after the visit by the Magi to prewarn him of such events while staying in Jerusalem. Herod was king of Judaea and, through his fury, had every baby boy born within the last two years in and around Bethlehem killed to ensure that Christ would not escape his wrath, seeing as he would have been roughly around this age. This was all down to God warning the Wise Men of Herod's plot in a dream, and when this came to Herod's attention, he ordered a killing spree to be initiated to safeguard his rule. Fortunate for the family, and through the warning from an angel, they survived. Concerning the birth of Christ, Mary's pregnancy obviously forbade any human sperm contamination from her husband (and within the genetic sense other than his mother's) to ensure that Christ's biological materialisation within this matrix was as close to the Father (God) as could be, untainted and having an apparent pure spiritual link to the divine, and which was also devoid of sin. Jesus Christ of Nazareth and *'King of the Jews'* was born via immaculate conception, and an idea heavily promoted within theologian circles who see human intercourse as sinful, but arguments raise that just such a process is essential within the progression of our species. Christ was crucified around the age of thirty-three, but his reign and presence were enough to affect millions of followers around the world, even to this day.

Are we all to be labelled as 'sinners' in this drama surrounding the fall of man due to one single act of apparent disobedience which played out in the Garden of Eden? This hypothesis is puzzling, to say the least, and was heavily enforced by the churches in the past to promote control and order. In Paul's Epistle, it reads as: *'Therefore, just as sin entered the world through one man* (Adam) *and death through sin, and in this way, death came to all people, because all sinned.'* Christ's incarnation was to bring deliverance and salvation, offering final rescue from the devastating effects of sin. Within much of the Christian teachings, every single human is considered a sinner, until they bequeath their love and allegiance to Jesus Christ. Sin occurred when, and in the bible's interpretation, both Adam and Eve ate from *'The Tree of Knowledge of Good and Evil,'* and had been tricked by a serpent. But I believe that much of the scriptures have been contaminated by those in governance in the past (and something which still holds firm within its convictions and faith to this day), and that the true interpretation is not what we have been led to believe. Adam and Eve are purely symbolic in nature, as our emergence was engineered by Gods and not the 'One' true deity, which we are all connected to on a higher level of spiritual awareness, and a force which has never taken human form.

So, we can see that Jesus, the son of God's incarnation, had entered our world through the womb, and not by some other method where Thoth and other Avatars are concerned. Christ's emergence in this way may well have been initiated so that as an elevated and supreme embodiment of divinity himself, he could be among his fellow compatriots as a mere carpenter (and a person who his people could associate with regarding empathy, love and compassion) and not elevated to the status of a god-like figure, unlike those within Egyptian antiquity. Thoth's incarnation is quite an altogether separate mystery, and far diverse from the normal way in which life is conceived. This may be one of the reasons why many consider Thoth to have been extraterrestrial in nature, as opposed to human. Such thoughts will be a real headache for those who categorise mythology and fact separately. But, consider this, those who believe in the bible are all too accepting of the enormous wealth of supernatural occurrences which litter its pages. Is this mere fantasy? Or are we to believe them as truth in the literal sense?

Our incarnation, along with many other apparent elevated souls, comes directly from God, the source of all that is, and a force we are all connected to. God is known as the light, and this is interesting when addressed within certain biblical texts. As described in John 1, the King James Version: *'In the beginning was the Word, and the Word was with God. The same was in the beginning with God. All things were made by Him; and without Him was not anything made that was made. In Him was life, and the life was the Light of men. And the Light shineth in darkness; and the darkness comprehended it not. There was a man sent from God, whose name was John. The same came for a witness to bear the witness of the Light. That all men through Him might believe he was not that Light but was sent to bear witness of that Light. That was the true Light, which lighteth every man that cometh into the world. He was in the world, and the world was made by Him, and the world knew Him not. He came unto his own, and His own received Him not. But as many received Him, to them He gave the power to become the sons of God, even to them that believe on His name, which were born not of blood, nor the will of the flesh, nor the will of man, but of God. And the Word was made flesh and dwelt among us (and we beheld His glory, the glory of the only begotten of the Father) full of grace and truth.'*

The '*Word*' comes from a thought, and thought is that omnipresent vibrational energy which permeates beyond our world within the creation of matter and is shaped no less by the infinite light of God. This leads us into areas surrounding the quantum issue, most of which are mere theoretical in nature at the moment. However, in the above passage, we can clearly see through this interpretation that 'light' is how Man was created, but there are those beings who were not made of flesh, blood, and bodies, and who did not come through any incarnation procedure. Within '*The Emerald Tablets of Thoth*', this particular deity refers to his uniqueness as a superior Avatar, and far removed from those of us as humans; '*Aye, different, yet one with the Children of Light. Custodians and watchers of the force of man's bondage, ready to lose it when the Light has been reached.'* Here, Thoth is describing his separateness from those of men, and that such spiritual bondage for us as humans, held within our temporary existence within the flesh, is reunited within the light once death ensues. He is also a *'Custodian'* and *'Watcher'* of humans, like an Overlord whose mission was to advance the children of Earth.

Thoth was generated from the lips of Ra during the beginning of time and is known as the god without a mother. According to sources, Thoth is self-created and, as an Ibis, lays the cosmic egg which holds all creation. Interestingly, the current model of the universe is believed to be shaped like an egg, but the question begs: what lies beyond the border of this apparent ellipsoid? Are we in a cosmic womb? One can only wonder as to this hypothesis.

Unlike Jesus Christ, who incarnated into the womb, Thoth appears completely separate upon his arrival on earth. This may explain why, and as humans, we do not have the capacity to recall any memories of our former self within those higher levels of reality because of the brilliant, but highly restricted biological form we are temporarily enmeshed within, unless explored by a past-life regressionist. An example would be a deep-sea diver who is confined in numerous ways within his temporary bodysuit while exploring the depths of the ocean, until he is freed from such restraints. Yet, many would consider that such self-replicating materialisation is nigh impossible, and seeing as all life must seemingly come through the reproductive cycle, there can be no other method of existence. Discovery into the nature of light may answer this question. As we know from the bible, Genesis 1:3, God said, *'Let there be Light,'* and there was light. We exist within a universe that is mostly structured by four elements: those of gravity, electromagnetism, along with strong and weak nuclear forces. Mass fundamentals such as dark energy, which amounts to 68.3% of the universe's composition, along with dark matter at 26.8%, and atoms at 4.9%, are the key components that are the building forces of everything. In the beginning, there heralded the Big Bang, occurring some 13.8 billion years ago, and which inflated from its initial state of high density and temperature, ballooning out faster than the speed of light within its period of rapid expansion. As the cosmos began to cool, light was born between 240,000 to 300,000 years after the initial discharge which thus creating the stars, galaxies, and everything else. As anyone would come to expect, within any explosion, the rate of expansion would naturally slow. Yet, this does not appear to be the case at all. Our universe is actually accelerating within its growth, which has puzzled Cosmologists. Although the question of what was there before the Big Bang remains one of the most puzzling enigmas of all time. Can we envision nothingness? And what created this sudden blast and inflation process in the first instance within the universe's primordial emergence? This is still a hotly debated conundrum. The creation of light is another interesting area. As photons, protons, and electrons crashed into each other, this generated fusion, making light and energy possible. Such elegant interactions are what power our Sun, along with many other stars, and naturally occur when two atoms heat and compress so forcefully, their nuclei merge into an entirely new component. But what of the light God addressed? I don't personally feel he was just talking about the light of creation, but that of Man.

We are all in possession of a soul, and that soul is reported as being light. Indeed, when people who experience an NDE, and just before their crossing over to the other side, always report seeing an intensely bright, white light which does not affect their vision by any means. This is because, upon reaching the final stages of death, the real essence of their embodiment is now being removed from its temporary physical reality. As mediums, both Chris and I see these lights. They come in varied colours: silver, blue, white, pearl, and gold, and it has always fascinated us to know what exactly these are, and which appear not from peripheral vision, but directly in our line of sight. To begin with, I wondered whether I had some form of neurological issue, but knowing Chris experiences these too suggested we were both (like many other mediums) actually witnessing 'spirit' piercing through from within the quantum state. We can surmise, then, and as most mediums agree, that such intensely clean and brilliant lights must belong to the energies of those loved ones who have moved on to a higher expression of life, and of which, on varied occasions, can show themselves to any one of us. I have lost count of how many times, and when I've finished a reading, the sitter has told me of seeing these amazing luminosities. Such lights, now free from the flesh, exist within other dimensions of reality, no longer inhibited by a cumbersome body that held them within this matrix.

Beyond the material world, and when studying areas of quantum mechanics, we are currently aware that when scientists look to see what's holding the atom together, and even beyond those tiniest of particles, they discover space, and something which mirrors our universe. This, I believe, is the field of pure potentiality, and one wonders whether through thought (vibration) we actually created ourselves into being within the beginning of all time, as we know it. This is a fascinating theory, and tells us, perhaps, that our primordial foundations are not to be located here within this physical universe, but one which is entirely different from anything we've known while manifested as human. But can this be proven? Within all areas of science and technology, most of the progress made is founded upon the basis of theory, and usually, most of the time, such theories end up becoming fact, because it fits with other models created beforehand. It's a bit like putting a puzzle together. Eventually, you'll find those pieces that fill the missing gaps.

Does the soul really choose to come to earth? Is there a choice to be made by that soul within its current state of existence? My dear and closest friend, Chris John Mayes, walked into my life in December 2022, having read one of my books, '*Guardians of the Dead.*' From our first meeting, I knew I'd connected with an extremely elevated soul, and we just hit it off. Our many long hours of debating genesis, the afterlife, and our own personal psychic experiences fuelled the way forward in at least trying to tackle such a difficult subject, and it was Chris who seeded the idea for this book, no less. I have him to thank for his incredible poems and writings channelled from 'spirit' which graces each chapter heading, along with the Preface and healing energies. Indeed, he has been instrumental in the development of this project and contributed much of the material. Our understanding of the big question surrounding soul survival is an enthusiastic drive towards a greater truth. He is also a brilliant and extremely gifted artist. Gentle, kind, but also fiercely intelligent, I have him to thank for turning things around in my life, literally. They say angels walk among us, and I'm sure he's one of them, minus wings! Chris recalls his own 'incarnation' process before his life on this planet developed, which is rare, unless you've had regression, which he has not. His memories are raw, yet fascinating within the extreme. It's interesting to note that in cases of NDE, nearly all those who have died and come back through resuscitation (or by other means) do remember every fine detail of their subsequent spiritual crossing, but within the development of incarnation, this is not always the case. Since consciousness has temporarily severed its link from the other side may indicate why we do not have clarity when entering into the womb, and which we have already touched upon.

Chris recounts a memory which, ironically, mirrors the Egyptian deity Thoth when detailing his own journey through the ether before his incarnation on earth described in '*The Emerald Tablets*', took hold. Although Chris had come into the womb as we all do, Thoth's was altogether different in terms of his apparent process of self-replication, bypassing the normal gestation period we all experience on a biological level. The importance here is to understand that a '*choice*' by the incarnating soul does appear to be part of the agreement before entrance upon this planet occurs, and for numerous reasons decided by that soul. As a child, Chris recalls a distinct and repeated memory which would make him cry, and on every occasion, he had to be consoled by his parents, telling him that everything would be fine when these incredible recollections emerged, but something he knew they would never come to understand. These shocking and clear visions, which continually surface within his mind, tell of his soul journeying from another place and time, and so removed from the corporeality in which he currently resides. His feelings of isolation and helplessness, and a yearning to return to where he'd originated from beyond this veil, is apparent when he reminiscences about this episode. Before his separation from the other side, Chris remembers having a conversation with '*others*' (which he considers were highly evolved masters) and of the vital importance his soul mission was in his choice to incarnate. He was primed before his parting from this realm that if he was to remain true to form, to be more than he was in terms of *himself*, to remain steadfast within his own convictions of retaining who and what he embodied on a soul level, then his mission he was about to undertake would be successful upon his return. It was also explained what the procedure would be like, which he had agreed upon. This seemed vital to Chris. He remembers a moment of anticipation, as though once his agreement had been met, he was actually going to go through with it, but also acknowledging the fact that, although he'd be alone once his severance took hold from those within the higher planes of reality, he would, nevertheless, be guided all the way. It's as though he was at the cusp of knowing he would forget himself through this temporary departure from the '*real*' world, but it was, he feels, a component essential to his development on a spiritual level. Somehow, he felt sure the assignment he was about to undertake would make his soul grow much brighter, contributing towards a vast unity of love, understanding, and helping those within his group evolve on a grander level.

Chris felt a flash of exhilaration mixed with dread. In the instant of disconnection, everything happened so fast. He was no longer met with light, but darkness, along with a perception of unbearable loneliness. The glowing illumination and warmth he'd previously felt were gone. There now came an awareness of no substance in terms of embodiment, along with the sensation of not belonging anywhere, only a feeling that he was somewhere else, where a new place and time were about to be born. His confrontation with the void gave rise to trepidation of what he was about to experience, yet again! To Chris, he knew this was not the first time such episodes of personification had taken place. Another incarnation which he had agreed to undergo, as well as the knowledge that the true nature of himself would be sacrificed for a time, forgotten, but with the understanding that he would be able to recall upon his return once his vocation had been accomplished. Within this journey, the greater part of his higher awareness would diminish until the unification of his soul was restored, and he was back home on the other side.

With no physicality, and also being aware of the immensity of space around him, Chris was shocked to realise that things were much larger than he'd imagined, as though the enormity of the void would consume his very essence. He describes this as literally overwhelming to his senses. Previous to being in a state of '*all that is,*' he was horrified to grasp that he was now but a component to many other parts, a mere speck within the grand scheme of creation, and no longer an aspect of pure and blessed excellence on an elevated level of super-consciousness. This new 'separated' reality meant that it could have influence and control over him; this vulnerability was an uncomfortable and scary concept. He also believes, as I do, that within the process of severance, there comes amnesia, as though these functions serve as a vital element within the incarnation procedure. The only security he had was the knowledge that he was destined for '*somewhere*,' but he had to pass many other realities within the void before reaching his intended target. He cannot recall if he knew where he was going, but the feeling that his acceptance in this mission remained prevalent, along with the fact that this was neither random, because he was very much aware he was being carried, guided, and followed by some other force throughout his journey. The further away he was pulled from his primary location, the less he was able to recollect. As he was wrenched with incredible speed through light-structures which now formed within the distance, and which also materialised as solid in nature, his approach to them indicated he was actually hurtling through the very atomic structure of these coloured sources of illuminations which he knew were planets, while all along experiencing an uncomfortable wrenching and tugging sensation. He also describes that he knew on a deeper level all there was to know about those worlds he passed as his soul was projected forth through the immensity of space. He was made aware that there were a multitude of intelligent systems other than Earth within this vast chasm of the void.

There came a point of light, a golden speck which appeared dominant within his perception, and something he felt sure was his intended destination. But while this was occurring, his sense of identity was being stripped the further he got from his original locality. This overwhelmed him even more, realising his former *'greatness/being/self'* was being diminished, temporarily losing the very essence of his entire prominence. He recalls that the whole scenario was a nightmare to behold, replaced by trepidation and loneliness. As Chris described this to me, one of the most profound features within his recollections was just how enormous everything appeared to him, giving him a complete sense of no longer being *'great,'* but shockingly so much smaller than he'd ever known.

The point of golden light, which at first appeared as a mere speck to Chris, now came into view as being enormous. It was during this instance when he felt like he was being sucked into it. He reiterates, *'...this is it? Wham! Everything happened so quickly, and within the blink of an eye!'* As soon as he made contact with the enormous golden light, the feelings of helplessness and no longer being separate overwhelmed his awareness. This concluded his emergence into the world of matter.

Chris knows that this haunting memory heralded his physical emergence on planet Earth. He has sentiments of melancholy when relaying his clear memory of what he'd experienced as a child, and does not feel like he belongs on this planet at all. Interestingly, I feel very much the same, as though this *'mission'* we have elected separates us from our former glory, something which appears to be an essential ingredient within our own spiritual enlightenment. To forsake heaven within memory throughout our incarnation may also assist us towards a grander evolution beyond the physical universe we currently inhabit. It is plausible to consider that Earth is a school for the developing soul, but a harsh one at that, and our *'forgetting'* is vital, where we can learn to work upon our chosen assignments before our return and overall *'awakening'* comes into effect.

We can clearly see the emergence of the soul enters this physical universe after it has made a choice to incarnate. This proves there is order as opposed to chaos within our sovereignty. Chris describes that his decision to come to earth is based upon remaining *'true to himself,'* to endure the purity of his own being. That is his overall mission. Thoth also states within *'The Emerald Tablets'* and acknowledged by author, Danielle Rama Hoffman in her book, *'The Tablets of Light'* (published by 'Bear & Company') *'It is time when the more that you are being you, the greater is the unlocking within you of the you-ness of you.'* Chris has always told me that I have to be me, as he is himself, and I know exactly what he means. The material world in which we live appears to have no mercy when it comes to certain challenges we face, and he also informed me of this fact long before I'd found that Thoth's journey within his incarnation was almost identical to Chris', along with his message about the importance of building upon your uniqueness as an individual. So many people are not themselves because they live under the shadow of others. Only when we are true to who we really are can we shine our light brighter for others to see and to assist them in their journey.

Chris recalls a conversation with *'others'* before his journey from the other side began, and which tells us a lot about the experience once his choice to incarnate had been made. His tears as a child as he recounts the experience to his parents had been for a yearning to go back to his real home, and not that of earth, because the memory imprint had somehow remained with him, as is often the case with many others who have no previous knowledge of their existence within the actual incarnation process. Also of interest was his passing through the atomic structuring of other star-like systems within the last stage before being sucked into a vast, golden light of the womb. Perhaps we can speculate that this is how the soul gains entry in the biological sense. The soul goes through a transmutation from a higher vibrational state to a lower one to attach itself within this material existence so that it is matched by its density, carrying with it the germination of seeds it has implanted within its own, unique blueprint. This blueprint would be deeply ingrained within the nucleus of the etheric body.

Thoth's account of his voyage makes for interesting reading indeed. Within the interpretations of '*The Emerald Tablets,*' there are some revealing anecdotes. I have included the section relevant to the subject at hand, which highlights Thoth's clear recorded memories surrounding his journey from light.

*'I was free from the bondage of Earthmen. Free from the body, I flashed through the night. Unlocked for me at last was the star-space. I was free from the bondage of night.*

*Now I sought wisdom to the end of space, far beyond the knowledge of finite man. Far into space my soul travelled freely, into Infinity's circle of Light,*

*Strange beyond knowledge were some of the planets, great and gigantic, beyond the dreams of men. Yet I found Law, in all of its beauty, working through and among them as here among men.*

*There were shapes, moving with Order, great and majestic as stars in the night, mounting in harmony, in ordered equilibrium, symbols of the Cosmic, like unto Law.*

*I passed many stars on my journey, passed many races of men on their worlds. Some reached as high as stars of the morning. Some fell low in the blackness of night.*

*Some I found who had conquered the ether. Free of space, they still yet were men. Using the force that is the foundation of all things, they constructed a planet far out in space.*

*Drawn by the force that flows through the All, condensing and coalescing the ether into forms, it grew as they willed. Surpassing in science, all of the races were mighty in wisdom, were sons of the stars.*

*For a long time, I paused, watching their wisdom. From out of the ether, I saw them create gigantic cities of rose and gold, formed from the primal element, from the base of all matter, the ether far flung.*

*Far in the past, they had conquered the ether and freed themselves from the bondage of toil. They formed in their mind only a picture, and swiftly created, it grew.*

*Then my soul sped forth through the Cosmos, seeing ever-new things and old, learning that man is truly space-born, a Sun of the Sun, a child of the stars.*

*O man, know that whatever form you inhabit is surely one with the stars. Your bodies are nothing but planets revolving around their central suns.*

*When you have gained the light of all wisdom, you shall be free to shine in the ether, one of the Suns that lights outer darkness, one of the space-born grown into Light.*

*Just as the stars in time lose their brilliance, their light passing from them into the Great Source, so, O man, the soul passes onward, leaving behind the darkness of night.*

*You were formed from the primal ether, filled with the brilliance that flows from the Source, bound by the ether coalesced around, yet ever it flames until at last it is free. Lift up your flame from out of the darkness. Fly from the night and you shall be free.*

*I travelled through the Time-Space, knowing my soul at last was set free, knowing that now I might pursue wisdom. Until at last I passed to a plane hidden from knowledge, known not to wisdom – an extension beyond all that we know.*

*O man, when I had this knowing, my soul grew happy, for now I was free. Listen, you space-born, hear my wisdom. You do not yet know that you, too, will be free.*

*Listen again, O man, to my wisdom, that hearing you, too, might live and be free. You are not of the earth – earthly. You are a child of the Infinite Cosmic Light.*

*O man, do you not know your heritage? Do you not know you are truly the Light? Sun of the Great Sun, when you gain wisdom, you shall be truly aware of your kinship with Light.*

*Now to you I give knowledge, freedom to walk in the path I have trod, showing you truly how my striving, I trod the path that leads to the stars,*

*Harken, O man, and know of your bondage, know how to free yourself from the toils. Out of the darkness you shall rise upward, one with the Light and one with the stars.*

*Ever follow the path of wisdom. Only by this can you rise from below. Every man's destiny leads him onward into the Curves of Infinity's ALL.*

*Know, O man, that space is ordered. Only by order are you one with the ALL. Order and Balance are the Law of the Cosmos. Follow and you shall be one with the ALL.*

*He who would follow the path of wisdom must be open to the flower of life, extending his consciousness out of the darkness, flowing through time and space in the ALL.*

*First, you must linger deep in the silence until at last you are free from desire. Free from the longing to speak in the silence, conquer by silence the bondage of words.*

*Abstain from eating until you have conquered desire for food, which is bondage of the Soul. Then lie down in the darkness. Close your eyes from the rays of the Light.*

*Centre your Soul-force in the place of consciousness, shaking it free from the bonds of the night. Place in your mind-place the image you desire. Picture the place you desire to see.*

*Vibrate back and forth with your power. Loosen the soul from out of its night. Fiercely shake with all your power until at last your soul is free.*

*When you have freed your soul from its bondage, know that for you the darkness is gone. Ever through space you may seek wisdom. Be not bound by fetters forged in the flesh. Onward and upward into the morning, free flesh, O Soul, to the realms of Light.*

*Move in Order. Move in Harmony. Freely move with the Children of Light. Seek and know my Key of Wisdom. Thus, O man, you shall surely be free.'*

Thoth's mention of being free from the bondage of '*Earth-men*' clearly shows that he was not of '*Men,*' and that his journey across time and space gave him the freedom to note those civilisations who had freed themselves from such material constraints, and those who had not. His incarnation allowed him to be free of material substance, and something he could fashion within his own mind. He also makes clear the importance of us as 'humans' to escape this corporeal existence through the light of all wisdom, as though within each incarnation we take, there comes a choice to open ourselves up more to the realisation that we are of dust in the biological sense, and that of our true heritage within the Light of All that is. Thoth also appears to have been the incarnate of Hermes Trismegistus (the legendary figure who existed within the Hellenistic period) and a teacher himself of Hermetism. He is also attributed along with Thoth regarding the writings of '*The Emerald Tablets*' within the 2nd Century B.C. But what of Thoth's self-replication from light? Can this be achieved?

According to discoveries in science, this may indeed be a possibility. Scientists studying particle collision at the 'Relativistic Heavy Ion Collider' (RHIC), which is a United States Department of Energy Office of Science user facility at Doe's Brookhaven National Laboratory, have been able to generate matter directly from light. The primary discovery comes from pairs of electrons and positrons (particles of matter and anti-matter) which can be assimilated directly by colliding energetic photons together, which are quantum 'packets' of light. Although slightly technical within its terminology, Einstein's famous $E=mc2$ equation dictates that energy and matter are interchangeable. Rather like a wave becoming a particle when such conditions are right, and vice versa. The process of incarnation teaches us there is indeed intent and purpose to our existence, and that we are born not only of the flesh, but also that of spirit (light) which has journeyed from its original source of origin to be here. I believe, however, that such information has been deliberately hidden through other forces here on earth intent on not allowing us to reach for the stars in the spiritual sense, and consciousness overridden with an altogether lower form of understanding surrounding our '*actual*' origins. The material we have been fed through the system we serve is merely a watered-down version, which does little or nothing to truly inspire the soul on a deeper level when it comes to those true answers we seek. This also confirms why the system persecuted anyone back in the past getting in touch with so-called esoteric practices, for the simple reason that these very areas of enquiry paved the way forward to amazing knowledge about us, the soul, and creation. I believe this is still happening today, but on a psychological level of implementation.

So, what's the reason behind our incarnating upon a challenging planet? Why are we here? Perhaps those answers lie deep within us, and we have only forgotten. The etheric body is another area of fascination and may lend credence to the revelation that we are not just biological creatures as we have been led to believe, but far more. Are we not also a composite of the cosmos, too? The terminology that Man is born of '*dust*' is interesting, because we are aspects of the very essence of what the universe is made of, and in every respect.

# 'The Eternal Avatar'

## Chapter Five

## Reincarnation

*'This Earth we wake from day to day,*

*A life, a dream, a role we play,*

*Has our times before expired here,*

*Or on other worlds and realms, our souls appeared.*

*As we age, our footprints appear to grow,*

*That mark our past and often show,*

*The loads we carried and the stops we make,*

*Could this life be one of many along the path we take?*

*From source we become a greater part,*

*Of life's eternal expression of the love in our heart.'*

Chris John Mayes

The idea that we continually go through a process of incarnation as a human appears to be evident within certain areas of past-life regression studies. Yet, the question begs as to why we would put ourselves through such challenges, and in some cases, terrible life experiences. People have asked me if it is true that we plan our journey on the other side before our emergence on this one takes hold, and there is every reason to speculate this occurs, but not always in the way we intended in the majority of cases. Life poses many trials within our incarnation. The advent of free will may also create issues which could hinder growth through the choices we, and others, make along life's path. Chris' recall of his entry seemingly from source before being sucked into the material realm which was described earlier has always haunted me; more so because, in the majority of cases, our inability to remember anything of our former life in spirit when it comes to actually entering the physical world. Amazingly, he has total recall of the experience as it transpired, and just before his entry into the womb. Not surprisingly, he can also remember being able to come out of his body while in the developing stages as a baby, and soon after his emergence into Earth's reality.

As a baby, Chris discovered that if he could lift himself and bring himself forcibly down in his cot, the impact generated would somehow release his soul from his body, and he knew it was working because he would invariably see and sense things not of this world; of flying, escaping his body's prison, creating a sensation whereby he knew his spiritual essence could easily detach from its physical counterpart. After a while, Chris became aware that he could periodically replicate this sensation through such an action and was eager to explore more of this disconnected state, which invoked other sensations like freedom, calmness, peace, and a knowing that he was somehow indestructible when this severance occurred. The indestructible feeling was a realisation that he was, in fact, spirit, and not the biological matter he now found himself in. Because of his periodic rocking, it caused his cot to lift and bang in a rhythmic motion, so much so that the neighbours could hear the commotion from their side of the adjoining house, and who'd come round to see Chris' dad, John. The neighbour thought John was doing DIY work at night, and he had to explain that it was his son who was responsible for the commotion, and that, perhaps, the only way to stop him might be to chain him down in his cot!

It would appear that even from such a young age, a deeper knowing within Chris' psyche informed him that he did not feel comfortable being in such a cumbersome body and wanted desperately to get out of it. He would invariably find any method at his disposal in escaping the cot other than his forced out-of-body activities, and through the realisation that he was more or less stuck here, due to his other exotic spiritual travels, which did not afford him total severance. He'd cleverly worked out how to dismantle a metal rod which held the main frame of the cot's enclosure together, causing part of it to collapse and enabling him his freedom, which was always short-lived. His parents couldn't understand why their son seemed so determined in his exploits, and he was too young to find the language to explain his reasons. They recall the apprehension they often felt of opening the bedroom door in the morning to discover what damage they might find, usually accompanied with tools in hand for the repairs. He recalls being unyielding in not only escaping his body by way of stimulating an OBE, but also dealing with those physical obstructions he faced while his biological imprisonment ensued. As a child, this world puzzled him because such barriers were not evident from the place from which he had originally incarnated. Chris likens the feeling of body/soul separation to that of the North American Indians' dance which they would perform in ritual, inducing an altered state of consciousness, and whereby they were able to invoke the summoning of '*Spirit*' within their trance-induced ceremony by way of a repeated motion of the body, sending them into the Alpha state.

Memories of our sovereignty beyond the physical realm begin to diminish when we reach the age of five, where a new set of mental programming is initiated on this side of life. We know that within NDE research, many who have crossed over have no wish to return to their body after being touched by the light, and this tells us categorically that we are not 'human.' We are all spiritual entities going through a human experience, and only temporary at that. We discovered in the previous chapter that Chris remembers having a conversation with others in spirit before his incarnation took hold, and his mission was to remain true to himself, as well as working towards a larger version of what he currently represented. It is conceivable to assume also that our inherent memories from source are stored within the Akashic Records (the etheric body) while a new imprinting of experience is governed without any form of emotional, mental, or spiritual disruption while we set about creating a fresh (and in some cases) enhanced version of ourselves.

There are classic cases of individuals who have clear recollections of their former lives in spirit (but seldom with the process of incarnation, like Chris' account), and too numerous to mention within this book, without any form of regression on their end either. I have numerous memories of past incarnations as a human myself, all of which are from separate time periods, and none of them very enlightening, I'm afraid!

**Earth Past Life Memories**

One clear memory was of me as a young child in India, and I can recall this very lucidly. Within this incarnation, I can see myself aged around five, maybe seven, wearing nothing more than a dirty, white tunic outside my home. The house itself is a small, white building with a door, and my bedroom had been tiny, consisting of nothing more than a shabby, wooden bed, which was the only feature within this somewhat hot and depressing environment. I can see elephants from a vast distance, crossing a river and carrying within their trunks the remnants of cut-down trees. Here, there is progress in work on the development of a magnificent building in construction not far from my home.

The next image is of me in my mid-twenties, or early thirties, walking towards an ornate, metal gate. At this stage within my incarnation, I have developed into a man, and I know my parents have long since passed. My life as a peasant boy has somehow changed to a slightly elevated position within society. The gate I approach leads to a bathing area of sorts, and I see an elderly Indian gentleman wearing a turban who is deep in the water, inviting me to join him where we can discuss matters of importance while we have some free time on our hands. I have the feeling this man is my friend, and in service to a person of nobility. I am also aware that I'm in assistance too, and to the very same employer as my friend.

My master, whom I am in service to, is very kind, but often sad, and gives me food, clothing, and accommodation in return for my duties. The huge building where I am employed is sparse, but its magnificence is nothing less than awe-inspiring. In one memory, I am in my master's office, and there lies a decorative box on his desk. It has been agreed that in order to maintain our friendship and trust, this box must never be opened by me, and something I knew within this incarnation, I had never done. Finally, I recall lying on a mat in a huge, stone basement of some kind. My master is with me, along with a few other men, and I am dying. They are there to comfort me and stay with me until I have passed after contracting some illness of one kind or another. This demonstrated to me the strong bond both my master and I had for one another, and the loyalty I had demonstrated on my end.

When I was in high school (in this present life), I remember looking through a history book, and of those images of the famous Taj Mahal. The moment I clocked eyes on this incredible edifice, I knew this was where I'd been in service, or very much within the perimeter of this ornate tomb. I recall another entrance to the building, and very different from the famous scene of the Taj Mahal's Lotus Pond, which is most commonly illustrated. I distinctly recollect an entrance gate to the West, and upon searching other books, I found it! This had been in the days long before the internet. The question is, had I been in service to the fifth Mughal Emperor, Shah Jahan? It was he who had commissioned the assembly of the Taj Mahal back in 1631. Construction began in 1632 and was completed in 1648. There had been another five years of work after this period around the site, which had been created by the Emperor in memory of his wife, Mumtaz Mahal, who'd sadly died in childbirth. No less than 20,000 artisans, labourers, and painters had assisted in the creation of the Taj Mahal, one of the world's Seven Wonders. I also have a deep affiliation with the Indian community and feel very much at home in their company. Perhaps those inherent memories stored within the etheric body occasionally seep through from our past lives and, I'm sure, combine with the shaping of our personality as we develop through each incarnation.

Another equally sad memory is of me being a tramp, living in a small, brick shelter somewhere up North in England. I can see the faint lights of a fenced-off factory in the distance, and my makeshift abode is within an expanse of rough grassland. Ahead of me, I can see a hill where a row of suburban houses sits. I know within this life that I am not a drinker, or in any way troublesome. A kind lady comes down from the hill every day with her two children to give me food, drink, and books. It is evident that I liked to read back then, but the depressing view of the factory and the smell of a sort of electrical/sulphur odour in the air, along with the appearance of fog, gave rise to a feeling of no prospects for my future. I was evidently a hermit with no family. Even today, when I see fog or get that occasional smell in the air of sulphur, it invokes deep feelings of sadness.

I vaguely recall living as a monk in what I believed was Tibet. I can still see high, rolling mountains with the early morning mist, and know that our monastery is isolated and at some height within a mountainous area. I feel a great peace and connection with the land around me. The visual memory is beautiful.

In yet another of these past-life memories, I am a rich, Italian boy. I can actually recall the details of the large house I lived in. As you enter from the street, you have to climb down some ornate stairs, as though going into the basement of the house. Here, I have a mother who is cold and unloving, and I find I have to spend a lot of time running errands for her. She is a plump, but magnificently dressed lady. Within the house, there is a long, marble corridor which opens up to several other rooms. The house holds expensive furnishings, but I feel sad because of my mother's lack of love or attention. I have a feeling I am without a father.

I believe I had also been a Cowboy in a past life, too, which I have illustrated in a later chapter, namely because this ties in with my spirit guide, and may indicate how the past can indeed affect our future.

One other recollection is of me residing in Gloucestershire, England, and I'm a small, old, and bespectacled man living in a room filled with books. I am alone and sad, but find comfort in the literature that surrounds me. For some reason, I get that depressing feeling that my life here is filled with emptiness, with no family or partner to share with. When such memories surface, I find myself deeply troubled by these incarnations because each of them denotes a level of emotional and material subjugation.

I have a few more past life recalls, but not as strong as the one in India, or the other of me living up North as a tramp. We assume that our development as souls is exclusive only to Earth, but this is a big misconception. There are two other memories I have, and I am certain not from this world.

**The Glass, Alien Tower**

This recollection is the most suffocating of all. Here, I find myself trapped inside an enormous glass tower that has every amenity for survival, but also feels like a prison, nonetheless. I can see through thick glass panels to the right of my cramped living quarters a reddish, desert landscape outside, complete with a crimson sky, and am aware that the atmosphere on this planet is inhospitable. There is no other sign of life as far as I can observe, and I notice that from where I am positioned, I am at a great height. Giving a simple example and using a block of high-rise flats as an indication tells me that my position in this object would be around mid-section within elevation. It's also puzzling to me to know whether there are other people in this complex besides myself, but if this is the case, they are completely sealed off from me. I have a feeling that I'm inside a ship that has marooned itself on this alien planet. I can move up and down within the small compartments of my sleeping quarters, kitchen, and bathroom, all of which are positioned in close proximity within the varied chambers through a long, narrow opening. Imagine a tube, and on either side of that tube are tiny rooms with no doors. It seriously is cramped here! I can float within these varied sections of my abode via levitation from one compartment to another, which would denote a vast decrease in gravity. The sensation of knowing I'm confined and helpless to do anything about the situation terrifies me. There is one sure fact which I do know; this is where I die!

**The Alien Planet**

The other clear, yet brief memory I have is of viewing a room filled with computer technology. The walls are littered with screens and lights, but upon the floor, within the centre of the room, is a small, rounded basin which appears moulded in nature. Inside this circular basin are more lights, and I know this is primarily a modern crib where I was born. From my vantage point, even though I am enclosed within this incredible compound, there is a feeling of total exhilaration. I somehow know that I'm in a structure that reaches way beyond the clouds of this planet, and its beauty is beyond comprehension. I cannot emphasise enough such sensations which fill me with wonderment and joy. There, the image ends.

There are varied beliefs from numerous religions and faiths, which have their own spin on reincarnation, and others who take the viewpoint that we only have one incarnation, and that's your lot! However, whatever side of the fence you prefer to lean on, the soul of the individual appears to come to earth (or any other number of systems) for a reason.

Those who are able to recall fragments of their previous incarnations, whether through memory or regression, indicate a somewhat puzzling trait. For instance, you could find yourself as a rich man in one life, and then as a poor woman in the next. The sex of the individual, however, matters not, as the soul is completely androgynous in nature, and serves only as a template for '*experience*' while incarnation on this planet (or any number, for that matter) takes hold. It makes sense to assume that the very essence of the spirit is what's important as it moves through its varied journeys. The physical matter is discarded when its mission has been completed. Many believe that our soul progression must elevate us materially within each spiritual evolutionary cycle, but this is not the case. Those who walk among us now in the flesh and who are themselves rich fear, through the act of death, losing everything. Well, they do say that you can't take your money or possessions with you when you cross over to the other side! For this reason alone, many are horrified by the idea of reincarnation as a whole, simply because they're currently experiencing a life which fills them with all the luxuries possible. The very thought of coming back as a vagabond, or in a third-world country, would be their own horror story realised. However, there have been many cases within a near death experience where such wealthy individuals have come to realise when crossing over and going through what is commonly known as a 'Panoramic Life Review' that all their wealth imaginable means nothing when addressing the real nature of the soul, and of its subsequent inherent purpose.

**The Panoramic Life Review**

The 'Panoramic Life Review' is a process whereby the soul of an individual recounts the entire episode of their life journey in minute detail. This is to say that every thought, emotion, and action is taken into account and clearly displayed in a type of holographic image around the newly departed soul. They will be immersed within their own journey as though they are reliving their life all over again, and are shown how their actions affected others around them. Not only this, but they will come to realise how they made others feel. This, I believe, is what they refer to as 'karma,' but one which does not send the soul of the person into the depths of hell. Far from it. Hell is only a state of mind, but a reality, nonetheless. In the majority of cases, and when some souls do experience seeing demons, or abhorred creatures, they are normally saved by a higher force which pulls them away from that environment. The Panoramic Life Review clearly demonstrates cause and effect, good and bad, love and hate; the very qualities which we are all equipped with while in human form. The experience also lets the soul know how others thought about them while on earth, so there is a united understanding of the hows and whys of life. Once the review is over, the soul then gravitates to the astral planes. There are higher and lower dimensions of awareness, but the astral is, so we understand through regression and near-death studies, the main entry point of any soul when death ensues. On some occasions, no review is initiated, but I am sure one is undertaken at some point within the journey.

We can also consider that just such a life review is undertaken purely to decide if that soul wishes to reincarnate back into the earth system. There is a choice, or so it seems. Although now absent of time, many spirits do not fear making a decision in reincarnating. Indeed, their awareness that life is eternal while in this higher vibrational state of being doesn't seem to concern them in the least. Seeing as they are no longer inhibited by a process of restricted consciousness, and having access to a greater mental awareness assures them that another physical life is perceived as a step further towards their spiritual evolution. That said, it's a very different story while in this current incarnation. Because of the uncertainty, there is no question of our doubting what happens when we have left this life well and truly behind. In varied cases in near-death experiences, a soul is usually given a choice as to whether they wish to stay on the spirit side or return to earth to complete their mission. Normally, the returning soul is met by elevated masters, or loved ones who will allow them to see the overall results of their decision if they want to remain, especially for those they knew or loved back on earth, and how their absence would seriously hinder the growth and development for them. This is interesting because here we can see that some form of future *is* set in stone, and one the spirits can clearly see in terms of an '*outcome.*' The famous American author and regressionist, Dolores Cannon wrote of one case in her book '*Between Death and Life, Conversations With a Spirit*' (Gateway 1993) where a lady who'd crossed over after complications during a lung procedure wanted to stay in the afterlife after repeatedly being questioned by elevated souls who gently reminded her of the serious repercussions this would have on those back home if she decided to exit the physical realm altogether. She'd been insistent she was to remain and was never forced by those who'd greeted her within the light, but stated that if she was to reside here, then she would have to remain '*close to the edge*' and help her children, along with others, with their own lives on earth. The lady knew instinctively that this so-called '*edge*' would not permit her to fully remain in heaven until her guidance from spirit to those in the material had been accomplished. Naturally, she agreed to return to her body, which made everyone on the other side happy. This '*edge*' is perhaps a slightly lower field of vibrational reality which brings the departed much closer to those of us here on earth, and whereby a complete crossing cannot be achieved. I would not consider this a suggestion that the soul would be earth-bound, but I'm pretty sure it's as close to this as one can get. An earth-bound spirit is someone who (and in the vast majority of cases) does not realise they've died and are themselves in some kind of spiritual limbo. They will drift around on earth until a realisation from their end kicks in and they are thus helped back to the spirit world.

**Life Planning on the Other Side**

A life planned by a soul before its incarnation leads us to consider that an enormous level of action and intent is foreseen not only for the evolving soul but every life touched by each spark of awareness that decides to reincarnate within the same timeline. I have always postulated as to the overall purpose of this eternal progression beyond the material, but know on a deeper level it makes sense. We tend to complicate matters while in the here and now, yet for those on the other side, it's all quite simple in terms of understanding. While writing this book covering the subject surrounding planning our journey before we come to earth, I had a very startling and crystal-clear vision while in meditation of a large circuit-board, and upon this advanced looking component, I could see six wires which appeared slightly jagged to the left, but more or less in straight lines the rest of their width across the board to its right. These had been highlighted in an electric blue colour. I messaged Chris and told him, stunned by the clarity of this clairvoyant image. Had spirit been giving me a message in a symbolic fashion for me to know *they,* on their side, were aware of my questioning this?

Or was I seeing my own life's blueprint? I found the whole thing fascinating. The vision had been met with another scene directly after the manifestation of the circuit-board, and which had left me equally shocked, namely because I felt sure I was being shown something of my future here, and that my constant asking for things to change within my life may well yet be realised. Here's hoping! However, those souls who have experienced an NDE have stated that they have seen more or less the same image when asked about their life planning. In the film, which was made into a trilogy, *'The Matrix,'* a similar object was shown to one of the central characters. This does not mean to say that we all carry such *'physical'* circuit-boards in our biological form (well, not yet anyway!), but this best illustrates how detailed and complex going through the human journey is. It's not clear how exactly a soul reincarnates, or the process involved, but we may have some clues. I often wondered if there is some reincarnation chamber in the spirit world, or that, perhaps, we just fall asleep in heaven and send a part of our consciousness into its new, awaiting Avatar. How do we choose a physical body, along with the family, as well as the life ahead? Chris' recall of his incarnation serves as a template and gives us varied clues as to the process involved. It's not just about visually seeing the events as they transpire, but the feelings and sensations appear to be the most important part of it all.

The only memory I have (if indeed this was my decision to reincarnate back on earth) was of sitting in a beautiful room which had enormous windows, adorned by thick, red curtains tied neatly back to give a clear view outside. Warm lights came from above, and I found myself seated with a dozen or so other adults around the room's perimeter who remained in complete silence. What's interesting is that when looking out of the window, it appeared the building we were in was directly atop a small cliff elevated just above sea level, and from which a storm was brewing. The clouds were a dark grey, and I had the feeling this was the waters of life, and that our prevailing silence was an indication that the incarnation process was about to occur.

Most NDEers describe having a meeting with elders (a council of wise souls) on the other side who discuss with them their return to earth. Although each encounter with these Elders is unique to the individual, it nevertheless informs us that we are helped to some degree by elevated beings who know of future events which are to occur in the soul's journey, and all within this timeless province we call 'h*eaven.*' Writer, producer, and director of '*The Lossen,*' Colin Skevington recalls just such a moment when he had been taken back to his existence in the afterlife during a Life-Between-Lives regression session. This process of regression has proven to be most interesting when accessing memories of life in the spirit world. Colin is a filmmaker and developed an incredible spiritual film starring well-known actors, Sean Knopp, Albert Welling, and Linda Marlowe, and a story that demonstrates how our actions on earth can affect the life's path for others. His film has an uncanny twist at the end, which will most certainly get you thinking.

Long before he'd set about creating his own films, Colin never felt comfortable with the world he was in, an expression felt by many on earth that we hear so often. He knew on a deeper level, after experiencing many synchronicities, there had to be more to our existence, and that certain areas within our lives demonstrate this through the advent of remarkable 'coincidences' he has personally experienced. Colin discovered there were no such things as mere coincidence, but that a pathway appears to be mapped out for us in all our lives, leading us, perhaps, to our ultimate fate. He wanted to discover whether we'd been on earth before, and if there was any truth to the claims of previous lives, and not just through incidents such as Dèjá vu, which gives the impression we've done something before, but that the world around us is a reflection of ourselves. As a filmmaker and writer, he considers that the world is translating hidden messages to us from spirit in an effort to help us along our journey. Colin believes it's up to us to look at these messages and see what it is we need to change within ourselves, along with embracing more of our spiritual nature than the physical make-up of our reality.

Is there a supernatural world influencing our natural one? Colin's film '*The Lossen*' came about because of his need to explore the spiritual realms, which had initially developed when he'd suffered writer's block. Through a mutual contact, Colin was put in touch with a hypnotherapist named Deborah, who suggested over the phone that he may have to go through two sessions to try and counteract the block he was having. During his first hypnosis session, his writer's block disappeared completely, as if the floodgates had opened and he was now able to create with ease. Also in this regression, Colin recalls having a past life experience where he found himself living in a small cottage by the coast in Scotland. He's not sure if this could have been in or around the 17th century period, but in this life, he'd been a married man and was having an affair with another woman. Unfortunately for him, Colin's wife found out and, in a rage, stabbed him in the neck, thus ending his life. His wife explained to him, before his death by her hands, that if *she* couldn't have Colin, then neither could his girlfriend. Once his wife had executed her foul deed, she then committed suicide by throwing herself off the cliffs near their home. The weird part to this is that Colin had a birthmark on his neck. Is this (as is discovered in so many reported cases when dealing with past life investigations) a mark which appears to be carried through to the future-self due to some type of '*Past Trauma Blueprinting*' being physically transferred through the body within a previous incarnation? We hear so often about birthmarks and finding that someone had either been stabbed or wounded in exactly the area where such marks are located on the body. Ever since Colin's regression within this life, his birthmark has completely disappeared! He recounts a story from a boy in India who'd been run over and killed by a car in a previous incarnation, and within his regression, the boy kept repeating, '*I've been run over!*' In the exact spot where he claimed to have been struck by a vehicle, he had a birthmark.

Deborah asked him if he wanted to still go ahead with the second session he'd booked, seeing as his main objective had now been cured. Colin agreed but was unprepared for Deborah's response. She wanted to try out a past-life regression on him, seeing as she was training as a 'Life-Between-Lives' regressionist within the '*Michael Newton Institute.*' Dr Michael Newton had been a pioneering clinical hypnotherapist based in the United States, and had authored '*Destiny of Souls*,' along with '*Journey of Souls*.' His work came about accidentally when he'd been trying to help a man who'd been suffering intense pain to his side, and upon taking him back to childhood where no such memory of the incident could be found, his patient started relaying information of him being a young soldier who'd been killed in the First Battle of Somme in a past life, and where 20,000 young men had been wiped out on the first day of the battle in the year 1916. This had been a joint operation between the British and French forces intended to achieve a crucial victory over the Germans on the Western Front. Newton had been shocked when asking for the man's name in his previous life, along with rank and number, all of which checked out as accurate when the doctor had made his own inquiries with the War Office. This led Newton in a full-time capacity to study the subject, if only to help others within their healing, as well as exploring those Life-Between-Lives states.

Colin recalls he'd had a mind-blowing session which lasted for three hours. He describes the experience of being put into regression like someone having had too many drinks. He was aware of what was going on as these memories surfaced, but at the same time, felt completely detached from his body. For the therapist to get their subject to a Life-Between-Lives condition, Colin explained that they need to move you through time to the end of an incarnation relevant to the theme of the Life-between-Lives session, whereby the episode of your life in spirit can then be explored. Within his altered state of consciousness, Colin saw a row of doors presented within his mind, and these he assumed were varied entrances to a multitude of past lives he'd previously lived. He chose one and as he opened the door, found himself in an ornate wood-panelled study which he felt was from the period surrounding the early 19th Century. As he entered, he saw varied glass cabinets in which lay jars of herbs. Instantly, Colin knew he'd been a doctor who'd used herbs to treat his patients. Deborah asked him to take himself to the point where he was about to exit this life as a doctor so that they could explore the afterlife. Colin describes this part as rather similar to watching a film, and where he was both the observer and the person at the same time. Immediately, the scene switched upon the regressionist's instructions, and Colin saw himself in bed, dying of pneumonia. He could see his wife, along with his son and daughter standing close to his side and recalls many people entering the room who he feels were those patients he'd treated coming in to pay their last respects, many of whom clearly stating that they wouldn't be here if it hadn't been for his medical know-how. Colin had been overwhelmed by the amount of visitors he'd had. When the regressionist had asked him to move forward to his death, he suddenly found himself in a deep, emotional state, crying uncontrollably. He didn't want to die because he'd been blessed in the life he was reliving, but at the same time, and while lying on the couch, Deborah had to try and remove his emotions so that clarity could be attained, asking him why he was crying so much. Colin replied that while in this incarnation, he'd had the perfect life and didn't want to die. He could see this all happening from above, as though being a witness to his physical end as a detached observer. His wife and children began to cry, and then, as this scene ended, Colin, who'd been previously distressed, suddenly found himself laughing and feeling elated. Deborah asked why he was laughing, and he replied by stating that he was excited to now be reunited with his father and grandfather in spirit.

Once his reunion came to an end, an equally colourful man suddenly materialised. Colin likened the individual to one of the character creations from J. R. R. Tolkien's famous *'Lord of the Rings'* and wondered as a writer himself whether this was purely all down to his imagination, or that this little fellow had revealed himself in this way so as to appear different, and as we know spirit guides often do. Their guise informs their subject that they are helpers from the other side. He'd been equally shocked when this seemingly pleasant and jolly man told him that it was now time for his life to be reviewed. Colin had a strong feeling this was indeed his spirit guide (although he couldn't be sure) and duly followed him into a beautiful garden towards a stone bench where they both now sat. Upon seating himself, he was overwhelmed by a distinct but strong smell of Orange Blossom and Jasmine, and he explains that whenever he comes into contact with these smells, it feels to him like he's been transported to heaven, and long before his session with Deborah had taken place. It is obvious that certain aromas trigger memories deep within the human psyche, but such recollections are too embedded while we remain within the conscious state, in being able to understand where their roots lie within cognizance. Many people have more or less the same feelings they are unable to translate due to their senses being overwhelmed in this manner, and are, in most cases, clear indications that varied recalls of past incarnations, as well as those lived on the other side are multi-layered and hard to access, unless brought forward by a qualified regressionist. There had been no Orange Blossom or Jasmine in the room while Colin's session was taking place. The spirit guide went on to explain to Colin that he'd had the perfect life and asked if he'd remembered why he'd chosen this almost flawless incarnation. Colin replied by stating that he couldn't remember why this was the case, and at this point the guide asked him to follow through to some large doors within a hallway and into a separate chamber where he was now presented by a group of seven people (a mixture of males and females) seated behind a semi-circular table. He'd felt they were more akin to a council of wise souls, or what he termed as *'Elders.'* These Elders viewed him with compassion, and Colin's attention was drawn to a lady seated directly at the centre of the table. She wore around her neck a gold chain, at the end of which hung the letter 'S.' Colin wondered whether this was linked to his surname in the here and now, '*Skevington*' or whether it had some connection to the British television and film producer, writer, voice actress, and costume designer, Sylvia Anderson who'd been married to Gerry Anderson, famous for the children's series '*Thunderbirds,*' among countless other incredible productions. At the time, Colin didn't associate it with Sylvia Anderson. It was years later when he happened by chance to see a photograph of her wearing a chain around her neck with the initial on it. Were these Elders giving him a sign that his future life's work would also be linked with writing, television and film making? Colin himself had been a great fan of the late Gerry Anderson's work and met him once. As a young kid, he'd written to Gerry and got a reply from the great man himself, especially with his creation of '*Space 1999*' which Colin loved so much. Upon discussing these memories, he has kindly allowed us to use his experiences in our book and sent me two pictures of Sylvia Anderson at a function. Around her neck she is clearly seen to be wearing an identical gold necklace, complete with a large 'S' initial attached to the chain, which Colin had seen around the Elder's neck. Coincidence? A prediction? He was not sure.

The female sitting at the centre of the table and wearing the necklace reiterated the same question which his spirit guide had previously asked Colin, '*You had the perfect life. Can you remember why we guided you to choose this perfect life?*' He replied by saying, '*I have no idea!*', but what he really wanted to say was that he wished someone would just tell him because he was beginning to get a little frustrated by the question. As though detecting his exasperation, the female continued by saying, '*You had the perfect life because you had many lives on e<u>arth</u> where you shared your spiritual knowledge, and you have a real insight into these matters. In varied lives, you have been persecuted for sharing that knowledge. So, we agreed with you that you would have the perfect life in order to share your wisdom without persecution. What happened was that the key part of your life, those coming in at the end of this, your last physical incarnation, was primarily to give thanks to you, and something as a clear indication to demonstrate the results of sharing your knowledge, and of the enormous impact it had on other souls. That's why you had that life.*'

It's interesting because this Elder had stated, '... *many lives on earth.'* Could this be a clear indication that the soul has the choice to incarnate on other worlds, other than Earth, too? Colin recalls becoming quite emotional by the Elder's last statement. Deborah asked him if they could go forward to see why he had chosen to be Colin in this, his present life, and asked what was now happening. He suddenly found himself back with the same group of Elders, and the lady wearing the necklace told him that, *'.... We'd like you to go back during a time of great change, because there's going to be significant transformations to occur on Earth. We need you to go and share your knowledge at this time.'* Colin was humoured and replied, *'Oh, do I have to?'* The Elder stated,' *'Well, not really, but we'd rather you did!'* After he had agreed to take on the mission, he finished by saying he would go, but on two conditions. The first being that he wanted to be completely physically protected, that he would have a body suitable for his next incarnation, which would not become ill and inhibit his ability to complete the mission, and secondly, that he'd do the job, go in quickly, and then get out. Interestingly, he'd been told by varied mediums that he'd have a long life, and when his passing was due, it would be quick. Deborah interjected and asked how he chose to become Colin. What was the procedure for deciding his next body? He explained that you are given choices for a suitable human form with which to incarnate, and this is accomplished by various 'models' which were presented to Colin energetically. We can imagine that such a method would be likened to some form of holographic imagery, and whereby Colin's astral body would slip into his available future self, rather like trying on a suit, thereby allowing him some insight in to how he would be able to adapt within his biological vessel (they draw the holographic body up from the place you could incarnate). He was given four bodies to choose from and rejected two of them instantly. The last two had been a male and a female, and he decided to go with the male because he wanted to be able to have a male voice vibration, and this vibration suited his needs in every capacity. This is not to say that females are not matched in terms of strength like males (especially within our modern times), but for the period of Colin's next regeneration in human form was essential towards his overall mission. He knows there are key points within our lives which we map for ourselves, along with free will, but ultimately, there is a blueprint of design and order. Colin believes we are experiencing all of ourselves through aspects of ourselves, rather like a central character in a story who goes on a journey, and on that journey are themselves tested. They will invariably come across others whom they will either love or dislike, but really, these are elements of yourself yearning to unite with the sum total of those parts of you which are seen within the reflection of others. Once we stop judging others and find tools that can help us connect with the divine, then we are well on our way to discovering a larger aspect of our illusory, separate selves. Many of us do not like the shadow side of what we term negative, but working with it can help us heal and progress along our life's journey. Colin took great comfort from a book written by Debbie Ford called *'The Dark Side of the Light Chasers'* (Hodder Paperbacks, 2001), which best illustrates how we can completely transform those destructive and negative energies around us and use these to our advantage in a positive light. Colin states that this is really about asking the question, 'Why am I witnessing particular situations in my life? If you come across angry people, perhaps we need to heal the anger within ourselves. What we see as negative in another, and if we respond emotionally to it, then we need to look at that shadow aspect within ourselves and heal it, and our outer world changes for the better.

In a future event organised by Colin's regressionist, Debbie, he was delighted to learn that she'd made plans for a weekend Life-Between-Lives assembly to be held in the Swan Hotel in Bedford, and right on Colin's doorstep. Although the seminar had been for up to forty-three people (most of whom were coming from all over Europe) who were also to be trained in Michael Newton's 'Life-between-Lives' program (forty-four, including Debbie), she realised she was one person short after someone pulled out and duly asked Colin if he would mind attending, not to train but, rather, be the one taken through his past memories. The group would work in pairs, and it was important that no one was left out. Colin jumped at the chance, if only to understand more of who he was and the journeys he'd taken in previous lives, seeing as his preceding sitting with Debbie had opened incredible areas of deep contemplation.

On this occasion, and once again taken into a Life-Between-Lives episode, Colin found himself being a victim of the Holocaust in Auschwitz (a genocide program which ran from 1941-1945). There had been numerous camps spread throughout German-occupied Poland, and a few others in Austria. In these devastating systematic Euthanasia extermination centres, primarily instigated by

Nazi Germany and by the ruthless dictator, Hitler, more than six-million European Jews had been annihilated. One and a half million of those had been children. Within this existence, Colin now saw himself as a Polish man, and interestingly, he had two children (the same as he'd had in his previous early 19th-century life as a Doctor of Medicine) along with a wife whom he knew had perished within the camp. He was also shocked to discover this incarnation was far removed from the one that had promised him a perfect life. Colin recalls being in a room where he was being experimented on. It is known that many years after the Second World War, varied extermination camps were used as a means for crude medical research to be tested on people in the most horrendous ways, too upsetting to include within the pages of our book. Auschwitz had been the base of the evil German doctor, Josef Mengele, also known as the *'Angel of Death.'* Although Mengele had not been wholly responsible for all 400,000 deaths through such gruesome experimentation (there being some fifty doctors based at Auschwitz in total), he was well known by those survivors as being the most notorious of them all. After the war, Mengele would escape detection, along with prosecution, and was the one who would select people within the camp who were too ill to work and who had been unknowingly sent to their deaths in the gas chambers. Mengele had been particularly interested in twins, so it is almost certain that any appearing on base would have been dealt with by his hand. Colin recalls being strapped down on a bed, having something pushed down his throat, which made him choke, and subsequently dying as a result of this. Whatever instrument had been used had obstructed his respiratory system. What's also incredible is that in this, Colin's present life, he used to have problems swallowing, and after he'd had his regression, where such details of his passing at Auschwitz surfaced, these persistent issues ceased.

In another Life-between-Lives session, Colin recollects being in another world. With the people here, he encountered balance and harmony and is certain this was another planet because Earth has always been met with strife and conflict throughout its long-suffering sojourn, where the human race is concerned. He found himself living a happy and joyful existence, which he finds hard to describe due to its perfection. The sky was a beautiful blue, and the temperature was just right. The people wore robes and went about their business of the day on a purely empathic level. The emotions he felt had been incredibly positive and at odds with those on earth. He remembers being by a beautiful bay looking out across a calm ocean. The townsfolk went about their business in a simple fashion around open markets, selling a multitude of items situated close to the bay. On a spiritual level, the familiarity and warmth filled Colin with an incredible sensation of being at '*home*' (a feeling many who have returned back to their original place of origin beyond the material usually describe) and considered this world to be as such. He remembered tasting a Mango at one of the stalls and can still recall its rich flavour; as though this fruit had been the real thing, unlike those back on earth where we can consider everything within its material sense is nothing more than a blueprint created from its original source within these higher states of awareness. The regressionist who'd been one of the workshop attendees asked Colin, while exploring this past life, if he was bored being in a world of perfection, and Colin replied that he had been. There was nothing further he felt he could contribute in the way of learning here, and he was on his way to see the Elders in the village to ask if he could leave this reality. Once among the Elders, they quizzed him, asking him if he was sure this was what he wanted. He'd been resolute that he was up for another challenge, and they, in turn, gave him their blessing. What's interesting here is that Colin then took himself to the beach where he duly sat upon the sand and began to meditate. Within this altered state of consciousness, his spirit rose. He saw the empty shell of his body he was leaving behind just sitting perfectly and as exactly as he had left it – on the beach! Just how the process of reincarnation is achieved varies, but we understand that when we talk of spiritual realms, our energy is matched by that frequency when we are there. While in this world, Earth to Colin would be as much a dream as we imagine such realms from our side to be. Taking into consideration the fact that within this existence, Colin had been presented with numerous body choices in which to incarnate, the reason is clear due to his being bored and could offer no more in the way of progression. This, I believe, depends on the assignment undertaken in the next life, or that Colin was sufficiently advanced within his own spiritual development that he could make that choice himself. He reiterates by stating that the body is not what we think it is. When he'd gone to see his father, who'd just passed in hospital, he says that upon viewing the body he knew that it wasn't him! The biological form appears mechanical in nature, robbed now of its spark of life. Once the life essence leaves its temporary vehicle, the shell begins to look identical to other cadavers, and something hospital staff explained to him when he'd made this observation. It is the soul that brings life into its Avatar.

Chris also has recollections of past lives, although in fragmented form, like many of those with regard to such deeply embedded memories within the psyche. Three of these are prevalent within his mind. One was of him running through a street in ancient Egypt, the other of living inside a damp castle, which he described as being cosy, and the other of being a soldier, drowning at sea when the ship he was on had been struck by the enemy. Interestingly, Chris's recall of the incarnation process, and of being able to experience an OBE as a baby, are more prevalent within his mind than those lived on this planet.

Regarding Earth being the only planet within the entirety of existence for the incarnation/reincarnation development appears questionable. Is this really the only physical system of reality within our vast cosmos where souls go through their rigorous learning and advancement within the process of rebirth? We are reminded so constantly within the media cartel that this planet is the only intelligent world which supports life, and if there is any suggestion that other 'lifeforms' could be present within the universe, then it's too far away for us to concern ourselves about. We know, however, that our world has been visited by 'non-terrestrial entities.' It appears strange when looking at the UFO phenomenon that many view these topics as completely unrelated within the spiritual subject. It would be interesting to know whether such entities we call *'space men'*, go through a similar procedure of incarnation as we do, and whether they are met with similar challenges we face on earth. The study of Ufology indicates that we may be dealing with an interdimensional singularity, and this is fascinating within its extreme. So, if we are to assume that there are indeed other planets which harbour their civilisations, then what's to say we haven't found ourselves incarnating within such worlds? We hear so much about the 'human' experience, and less of the extra-terrestrial reality in these matters, and an area sadly much frowned upon within the UFO community simply because of mental conditioning by our own system which is, in any case, seriously restricted within its current grasp of reality, and as discovered within the field of quantum mechanics which throws the majority of what we *'think'* we know right out of the basket where logical thought is concerned. Most will not address the spiritual nature to such contacts, preferring instead to go along with the theory that all extraterrestrials are coming from within our physical realm. Thankfully, others are taking the interdimensional hypothesis more seriously these days. There are some incredible souls on our world who have had direct knowledge imparted through to them, and not always within an 'alien abduction' or being a 'Contactee' as one would come to expect within the UFO department, but from another intelligence communicating directly through to its conduit using the mind, and with no external force or interaction. Such individuals are known as 'channels' and there are a number whose imparted knowledge and published work have literally astounded the scientific community in terms of theoretical content. One of these was author and medium, Jane Roberts, an American channel who discovered a personality called '*Seth*' while using a Ouija board, and which then developed on with Seth working through Jane as a direct voice-link. The Seth material came largely to the public's attention back in 1972 and has since gone on to sell more than eight million copies worldwide. The first in many books published surrounding the metaphysical teachings of Seth and titled '*Seth Speaks: The Eternal Validity of the Soul,*' (Prentice-Hall 1972) Jane's work through this incredible non-physical entity was to become one of the most important in understanding aspects of the soul, its origins, along with reincarnation. Seth is (in the sense that this personality is not dead, and never has been, for that matter!) a non-physical teacher who has informed his audience through his human interpreter that death is nothing less than an illusion, and that we move into varied spheres of reality upon our physical departure from this plane. His work through Jane has proven to be the most dynamic in terms of the philosophical approach, and many embrace today, especially through such other channels like Neale Donald Walsch, author of '*Conversations With God*' (Marcia Montenegro, 1995), among others.

**No Time Like the Present**

Artist, author, podcaster, filmmaker, UFO and paranormal researcher, Neil Geddes-Ward whom I have known for many years, and of such books as '*Faeriecraft*' (Hay House Inc 2005) and '*True Tales of the Paranormal: Spirits, Ghosts and the Hidden World,*' (Arcturus 2024) has been fascinated in the subject surrounding the afterlife himself. Here, he draws emphasis to reincarnation specifically:

*'When people die and go on to an afterlife and rejoin with those that have died before them, it seems straightforward. Well, to those that believe in that type of scenario, of course! You live your life and then you move on to another dimension of existence. It is the 'Kindergarten' explanation that works very well for most folk who consult mediums or visit spiritualist churches. It's a working model that suits us very well. But it is, of course, not the whole story.*

*Just as in a driver who jumps into their car to go to work and navigates their way through the busy roads to get to their destination, there is a whole lot more going on under the bonnet of the car and most drivers are too focused on the windscreen ahead, and rightly so! But when the car starts to run rough or makes strange noises, one of the first things to be taken into consideration is what is going on under the bonnet.*

*When your life may run rough, and not go smoothly, a doctor, or psychologist, or even a medium may be the first person to listen to you, and then lift the bonnet to see what is going on beneath. A doctor may tell you to take a rest and be prescribed medicine, a psychologist may suggest a course of therapeutic counselling to relax you. A medium may bring in a deceased loved one who send their support from the spirit world to help you through your difficulties. When things are too challenging to understand, people tend to point to issues that may have occurred to them before, not in their present lifetime but in a previous existence, and something they may not be aware of. Reincarnation is the term given to the belief that you are more than your present personality, and that in the past, you were born into a different time period. In that time period, say 1570, you lived in the Southwest of England as a man whose wife had died, and you live alone in your cottage, but get help from a young housekeeper who is only a 12-year-old girl. You have no clear memory of that life, but under the power of a hypnotist, they are able to relax you and take you back in time to that period to discover any difficulties you may have had then that affect you in your present moment. You may have a stutter in your present life, like a car engine that stutters. So, the hypnotist lifts the bonnet of your mind and takes a peek inside and searches out what might be causing the issue. The medieval existence reveals that you as that man in 1570 did not speak out in support of another man wrongly accused of a crime, and so this man was tried and executed. You held on to this guilt and subconsciously it affects your present lifetime so that you* cannot speak out when you need to. By revealing the cause of this guilt in the past, your present self then changes, and guilt is released and the stutter that so troubles you in the present then goes and you are heard more clearly.

That is a very simplified explanation of how previous lives may affect your present condition. Just as an engineer may tune up your car so that it no longer stutters, he may also adjust or replace the timing belt to ensure nothing major causes an engine problem. In reincarnation, there is a timing belt too, one that is constantly flexing and adjusting, you could say, due to the nature of time itself. However, with time, we are constantly used to the idea of one moment before another. In fact, it is quite handy, you agree to meet me at the town hall at twelve pm, and I also arrive there at the same time, where we discuss our business. We work to a clock. However, this is far from the truth!

Time, according to the spirit personality known as 'Seth,' occurs all at once. The present moment is all we really have; there is no past or future in the real sense. 'Seth' described himself as a 'Personality Essence no longer focused in the Physical.' Jane Roberts was a writer, and in the mid-1960s, Jane experimented with Ouija boards with her husband, Rob. After numerous attempts, a personality came through the board, calling himself Frank Withers, who had died some years before. He began to talk about various philosophical topics, most notably life after death, reincarnation, and so forth. Eventually, this personality dispensed with communicating through the board and began to speak through Jane Roberts whilst she went into a deep trance-like state. He then revealed that he was, in fact, a higher soul for the personality called Frank Withers, and could now be called 'Seth'. Over the following twenty years, Seth came through Jane and began dictating books on life, death, reincarnation, spiritual existence, metaphysical subjects, which included the idea of simultaneous time. They became bestsellers in their field and are hailed as classics in the New Age, Mind-Body-Spirit categories.

Seth explained that we create our own reality through our thoughts and beliefs. This explains why people might get into difficulties in their own lives, because the restricting beliefs are controlling them, and which they may hold on to. So, in order to change your life, you have to change your beliefs. He also explained that the idea of reincarnation was not correct. So instead of one life following another, all your lives exist at once. This for us, living in this apparent life of *moments passing by, turning into weeks, or months and then years, seems hard for us to grasp.*

*But if you try and imagine, say a record made of vinyl that we used to play on record players, this might give you a unique perspective in trying to understand it. On a long-playing record or album, you may get, say, five songs on one side of it. So, in order to play and experience those songs, you place the record stylus or needle on the outer part of the record, and it falls into a fine groove or track impressed into the record. The needle follows this path as the record rotates on the player. Eventually, it picks up the first song and you hear it playing through the speakers. After four minutes, the song fades out or stops suddenly and there are five seconds of silence before the next track begins, and so forth. If you imagine your lifetimes, one after the other like the songs on the record, playing with a short gap in between, the gap could be viewed as your moment of existence in the afterlife, the song ends, your present life, and then the silence begins, which is silence of a kind for those you have left behind on earth. After a time in the spirit world, you may reincarnate, and this is where the next song begins. If you held up the long-playing record to your face and tilted it at an angle, you may be able to see the tracks as lines on the record with darker lines between the tracks. The darker lines are where the silence is between the songs. But you are looking at all the songs at the same time, including the silence or darker lines. You can see from this perspective that all those songs exist at the same time. But in order for you to hear or experience them, you have to position the record on the player, place the needle onto the record, and then hear the music play out.*

*Some songs are very upbeat and rocky. Others later in the album might be more slow and sadder in tempo, and you as the listener may change your mood subtly as the songs play out and change as it progresses. Your lives may also be upbeat and rocky, and also sad in others. Each song tells a kind of story, and the song writer and singer are yourself on every track. But you take on a different role in each song, singing it in soft tones with one verse and extremely high, strong tones in the chorus. In assorted songs, you as the singer will also be joined by backing vocalists, who also sing along with you in the chorus. Just as in the song with the choral backing, your own life may be joined with others who are also singing from the same hymn sheet, as it were, and assisting at certain pivotal points of your life. These singers may also sing on other tracks on the album, and again they may also join you in other lives, singing along with your tune of life. Everyone sings the same song, but each has their role to play in the particular theme. To keep everyone in time, sometimes a conductor raises his baton to indicate where he wants everyone to start, slow down or even stop. This conductor in re-incarnational terms, is an overall lead soul, who is in charge of the other lives, and with their agreement, heads the overall direction of the lives that are to be lived. These lives give experience in third-dimensional reality to those that live them. But they are also experiencing other lives in other dimensions at the same time. So, to go back to our record on the turntable, there is a B side to the record, yet with more songs, also all existing at the same time. Then there are other records in the collection yet to be played, and other songs are being conceived yet to be recorded.*

*Some of the singers on the record are fully aware of their roles as vocalists, whilst others are just humming along in the background, in a daydream, but dancing along without fully knowing the words.*

*Seth says we are learning to be co-creators of the universe, which is not fixed or complete but ever developing and changing, like a flowing river which is always moving. We are learning to manage energies that are within ourselves. Eventually, we will discover all we need to do in these cycles of reincarnation, and it is then when we must change the record and move on to a different time of medium or format to express our collective consciousness. Then a new song must be learnt and sung!'*

Time, in this respect, appears to be illusionary and for the simple reason that we can no more appreciate a moment before it is sent hurtling into the annals of memory. It is only through memory that we can gain access to the recordings we have made in this life thus far. They say that living in the moment is one of the most powerful tools at our disposal, where no expectancy permits more opportunities within the advent of potentiality, and whereby a releasing of hopes, fears, and expectancy no longer imprisons us. Easier said than done, though! We have all been guilty of hoping, wanting, wishing, and seeing those very things we desire slip through our fingertips like a bar of wet soap in our hand if held too tightly! However, it would seem this philosophy is correct because energy works in the same way. And, as we know, we are nothing less than an amazing bundle of pure, blessed waves and particles which are shaped into matter accordingly.

**Starseeds**

A Starseed is an advanced spiritual being who does not originally derive from Earth. Certain individuals can tell if they are a Starseed by particular traits they exhibit within their outlook on life, and usually go through an activation period where they ostensibly 'awaken.' These souls carry wisdom, special psychic abilities, along with creative gifts, but often find it hard to navigate within the earth environment, which appears so far removed from their own biosphere. Their empathic nature also leads them into varied roles of caring, but they do not function well in crowds or negative environments. They are extremely sensitive and wish only for the betterment of Earth's people, along with the fortification of Gaia and all Her other lifeforms. Starseeds are usually reclusive, but love being with nature. Perhaps you are a Starseed? Who knows! When dealing with this remarkable subject in addressing our true sovereignty of the soul on varied levels, absolutely anything is possible. Our understanding of the UFO phenomenon enlightens us to the fact that we are dealing with beings not necessarily derived from our binary star system. It would be foolish, then, to assume that our incarnation is merely random in nature. How can anyone learn anything within the brief lifespan we are afforded on this side of life? It seems fitting that the soul has intended to gravitate to this reality for a particular reason. Yet, the problem lies within the very network of the Earth system, and something I feel has been corrupted on a monumental level. As we are aware, there is still controversy surrounding this subject, as well as those encompassing our spiritual nature. And there is every reason to assume that advanced beings from space have continuously visited Earth on varied occasions throughout the epochs to help steer the human race in the right direction. Unfortunately, and in light of our 'System's' tight grip on the economy, among other areas of progression, such new and free, innovative ideas brought forward by many souls to help within the advancement of our species from Starseeds go unnoticed, simply because no profit by the 'System' can be had. This world is all about money, and less on those areas which could propel us forward into an incredible, spiritual future.

It's interesting when looking back into the past, and of those civilisations which knew about planets such as Orion, Pleiades, and Andromeda, to name but a few. As illustrated earlier, the Great Pyramid of Giza's main star shafts link directly to Orion's belt, meaning that on many levels, they knew about these systems, which in all probability could support an advanced civilisation. Much of this knowledge, which informs us of these facts, may have been lost through time or hidden from the public. Thank goodness for free-thinking researchers who continuously dig away, questioning the official narrative and have discovered the true genus of our ancestors. Such remarkable feats of structural engineering betray these facts as to why Man would create such edifices in the first place, and not primarily as mere tombs.

Starseeds carry within the blueprint of their DNA activation encryption codes, which rise to the surface of their conscious mind. These can normally trigger at any point within their human experience, and upon doing so, occasionally cause mild emotional and mental disorders before a complete balancing and reprogramming within their psyche has initiated, overriding the already limited programmed narrative. The reality of any Starseed would inform us that the 'Human' is only one lifeform among many taking temporary residence in this universe. And in those cases of individuals experiencing UFOs, along with their occupants, who is to say that such intelligences haven't come to check up on their temporary human Avatar while going through their current incarnation on earth? It makes sense to consider the enormous misconceptions created surrounding this field of investigation when we take into account the larger picture here.

We now turn our attention to the incredible etheric and astral body in an effort to see just how amazing you, as an Avatar, are.

# 'The Eternal Avatar'

## Chapter Six

## The Incredible Etheric & Astral Body

*All entwined with energy,*

*Are many different parts of me,*

*We are made of elements that make us be,*

*More than just the flesh we see,*

*As particles and waves in duality,*

*On planes of existence beyond our reality.*

*By Chris John Mayes*

'The soul is always connected with the main spirit source. Our bodies are conduits that lock the God-source to this earthly experience. But the body is not a simple shell that we inhabit. The body is of a frequency that is sustained by this earthly level of vibration, as any other physical form that exists within this reality. Our soul and body are two entities of the same source, but resonating at two distinct levels. The etheric body is an echo of the two. It is the product of the marriage of both. A mid-point for the two to connect with. The etheric body reminds me of the double-rainbow effect. The main rainbow, the soul, is the *brightest and the result of all the light passing through to show all the colours of its source light. But the other rainbow, the etheric body, still gives the same effect, but it is much darker due to the rebound of light reflecting back. The etheric body is a product of the soul existing within the body. Like the light continuing to reflect through the droplet to give a second rainbow image, the etheric body is the product of the soul and body being together. It is not detached, or less. So, what purpose does the etheric body have? I think to answer that question, we need to ask ourselves a slightly different one first. What if we didn't have the etheric body? Without it, I don't think the soul could link with the physical body. The soul is of such purity and high vibration, it would not anchor or stay within this dense fabric of space and time without the etheric. This also answers why we sleep. As much as our bodies rest, our souls are not meant to be in this low vibration. Babies sleep more because their souls are still needing to customise to the challenging work of sustaining their presence here. Without the etheric, it would be similar to expecting a butterfly to live happily in the depths of the ocean, when it is created for a more graceful and lighter environment. Not only is the etheric very much another essential layer of our soul, but it only exists because the body does. It is able to sustain our link between the two worlds and is another facet to even more wonderous aspects of ourselves we have yet still to discover.' Chris John Mayes.*

Chris' understanding of the soul being the primary '*source*' is correct, and that our bodies are merely conduits which lock the God-source into this plane of reality through its subtle counterpart (that of the etheric body) indicating that a record of our thoughts and actions, along with an incredible amount of other information is housed within the auric energy field. This facet is much more than just a secondary sheath that complements its twin host, the body. The double-rainbow streams through from its primary emergence from the spirit world and interconnects within the core of every cell within the lifeform the soul has chosen to incarnate within. This is demonstrated through the viewing of the aura, an astonishing combination of layered energies that moves like fire within and around the body. Here, and while 'locked' into this biosphere, the etheric has a complete recording of every aspect of your emotional, mental, and spiritual development, which is chronicled. Think of this subtle body as the hard drive, and the software you're punching in is continually being recorded throughout its physical journey. Nothing escapes its attention.

The etheric is also known as the 'vital' body and is the lifeforce (Prana) which invigorates the physical elements, thus forming our spiritual anatomy, and creating our link to those higher states of consciousness which can be achieved while we are anchored here on earth within our biological spacesuits. These connections can be accomplished during practices such as astral projection, remote viewing, healing, lucid dreaming, clairvoyance, along with various other methods when the mind is disciplined within such temporary extensions of the psyche. It is the etheric which also houses the main chakra system, creating both balance and order as the primary gestation period during the birthing cycle through to maturity takes effect within our physical, emotional, and spiritual state. However, there are a number of facets that can either corrupt or enhance our entire energy centre. Like any component, if care and all due attention are not constantly maintained, things will eventually break down. The same with our chakra system, also known as 'disk' or 'wheel' in Sanskrit, an ancient language from India. Ostensibly, the aura navigates the etheric body, and such colours which Chris speaks of (and are an exact duplicate of those hues within a rainbow) are seen surrounding the body by trained observers who can interpret these illuminations, the radiances of which indicate any number of positive or negative attributes filtering through from the subtle forces and into its biological unit. We know that the body has seven chakra systems, which are vital to our corporeal functioning from day to day.

These vortices of energy are in constant motion, generating stability within the distribution of momentum as the etheric is held in place within its biological body-suit, creating these light-waves which can be observed by a process known as Kirlian photography. All life is governed by this external dynamism, although most of the scientific establishment refutes any claims that we have a secondary light-unit and considers that Kirlian research is merely attributed to the body's temperature.

Kirlian photography was accidentally discovered by Soviet scientist and researcher, Semyon Kirlian, along with his wife, Valentina (a teacher and journalist), in 1939 while observing a patient who'd been receiving medical treatment from a high-frequency electrotherapy device. He'd witnessed a 'spark' of light being generated from the machine's electrodes coming from the patient's skin and wondered whether he would be able to capture this phenomenon on camera. This led to Semyon creating a technique used to encapsulate electrical coronal discharge by placing a living organism (most notably leaves) on a photographic plate and wired to a high-voltage source. He would first photograph a freshly picked leaf on his device, which resulted in an energy field being clearly seen surrounding the foliage, which defined what he believed was its aura. What was more surprising was that when the leaf had been cut in two, and only one half was placed on the plate, his machine would display a replica of where the leaf's missing part had been severed. He considered there was some type of energy blueprint that continued after the organism's physical decomposition. His work remained relatively unknown until a book was published in 1970 entitled '*Psychic Discoveries Behind the Iron Curtain*' and authored by American writers, Lynn Schroeder and Sheila Ostrander. Although Semyon had some fame from his discovery, he had been disenchanted by the medical profession, which refuted there being a secondary energy field encompassing the body. This is no surprise, considering any radical discoveries (and mostly centred around the betterment of our overall health) are severely challenged by the World Health Organisation (WHO), which frowns upon anything which counteracts any suggestion that alternate and cheaper methods of healing which do not always involve surgery, or drugs are available. Most notably, two other individuals who suffered this same fate of ridicule and ultimate ruin had been Wilhelm Reich (inventor of the 'Orgone Accumulator') and Nikola Tesla (Serbian-American, discoverer and futurist engineer). Indeed, Semyon had attended one of Tesla's conferences where he demonstrated high-frequency electrotherapy devices, and this further inspired Semyon to continue with his research, knowing that other acquired minds were already exploring such avenues in bringing betterment to the world. Tesla's work had been way ahead of its time, and upon the inventor's death, his laboratory and all his creations had been seized by the FBI (Federal Bureau of Investigation), and workshops were subsequently destroyed. Perhaps such innovations, which could benefit the world freely, would not ultimately profit those large corporations that seek only to gain from vast fortunes while draining the planet of its precious resources. Anything that invariably challenges the official narrative is immediately scorned and demolished. It's so easy for such companies to dismiss revolutionary discoveries when it doesn't line their pockets and keep the public in check! But the reality of such subtle vibrations of force has been proven to exist, and an area that those in governance are all too eager to reject. Wilhelm Reich was another visionary, and famous for creating an object known as '*The Orgone Accumulator*,' a device thought to be able to cure cancer, along with various other illnesses. Reich was an Austrian Doctor of Medicine and psychoanalyst, as well as a member of the second generation of analysts after Sigmund Freud. He'd been an immigrant to the USA and refugee from Nazi Germany in the 1940s, spending much of his time studying and, thus, capturing an energy he called 'Orgone' which he believed was present not only in outer space, but also within our atmosphere on Earth. This force could be directed within the human body within Reich's 'Accumulator,' thus correcting any ailments suffered, and something proven, in most cases, to work. There have been countless inventors within medicine who have found themselves as unwitting victims to a system which, without question, denounces anything that defies the World Health Organisation. Cancer has always been the biggest area targeted by those who believe they have an answer to a cure or helping towards finding one. And how can anyone stand up to these giants? Such revolutionists have had their entire lives literally devastated by just bringing a new idea or invention to the table without even considering an alternative.

**The Psychic Initiation**

Many years ago, I had gone to see a crystal healer who introduced me to the body's energy system, and it was an experience I would never forget. Her name was Carol Maples, and this had been at the time I'd started doing my own mediumship. I wasn't too sure what to expect when a friend had booked me to see her privately for a session of healing. I'd been invited to do a talk on UFOs at one of Carol's garden parties some months before, and she found the subject interesting, but other than that, I didn't know what to expect when I eventually arrived at her large house. My exploration into the psychic realm was leading me down some interesting corridors, and I knew I was barely touching the tip of the iceberg when investigating UFOs, the afterlife, consciousness, along with varied topics I'd been exploring, which our system of control informed us do not exist. Carol was a tiny lady, but her gift in healing made her a giant among the Gods in my estimation. I'd heard so much of her from my early days, but she shunned the limelight, fame, along with all its trimmings.

My friend, Polli, had driven me there, as I was told I could not drive because her healing was known to blow the socks off of anyone! Well, I thought, we'd see if this was true, and I walked into her house with no expectations at all. Carol greeted me warmly before giving me a run-down of the main chakra system. She did her work in a huge section of the house, which was on ground level. When I walked into the healing room, I was amazed at all the crystals sitting on tables. Some of these had been eye-wateringly enormous. I didn't stop to think just how much she'd spent on her prized collection, but she did inform me most of them had been purchased from other parts of the world.

Carol felt I needed 'tweaking' on a spiritual level and had noticed this with me immediately when I'd lectured in her garden on a beautiful summer's day. Quite how she did this, I wasn't sure, but I'm aware that on a psychic level, she'd been reading my aura. This had been the first time I'd really known anything about this secondary energy system. First and foremost, she had me relax in a comfortable chair. I'd noticed a medical couch ahead and in the largest part of her healing sanctuary, and she informed me jokingly that she'd be getting me on that for the last part of the healing. She asked if I'd ever suffered with my legs, and I told her this was correct. Now, I will just say here that Carol foresaw an issue that would eventually be sorted through an operation on my right leg many years later, but for now, she knew enough from her psychic deduction that something wasn't quite right. As I relaxed, she rubbed some liquid into both my legs and produced the largest wand-like crystal I had ever seen, along with a pendulum which had a diamond-shaped quartz on its end. Standing in front of me, she informed me that I was not to worry, and that she would first locate the source of my leg's issues by using the pendulum before applying the wand-like crystal's power to heal. Carol explained that my main chakra system would be balanced later, but for the moment, it was vital for me to trust her and not interrupt while she went about her work.

I distinctly recall the sensation of 'pins and needles' immediately surrounding my right leg as she used her pendulum, locating certain areas of the lower section of my knee for something. I saw the pendulum she'd had in her right hand gently swinging backwards and forwards in an almost hypnotic fashion, while she directed the wand in her left. Carol made mention for me to witness a most curious phenomenon. She asked me to pay close attention to the shadow on my leg, which was being cast from her pendulum's cord, and then enquired if I saw anything unusual. I had! And I was shocked. By all intents and purposes, there should only have been one shadow being cast, but there were two! She looked at me knowingly. The crystal pendulum was, in fact, locating not only the physical body, but also its etheric double. I remember being stunned, yet Carol only sniggered and continued her work on both legs. I began to feel cold, as if someone had suddenly opened a door to a freezer right in front of me, and she explained this was all due to the energies shifting. 'We have much work to do on you today,' Carol explained matter-of-factly, but I was incredulous as to the method she was applying, and actually feeling these so-called energies affecting my physical body had been staggering to my mind.

Once she had completed her work on my legs, Carol then went on to use the crystal wand above my head. It was here where I noticed another peculiar sensation, as though thousands of fingers had been prying into the top of my skull. The exact same phenomena permeated as she moved the device to my third eye, throat, heart, and then solar plexus, all along balancing the energies and creating a correction in the flow of my etheric body. This had taken around one hour, but we were, so she explained, far from finished. I recall saying how amazed I was by the entire process, but like a teacher, she merely acknowledged my understanding and, as a true professional within her field, focused on her mission to get my entire system equalised.

When the session with the crystals had been concluded, Carol directed me to the medical bed and asked me to lie down on my back, ensuring that I was completely comfortable. She clarified that during this second part she was going to be performing a spiritual initiation on me, and that she'd been informed by those in spirit that I was now ready for this new shift in vibrations within myself, and which, for this ceremony, would allow those guides on the other side greater access through to my mind, thus enhancing my own psychic development. I merely went along with the whole thing, trusting Carol completely. Her reputation was sound, and as a pupil, I would honour my teacher. While I lay there, Carol proceeded to line certain crystals upon and around my body, explaining that I was to remain as still as I could for over an hour while she directed her energy from a slight distance. Calm and rhythmic music was playing in the background, and she talked me through a meditation to ensure I was totally relaxed. I cannot for the life of me recall anything of what she'd said after this, but I noticed some incredible sensations, and also met with a powerful vision I was about to experience while in this slightly altered state of consciousness, as well as hearing a strange sound. My entire body began to 'tingle' as if I were now floating. During one part of the initiation, the top of my head felt as though it had been prised wide open, almost as if I had been deprived of my Calvarium. Shocked, I recounted this to Carol, who merely acknowledged this fact. I underwent a sensation of warmth, like being cocooned in a quilt, and for a time, I remained in this tranquil, almost dream-like state, half-in and half-out of my biological vehicle, or so it seemed. The room began to transform into something else. No longer was I in the sanctuary, but now in an antiquated temple from ages past. I could see large, wooden beams which gave structure to an altogether different building high above me, and which spread out in some ornate fashion like a spider's web. I had the distinct impression I was near an ocean. Then came a sound like a 'Whomp! Whomp! Whomp!' and I knew this to be a great, powerful source of energy. I quickly found myself back in my familiar environment, but continued to hear this low resonance. It was coming from directly above and outside the building where I lay, and Carol further stunned me by acknowledging that 'my friends were here!' I knew instinctively that she was talking about aliens, or that, perhaps, their UFO was within our space, but I had no idea why they had turned up.

Once the process had been completed, and Carol helped me off the bed, I remember feeling as though an arctic cold had engulfed my very essence. She immediately got a blanket and wrapped it around me. What a welcome sight, I thought. I'm six feet in height, and Carol is a tiny lady. If anyone were to see this giant of a man being helped by a diminutive lady from the bed would have been a class-act within itself! She prompted me towards a chair. Being an expert in such matters, she'd no doubt seen this countless times with her clients. I was shaking with cold, but was assured the effects would soon wear off. I told her of the building I found myself transported in, and she replied by stating that I'd been in an Atlantean healing centre. Interesting, considering another medium had seen both my twin and I existing as sisters in a past incarnation on Atlantis within its golden era some years before. There was no hesitation in her deduction, and she proceeded to explain that the three-hour initiation would take quite some time for my energies to balance themselves out. I quizzed her about 'my friends' whom she'd mentioned regarding the sound, and she merely smiled knowingly. I thought that some things are best left unsaid, but the sensations and vibration had been truly staggering. I wondered whether the 'visitors' had also manifested to help within this 'psychic tweaking.' Certainly, it had felt as though I was vibrating from the inside out (like a tuning fork which has been struck upon a solid surface) and Carol advised me on the procedure for grounding myself, along with making sure I was hydrated, an area which I have always failed to do most of the time.

Polli came to pick me up and wanted to know all about my experience. I remember distinctly feeling like I was wide open and sensitive to any sound around me. Gradually, these uncomfortable sensations diminished, but I discovered my psychic intuition sharpening. Some years later, Carol phoned me to tell me that she no longer wanted to be on this planet, and that things were becoming progressively worse through her eyes. I had no idea that she would soon pass over due to clots and several strokes to the brain. I had been heartbroken when the news finally reached me, but it was Carol's wish that I take her funeral, and I conducted her instructions to the letter.

This had been the first time I'd been introduced to a different kind of energy, and one I never believed existed, until the initiation was performed. During this point, I was aware of a greater power operating beyond the known laws of our physics. How was I to explain this to someone on the street? There was no way they'd understand, and this puzzled me when looking into areas of what is referred to as the quantum body. People mostly accepted the hypothesis that we are mere biological creatures who die, and that's your lot! Looking back on those cases where pioneers had brought something revolutionary to the table, which could only help towards correcting, or indeed, enhancing the natural body's health in areas of healing, puzzled me when we learn of our very own system negating, and thereby destroying such groundbreaking ideas.

Negative emotions can have a serious impact on our health. We live in a world which offers little in the way of hope for many, and the constant stream of destructive news within the huge media cartel, along with our system taking more in the way of collateral than caring for its own people which they see as nothing more than a commodity can have enormous detrimental effects upon our physical, emotional, and mental existence. The pressures of life never seem to ease either, or no effort made by those in governance to truly bring out the best in an individual within any one lifetime. It is a make-or-break situation for us all. However, there are ways we can practice tackling such negative circumstances, and which have been proven to have psychological ramifications in this constant drip-feeding of the system's need to mentally subjugate the masses.

**The Psychic Highway & Pathway to Healing**

If we think about it, we are all connected to one another in terms of consciousness. Using the mobile phone analogy always works well when describing this in an easier terminology; the illusion that we're all separate from one another, as many believe. This couldn't be any further from the truth. Energy (which we are entirely composed of, but in different variations) permeates all around us, the same as your communication device. Although our body appears to be restricted within its biological suit, our minds are very much on the move constantly, and oftentimes away from the physical plane we currently inhabit. We are all guilty of day-dreaming, fantasising, or taking ourselves off to some far-away land in order to escape the monotony of life. Let's face it, we've all been there, or still are, within varied moments throughout the day. There's not, I think, a moment that goes past where we find ourselves so far removed from what we consider to be reality. No longer focusing on the present, we partake in another reality altogether, and one within the mind. We yearn to be here, or there, or with that special person, or on another planet entirely! Yet, we are frustrated that such wishes appear only to exist within the mind. It is, however, precisely the mind which is more powerful than our system of control would want you to believe, and which YOU are in management of. The etheric body can be affected due to adverse conditions (emotions being the main category), whereby you are able to reverse such unhealthy influences via a change in mental attitude. So, taking travels within consciousness, and temporarily away from your present location, is indeed healthy, provided your thoughts are experienced within a positive light. How you think and feel will create changes to your biological system, whether positively or negatively. Your emotional and mental faculties help facilitate balance and order throughout your entire being, as opposed to chaos, which many of us are constantly met with in a troubled world. How many times have you found yourself in a tough situation that really got to you? This promotes an increase in stress levels, which can upset the entire equilibrium within the etheric and physical body. In such cases, your light will become progressively murky, and this is reflected within Kirlian photography, clearly demonstrating the differences between a healthy, vibrant system, compared to a corrupted one. Although consciously we are all linked within a universal mind (the Godhead), our bodies are not, as these are independent vehicles which have been created to exist within this time and space, which goes through a process of deterioration before expiration, so care of our physiology is paramount. As humans, we are met with varied health issues throughout life, and although most illnesses and diseases are brought on by a number of genetic disorders, a strong and positive mindset can, on occasion, bring about an entire correction that afflicts our organism, contrary to what the medical profession tells us. Of course, treatments must still be sought, but a change within our mental attitude can also influence radical alterations. This has been proven, even in near-death studies, whereby the person who has died and crossed over to the other side have found that, upon their return, there has been a complete reversal within the overall health of their body which may have been riddled with disease, or any number of other life-threatening conditions.

Something also to consider (but does not necessarily relate to the majority of cases where restorative intervention has led to the disfigurement of a foetus within the medical establishment while trialling new drugs) could account for how some souls are born with a missing arm, hand, leg, or themselves suffer severe physical disabilities while going through their incubation period within the womb. It's interesting to note that some children recall a horrific passing in their past life, only to find that the reason they only have one leg (taking an example from proven cases) is because they'd been struck hard by a vehicle in their previous life! This could indicate that the trauma of this has impressed itself strongly within the etheric body, and the memory is carried forward into the blueprint of their next life, unless there had been a grace period for healing, either emotionally, physically, or mentally. This is a clear indication that our memories are transferred from past lives, which can shape future ones. On top of this, it is clear that when such tragic events of this kind happen, where the incident has led to the immediate death of the person, the imprint has been carried forth, which alters the DNA of the child as they are reborn. They say that nothing happens by random, and I also contest that through past-life regression, we can heal the past and end this cycle of biological imperfection if that soul wishes to reincarnate at some future event.

**An Enhancement Within the Etheric Body's Energy-Field**

Some truly incredible cases are evident, whereby a person has been completely healed when their soul/spirit has returned to its body after an NDE. This may lead us into the assumption that the etheric, and while temporarily infused within its biological counterpart, does itself become weakened here on earth before its return to the other side of life. In such instances where, for example, a person suffering from terminal cancer, and who has themselves experienced the near-death state, finds a complete reversal within the composition of their cells and organs, as though their temporary existence beyond time and space has seen to an enhancement, as well as a correction, within their field-frequency of 'light,' (which we are all made from) and which subsequently regenerates the body upon the soul's return. This is merely hypothetical in nature when drawing upon such conclusions, but it would make sense. The facilitation of our light being revitalised within the greater light on the other side, while temporarily detached from its body, transforms the individual not only spiritually, but also biologically. Like a newborn coming into the womb, its light is untainted and pure, and this energy permeates for however long its genetic coding within the DNA permits on a biological level. As we know, our genomic material has a lot to do with the way we evolve, the light (soul) can dim but never diminish, until it has returned to source. The sad thing is that we do physically degrade over time, and science is trying to crack open the secret to physical immortality, and something locked within a gene called SIRT6 which has shown to extend the lifespan of mice, but it is clear we still have a long way to go before such revolutionary methods of life-extension can be found.

Within the original ancient codices from the past such as the mystical tradition commonly called Gnosticism, manuscripts discovered in a large storage jar at the foot of a cliff along the Nile River, near the city of Nag Hammadi by a farmer, and better known as *The NAG Hammadi*' found in Egypt in 1945 tells us a completely different story surrounding our genesis and makes us aware that such Overlords (who themselves had been brilliant geneticists) had incredibly long lives, but which they did not subsequently pass down to their creation of the 'human.' Of course, the orthodox churches did not want such revelations becoming public, and as is often the case, pushed aside because it does not fit with the preferred narrative. We have already explored this area concerning our Gods, but it is evident that we, as an entirely separate species from our original creators, hold something they do not – that of the spirit which we are also endowed, as well as a soul. This 'Tripartite' within the human (body, soul, spirit) is what differentiates us from our architects, who, it is understood, only had the body and soul, and not spirit. Of course, this will open all sorts of debates and anger within the religious sectors, but I do believe there is truth within these ancient manuscripts, and something which may answer a lot when exploring the current UFO/UAP situation which is another area of contention by our system which has always redirected attention away from this most perplexing matter.

The seven main chakras, which facilitate the distribution of energy, are listed below. What's interesting is that the separate colours emit light frequencies of the ultraviolet and infrared rays along with the sound notes of each chakra.

| | Chakra | Colour | Note | Sound Frequency (Hertz) |
|---|---|---|---|---|
| 1) | Crown | White/Violet | F | 344 |
| 2) | Third Eye | Indigo | E | 330 |

| | | | | | |
|---|---|---|---|---|---|
| 3) | Throat | Blue | D | 293 |
| 4) | Heart. | Green | C | 256 |
| 5) | Solar Plexus | Yellow | B | 241 |
| 6) | Sacral | Orange | A | 220 |
| 7) | Root | Red | G | 194 |

**The Astral Body**

Another fascinating area of these subtle energies concerns the 'Astral Body.' This component serves to bridge the gap between the physical and spiritual realms, whereas the etheric body pulls on physical quantum events and links the astral realms to our corporeal self. Both work in tandem with one another. The astral part of us is what gives us animation and life here on earth, but is connected to the universe and beyond. The astral also transcends all mechanisms of the physical, allowing a stream of vibration to flow between the material and mental realms. The astral is nothing less than an incredible transmitter of energies that facilitates communications between alternate layers of our being, such as our emotional and mental states.

One well-known individual who was instrumental in bringing this subject to the attention of the public was Robert Monroe. Monroe had been a leading expert and pioneer within this field and demonstrated such exploits of soul detachment within his books, *'Journeys Out of the Body,' 'Far Journeys,'* and *'Ultimate Journey.'* Although most individuals can suddenly find themselves outside of their carnal frame while sleeping with no clue as to how this may have occurred, Monroe demonstrated that he could control the process quite naturally and was even able to map certain parts of the astral planes. This proves that, in some cases, surrounding the dream-world, we often take trips to alternate levels of reality until we awaken, and at which point we think the whole thing had been nothing more than a dream! However, Monroe demonstrated vast differences from mere dreams to actual soul detachment. The classic definition of this procedure is known as 'Out of Body Experience' (OBE for short). Through controlled methods practiced just before the sleep-state, Monroe discovered he was not only able to free his *'real'* self from the constraints of his physical body, but also travel to people and places while in this etheric state, even proving events occurring while he was at home in bed, and after investigating these situations himself personally. Such exploits have been documented in his amazing books, but it is not something for the faint-hearted, by any means. Some of his experiences had been truly mind-boggling! Monroe established three 'Locales' within the astral planes.

**Locale One** is thought to be a direct link with our material world, along with events happening in the here and now, as one would expect while existing physically within this realm. It is within this area where much of Monroe's experimentation took place before he began to notice several other dimensions far different from this one. He established contact with people he knew within this Locale, and some he didn't, and even demonstrated that he could *'remote influence'* within this environment. One such event had him pinch a lady he knew while traipsing the ether, without her being aware that he'd been to visit her while she'd been on holiday, only to discover that she'd felt the pinch, and had the mark to prove it! Monroe recalls the lady being visited by two other females, describing the colour of their hair, along with other incredible details. Sure enough, his friend showed him the mark upon her waist, and in the exact spot where he'd squeezed her when he'd revealed his intentions while experimenting in his out-of-body state. This is interesting and may lead to some truly extraordinary revelations when dealing with a vast range of unexplained paranormal phenomena occurring around the world where such remote influence is concerned. Locale One is very much earth-based, although there appears to be some mistranslation while in this astral condition when processing information, because the second body is no longer working within its normal flow of habitual conscious interpretation. This is why, and within our dreams, the most bizarre experiences appear quite normal, until we return to our waking state. During these episodes of mental transmutation within the astral and physical, both sides appear ordinary until we awaken from one condition to the other. Yet, we must consider that whichever province we find ourselves, whether dream, astral, or in our full waking state, there appears to be no differentiation in terms of its overall reality.

**Locale Two** is an area which Monroe reported as being both heaven and hell, and existing within varied states of awareness, depending on how you personally view your reality. Locale two is also a non-material environment, where everything imaginable can come into instant manifestation. Although such conditions have no barriers in terms of time and space either, the geographical environments can change simply through the act of the astral traveller's thoughts. Everything which has been fashioned on earth appears as a byproduct of this dimension; however, such inventions only exist for a temporary period, depending on how strong the thought-form from the recipient is, whether in this reality, or one being generated from a mind on earth. Here, both good and evil are encountered, along with the materialisation of strange creatures, angels, spirit guides, and so forth. Travel is achieved by simply 'thinking.' There is no apparent bodily movement while in the astral planes, other than a sense that your second-body is being propelled from one realm to another. Monroe reported that it was far better to focus on an individual you may have known and who has since passed over, rather than a geographical location which may be of interest to you. However, this timeless and apparent spaceless dimension is multifaceted, and caution is advised when traipsing within varied parts of this realm if you have succeeded in the art of astral travel. The newcomer who is not 'clued up' as to how things operate mentally may find themselves in tricky situations, but there is no death as we understand it. Here, the deep-based emotional and mental state of a person's mind is prevalent in the undertaking of their journey. What one thinks, one will create. This process is inescapable and may give us some clues as to a person's actions while incarnating temporarily on earth, surrounding karma. It's interesting to note that when our deceased loved ones cross over to the other side, reports indicate they appear younger, and roughly around the age of thirty. Energy is transmutable, and since the soul of the individual is no longer inhibited by its developing biological counterpart can transform into anything it so wishes in terms of a projected belief. There are some remarkable theories we can address, which may offer some clues as to the many reported supernatural activities occurring on this planet.

**Locale Three** appears to be a warped version of our current way of life, yet with vast differences. Although this locale appears to be geographically similar to Earth (having people, animals, farms, cities, and so forth), there are indications of a somewhat backward development within its technological know-how. Monroe considered whether this was an alternate biosphere, although a disturbingly warped one at that! There have been theories suggesting that we create alternate realities within this present life, and which verge into such hidden dimensions. Of course, this would be too much for the average reader to accept, but areas of quantum study suggest this may very well be a possibility, if not hard to grasp on an intellectual level. After all, we are composites of conscious energy, and such energy may be able to exist in these parallel universes.

One of the most surprising discoveries by Monroe and his research team when investigating the astral planes was the realisation that many of the test-subjects who trained at *'The Monroe Institute'* in the US, while experimenting in their astral state, found themselves being helped by varied intelligences within many areas of these locales. The separation from the physical body through an enforced act (unlike the natural one which occurs through death) appears to allow the traveller to wander where they wish within such planes, with no fixed location which they know of. We're not left with a map while here on earth of the afterlife! The description from those who have learnt the art of astral projection describes seeing themselves as a subtle light-body, which carries none of the distinctive attributes that set us apart from one another as humans. Identity is achieved through the second body's vibrational field and not the outward appearance that we are so accustomed to here. Looks are of no more importance. Your individuality is recognised by the influx of dynamism and knowledge you have accrued throughout your existence, and information held within the very fabric of your entire energy-mass. Yet, you have a form which is able to bend and mould through the act of your thoughts alone. Energy, as we are aware, is transmutable and can manifest in innumerable ways while existing on the other side.

In 1975, Monroe created and patented the first in a series of 'Hemisphere-Synchronisation' programs (short for Hemi-Sync), which became known as *'The Gateway Experience.'* He, along with his research team, then went on to develop a set of audio tapes, using a series of unique binaural beat technologies in order to induce varied states in consciousness. Because the left brain (which is analytical in nature) and right (the creative part) appear to be in constant opposition with one another, 'Hemi-Sync' synchronises both hemispheres simultaneously, thus allowing for an increase in awareness. This, Monroe knew, was the very gateway to a greater understanding of not only the astral body, but also the cosmos and beyond. Through extensive study, Monroe and his crew discovered that unique sounds are able to render the user safely into deep, relaxed states of awareness, along with expanding consciousness beyond the known laws of our physical dimension. 'Hemi-Sync' can be exploited in a variety of ways, but was initially designed to introduce a more intense method of allowing the astral body to separate from its physical vehicle. The process requires much discipline of the mind, along with intense training. In 1978, the military approached the Monroe Institute to evaluate how this could benefit their armed forces. They arranged to send prospective officers for OBE training to the research facility. Monroe's institute has an affiliated professional membership and has gone on to publish scientific papers that explore alternate states of consciousness, along with 'Hemi-Sync's' overall benefits within the individual's ultimate well-being. Such acceptances by many concerning the astral body, along with the techniques involved in allowing temporary severance from the material into the etheric, may appear a little like science fiction, but such conditions have been proven to work, thus allowing for a greater understanding of what awaits us in the afterlife.

Spiritual teachers from around the world have known about the astral body since the beginning of recorded history, yet varied religious establishments refuse to acknowledge this fact and are more inclined to sway the public's already programmed mindset into the manufactured, yet seriously flawed understanding of what it is to be 'human' through indoctrination within all areas of mainstream education. As a species, we appear lost, with countless numbers of people having no real understanding of their true purpose, other than the basics of survival. When science is no longer tethered to those corrupted organisations which have deliberately held back much within the province of our true origins and nature, and something which will eventually open the door to a greater understanding surrounding the etheric and astral body, will we be able to excel as a species? However, these are areas which are by no means new in terms of our etheric and astral conditions. Throughout the late nineteenth century, the birth of Theosophy became known, and was created, no less, by the famous Russian and American mystic, Helen Blavatsky (1831-1891) in 1875 through the formation of the Theosophical Society. It was Blavatsky who brought an updated version of events forward, and not just around spiritualism, but also genesis. Theosophy is a philosophical movement and comes from the Greek words for 'God' and 'Wisdom.' Such hidden knowledge is thought to answer questions surrounding not only the human condition, but also the universe. Many high-powered individuals throughout the epochs may have tried to bury certain truths, but they eventually get dug up, and Blavatsky was no exception, even though she had been under enormous opposition from the churches and scientific community during her time. It was she who authored many works which opposed the official narrative, and took into consideration the esoteric nature of reality, an area which varied religious sectors saw as blasphemous. Charles W. Leadbeater (1854–1934) was another famous British clairvoyant and a high-ranking officer within the order of the Theosophical Society. Leadbeater wrote extensively on the subject of not only clairvoyance, but also the afterlife, most notably the second-body and its survival beyond the physical world. In his book *'The Astral Planes: Its Scenery, Inhabitants and Phenomena,'* the author describes the various manifestations and states of being within this most compelling of controversial subjects, along with varied levels surrounding the astral body. It's interesting to note that much of his theoretical work appears to mirror Monroe's exploits while he ventured beyond the material realm.

Leadbeater understood the mechanics within the astral state and considered the varied levels a soul is met with when crossing over. He speculated that the aura serves as the real 'You,' and that your life-recording determines which level within these alternate dimensions of awareness (and there are innumerable worlds within this sphere of existence) your soul will gravitate towards upon physical death. This brings into the equation karma, and clearly illustrates that you cannot escape your thoughts and actions while here, even if someone professes otherwise from their outward appearance. What you carry within the blueprint of your soul, you will invariably take with you into the astral. There is no escaping this fact. Your soul (the real essence of what you encompass on a universal level of conscious awareness) has walked varied lives in a multitude of incarnations, and these, along with your newly completed recording of the last corporeal life you have completed, will govern what juncture you have reached. The second-body is described by Leadbeater who stipulates that: *'It will save the* student much trouble if he learns at once to regard these auras not as mere emanations, but as the actual manifestation of the Ego on their respective planes – *if he understands that it is the auric egg* (second body) *which is the real man, not the physical body.*' He further explains that: '*Though the kâmic aura from the brilliances of its flashes of colour may often be more conspicuous, the nerve-ether and the etheric double are really of much denser order of matter, being strictly speaking within the limits of the physical plane, though invisible to ordinary sight. It has been the custom in Theosophical literature to describe the Linga Sharîra as the astral counterpart of the human body, the word 'astral' having been usually applied to everything beyond the cognition of our physical senses. As closer investigation enables us to be more precise in the use of our terms, however, we find ourselves compelled to admit much of this invisible matter as purely physical, and therefore to define the Linga Sharîra no longer as the astral, but as the etheric double. This seems an appropriate name for it, since it consists of various grades of that matter which scientists call 'ether,' though this proves on examination to be not a separate substance, as has been generally supposed, but a condition of finer subdivision than the gaseous, to which any kind of physical matter may be reduced by the application of the appropriate forces. The name 'etheric double' will therefore for the future be used in Theosophic writings instead of 'Linga Sharîra': and this change will not only give us the advantage of an English name which is clearly indicative of the character of the body to which it is applied, but will also relieve us from the frequent misunderstanding which have arisen from the fact that an entirely different signification is attached in all the Oriental books to the name hitherto been using. It must not, however, be supposed that in making this alteration in nomenclature we are in any way putting forward a new conception; we are simply altering, for the sake of greater accuracy, the labels previously attached to certain facts in nature. If we examine with psychic faculty the body of a newly-born child, we shall find it permeated not only by astral matter of every degree of density, but also by the several grades of etheric matter; and if we take the trouble to trace these inner bodies backwards to their origin, we find that it is of the latter that the etheric-double – the mould upon which the physical body is built up – is formed by the agents of the Lord of Karma; while the astral matter has been gathered together by the descending Ego – not of course consciously, but automatically – as he passes through the astral plane.*'

The 'karmic' attribute is also interesting, and something which originated from Indian philosophy, but also integrated into many other cultural belief systems around the world, most notably in Buddhism. Karma is 'action,' and whereby it is believed your words, thoughts, and deeds (both positive and negative) lead to cause and effect which create ripples that influence your future experience, whether in this life or the next, through the process of reincarnation. Within varied cultures, karma is the forefront of what is to become of the soul, which has enlightened or corrupted themselves, along with others, and which determines their place within either the lower or higher planes of the astral. There are even upper levels which will be explored, but it is this dimension of the astral which is much closer to us in terms of our physical sphere. This may indicate that, for instance, a seriously corrupted soul may go through a complete transmutation within their composition of energy it has manifested, thus descending to lower levels within the astral planes. Indeed, this may answer some interesting questions when dealing with the supernatural elements our planet has been plagued with throughout the ages.

**The Silver Cord**

Many individuals who have journeyed within their astral body also make mention of a silver cord, much like the umbilical cord, which attaches a child to its mother while in the primary birthing cycle. Within metaphysical studies and literature, the silver cord is known as 'Sutratma' (a life thread of the Antahkarana - internal organ) and connects to the higher self. However, such binds are fixed like roots to a tree between the shoulder-blades of the astral body, extending out into a silver-grey colour and appearing roughly two inches in width. The cord itself acts like a rubber band and is reported to be quite strong and flexible in nature. This connection is linked from the astral to the abdomen of its organic counterpart. As we know, a foetus draws all its necessary vitalities from the umbilical cord while in the mother's womb, and the severance of this cord occurs once the child is sufficiently developed and has entered the physical world from the confines of its watery and dark cavity. We could suppose that the silver cord works in much the same way, but feeds the biological form from its eternal, ethereal self to create the temporary life-force necessary for its development on earth. The silver cord is also thought to serve as a kind of lifeline that directs the soul back to its worldly body once the astral traveller has completed its exploits within the ether, thereby anchoring it firmly in place.

It is theorised that if someone goes too far out within the astral planes, thus stretching the cord to its maximum, and away from their corporeal self, it will snap, thus ending the physical life of the said explorer. However, such notions regarding this thought are mere conjecture. Many of us are completely unaware of this cord, let alone having a second body. Yet, reports indicate this is very much a reality, and highlights that just such a thread must serve as a vital component on some level while we remain within our biological bodies.

Monroe considered this and discovered that just such a cord is indeed present, much to his surprise, but not in the location of the umbilicus. One of his diary entries recorded in 1961 in his book '*Journeys Out of the Body*,' shows that the author tests this theory while in his astral state and explains that: '*...I turned to look for the 'cord,' but it was not visible to me; either it was too dark or not there. Then I reached around my head to see if I could feel it coming out from the front, top, or back of my head. As I reached the back of my head, my hand brushed against something, and I felt behind me with both hands. Whatever it was extended out from a spot in my back directly between my shoulder blades, as nearly as I can determine, not from the head, as I expected. I felt the base, and it felt like the spread-out roots of a tree radiating out from the basic trunk. The roots slanted outward and into my back down as far as the middle of my torso, up to my neck, and into the shoulders on each side. I reached outward, and it formed into a 'cord,' if you can call a two-inch-thick cable a 'cord.' It was hanging loosely, and I could feel its texture very definitely. It was body-warm to the touch and seemed to be composed of hundreds (thousands?) of tendon-like strands packed neatly together, but not twisted or spiralled. It was flexible and seemed to have no skin covering. Satisfied that it did exist, I took off and went.*'

Interestingly, the silver cord brings into question the *actual* nature of its purpose on a universal level of current conscious awareness while we exist in the material. We are born of earth and die as such, with little or no awareness of the astral body, let alone its silver cord, which merges (if only temporarily) the spirit and genetic vehicle together. Have we, as a species, lived in ignorance of this fact, save for those brave explorers such as Monroe, among others, in bringing this information our way? In light of this least known and understood truth, there is evidently a much greater purpose for such attachments, and something which mirrors the development of a child within its womb during birth. It would make sense to assume that the spirit needs fastening while existing within a lower spectral level of reality, considering that our etheric nature is more real than the body we currently inhabit. As humans, we dream. The dream-state is another interesting area, and to many nothing more than a random release of images generated from our desires and experiences as we go through life's journey within the recesses of our subconscious mind. Yet, there have been moments when we most certainly have had some form of prophetic vision, which we find incredible to explain in terms of rationality. This may indicate that a significant percentage of our trips within the astral go completely ignored, save for those few events which stand out within our occasional mental recall. It is evident that we make varied trips into the astral and connect with those who we have lost from this side of life, along with spirit guides, masters, and other elevated souls.

**A Manifestation of the Astral**

I was to be given direct proof of this astral body, and in a way I could never have imagined possible. Although when such feats are performed by those initiating an OBE in order to roam the astral planes while in an altered state of consciousness, they are still tied to their material body. They have not gone through the process of death, so to speak. However, upon an individual's passing, it is apparent this second body continues to exist as an exact duplicate of the one it had once occupied, matching their physical detail in every way while they had walked on earth. This had all been due to a working colleague I had known back in the late 1990s.

Gareth had worked as a trainee manager in the department store where I worked, and we got along quite well, as most people do when you're in close proximity in such environments. He started at the age of eighteen, but less than a year into his employment, he developed stomach cancer, which came out of the blue. He'd been fit and healthy, competing as a swimmer for the Luton and Bedfordshire County. During this time, I'd began exploring my psychic gift soon after my maternal grandmother's death in August 1997 and had completed working on a manuscript tentatively titled '*The Eternal Cosmic Corridor*' which explored clairvoyance, along with spirit communication, and which I later received a contract from Capall Bann Publishing Ltd in mid-2007 after being retitled and major re-writes advised called, '*Reaching For the Divine.*' Knowing that Gareth was terminally ill, and even though he was still coming in to work through his gruelling chemotherapy, I gave him a copy of my manuscript to read. I didn't know what he'd make of it, but decided, above everything else, that, perhaps, it would bring a little comfort his way. At one point, I'd asked him to do me a favour (even though I knew I was pushing the boat into uncharted waters) and see whether he was able to appear to me after his passing, if only to prove there was life after death. I know that most people would frown upon such a question, but I dared it, under the right circumstances, when we'd been alone and in deep conversation about his illness. In desperation, I tried all I could to allay his fears (and not in a preachy way either) that there was more to our existence, and much literature proved this point in question. He seemed humoured by my request and asked how he would be able to perform such a feat. I told him I wasn't sure, but he replied in kind by stating that he'd 'beam down' like they did in 'Star Trek,' seeing as this was his favourite sci-fi program. I guess he just shrugged that one off as a joke, but there had been something more to his statement, which would later shock me to the very core. A series of synchronicities began to play out after my grandmother's passing from cancer in 1997. I was certain those in spirit were gearing me up for something other than the normal toils of life, and which would open my eyes to an altogether different reality.

My maternal grandparents moved to Somerset in their later years, and grandma was terminally ill in hospital with cancer. My twin brother, Ronald, along with my mum and me, went to visit her in hospital a week before she passed. It's funny, because when I gave her a last kiss on the cheek, and turned to walk away, taking one last glance as our eyes locked, I knew that would be the last I'd see her alive. I can still remember the event as though it happened yesterday. Back in Kempston, Bedfordshire, I lay awake in the early hours of the morning, around a week later, and suddenly found myself crying. I saw within my mind an image of Grandma cradling my brother and me in her arms as newborns (a photo that was taken back in 1969 in an old album we have in our house). Then, as if she'd been in the room with me, I heard her voice saying, 'Why are you crying?' She repeated this twice, and it had come into my head loudly. I was shocked and sat up. At this point, the phone rang (always serious when a call comes through during the early hours, especially in the days before mobiles), and news informed us that Grandma had given up her battle with cancer. It must be noted here that my Grandmother had also been psychic, and even on a late summer's evening in 1982, we three witnessed a silver orb, no larger than a football, which had presented itself to us when aged thirteen. Had this been a UFO? One wonders as to this possibility, but it had appeared over our grandmother's head silently, having no markings on it whatsoever, bar from its silver, reflective skin, and hovered in line with the second-floor window to their big house in Feltham, Middlesex. Upon asking what it was when the object made its spectacular appearance, she merely stated that, '...*the fairies have come to take a closer look at us!*' For kids, this was a bizarre statement indeed, but we both considered that she was protecting us from a greater truth and didn't seem at all surprised by the object's fast arrival. Had she seen one before? I'd never thought to ask her when she'd been in this life. The episode has been documented within the UFO community and serves only to add to such mystifying areas of high strangeness. Back in the day, folks didn't talk about UFOs because they thought you were either a crank or an outward liar!

From the moment my grandmother passed, I had this compulsion to find the truth surrounding evidence of life after death. Although I had been heavily involved with UFO research then (and still am today), from that moment onwards, I was hooked. Grief can affect us badly, and that's what happened to me, but not on a gullible level. I am known for my down-to-earth approach, especially surrounding UFOs and psychical investigations. This was the first time in my life I had booked to see a medium who worked in Bedford. The medium's name was Pearl, and she had been an incredible instrument, not only in bringing my grandmother through from the other side, but also information pertaining to my past, present, and future, even going so far as to acknowledging a few of my past lives! Her reading was spot-on, and there was no way on earth she could have known such things about me. However, during the reading, she told me I was psychic and would be working with spirit myself. I must admit, I found the idea amusing, but during this point in my life, seeing myself as a medium never really appealed to me. However, the clairvoyant was firm in her response. She looked me square in the face and said, 'Within the passing of two years, you will change your mind. Certain events will lead you towards a greater truth!' At the time, I didn't pay too much attention to what she had told me regarding this point, but it forever remained in the back of my head.

The events of Gareth's illness, which began in 1998, eventually led to his passing on the 25th of June 1999. This was more or less within the time frame Pearl had foreseen. His death was a great shock to us all, especially for a twenty-year-old who had so much life ahead of him. I was numb with shock, because tragically, within three months, not only had we lost Gareth, but also my aunty Betty, along with a dear friend, Margaret Heining, whom my brother and I considered as a grandmotherly figure.

In the winter of 1999, I took myself off to a second-hand bookshop in Bedford owned by a locally well-known author, Richard Wildman. I would constantly devour the occult section of rare books and grab anything which fuelled my interest. Mr Wildman was such a wonderfully kind and patient man, and knew the instant I turned up at his shop what I was after. On this occasion, I'd made my way over to the occult section, and immediately, a hardback book fell from several shelves above onto the floor. Picking the book up, I was surprised to see it was called '*Reunions: Visionary Encounters With Departed Loved Ones,*' by Raymond Moody, MD. In this book, Dr Moody explained how you could contact the dead by way of mirror gazing, and something of an art the ancient Egyptians used. I purchased the book, devoured its contents, and set about the experiment you had to perform in trying to communicate with those on the other side of life. The process required a large mirror, a semi-darkened room, and time alone to focus one's thoughts clearly. I used the sitting room at night when everyone else was asleep. As suggested by the author, it was important to position the mirror directly in front of you, roughly five to six feet in distance, and tilted at a slight angle so that your reflection wasn't seen within the glass. Then, relaxing my mind, I asked for Gareth to make himself appear through the mirror. You also had to stare into the glass within the blackness and make note of anything seen or felt. Several key factors must also be taken into consideration, such as the physical, psychological, and aesthetic principles, along with a clear indication within the mind of '*who*' you'd like to make contact with. Although this does not always present the results one would expect (some experimenters finding the apparitions can summon those they least anticipated), it is thus essential that your mind has the '*intent*' which appears to make a connection within the etheric dimension stronger. The only thing I got after around forty minutes was the face of '*Thomas the Tank Engine,*' a children's TV character which had been popular in England for kids. I had no idea why I saw this or the meaning behind it, so I put the mirror away and forgot about the whole thing.

It wasn't that long afterwards when I came back from work and sat in the kitchen. It had been late in the evening, and all I wanted to do was take the weight off my legs and relax. I idly stared through the conservatory glass doors and marvelled at how much like a black mirror they appeared. I could see our small, enclosed garden through the other set of doors leading out back. Our property is enclosed by high fences and brick walls, and there is also a door outside leading directly to our garage, which was always locked, so there was no way anyone could get in, unless they had a ladder! As I sat there, I suddenly saw a young lad coming directly from the garage door. I stood up, thinking we had left it unlocked and that someone had gained access to our property, but I hadn't heard the garage door being opened, or the side one, for that matter. As I stepped forward to see who it was, the young lad now turned in my direction to peer directly through the glass at me. It was Gareth! His appearance had been how I'd remembered him just shortly before his illness took effect. There was no mental communication (something which often occurs within this type of contact), but he merely raised his hand up at me, as if saying, '*What's up?*' I then watched as his entire, physical form began to disperse into hundreds of different lights, like the way the crew from '*Star Trek*' beams up on television. I had been shocked and awed at the same time. He'd done it! This had been a pivotal turning point within my investigations concerning life-after-death research, and there was no question at all in confirming the continuation of life beyond this world of matter.

I cannot emphasise just how incredulous this occurrence had been. It appeared that greater forces beyond our world were now leading me into an altogether different level of understanding, and had the event with Gareth not taken place, I am certain my future would have steered into an altogether different direction. Years later, I came to appreciate much more the nature of the human spirit, along with its transmutation beyond the physical laws of what we consider reality. Other pioneers, such as Monroe and Moody, are a clear indication that we continue to house substance, even when we pass over, and that the etheric and astral are key elements that prove this beyond any shadow of a doubt. I cannot imagine how Gareth was able to project himself temporarily back into the world he had departed, but I am certain that had I the opportunity to shake his hand, mine would have gone straight through his! This is because we are, and as described, operating on diverse levels of frequencies, but the event categorically assures me that death is not the end, but the beginning of another great adventure.

Now we shall explore the mechanics of how those on the other side are able to communicate with us, using the mind as a direct link to prove their existence within the astral planes.

# 'The Eternal Avatar'

## Chapter Seven

## Clairvoyance & Healing

*'I see no wings of feathered beings,*

*To guide me through this day.*

*I rest my head each night to bed,*

*And ask you hear me pray.*

*For all the years of joy and tears,*

*I've wondered where you stand.*

*The pitfalls and the perils do you give a helping hand,*

*When the bad days were against me,*

*Were they better than it could have been,*

*Are your gentle whispers in my head,*

*And is your work all done unseen.*

*High above, down below, or within the space I breathe,*

*Your presence resides beyond the veil,*

*And yet I do believe.'*

Chris John Mayes

We are evolving Avatars ourselves. As mentioned earlier, we are blind to our own brilliance, and something which has been denied us by a system of authority which redirects our 'thinking' down a mental cul-de-sac. Yet, when varied souls on planet earth demonstrate extraordinary super-human abilities, we imagine such powers are unique and exclusive only to them. This is false thinking within the extreme. Avatars like Thoth, Christ, Mohammad, Buddha, among others, had exhibited not only unrestricted access to universal information beyond our material world, but also abilities which others had seen as miracles within their time. It's also interesting to consider that civilisations from our past appear to have been more advanced on an intellectual level than we find ourselves today, but that some kind of catastrophic events saw to their eventual downfall. I have always believed that certain timelines of our past ancestry have been deliberately falsified to fit that famous preferred narrative. For example, the pyramids of Egypt are far older than once considered when analysing the water erosion which had once been prevalent around the Sphinx. Most people imagine this era to have always been a mere desert, but this is far from true. Egypt had once thrived within a tropical climate, and was more than capable of developing its own food produce. As a species, we are never able to truly make any advancement before that civilisation is brought crumbling down. Are we within this same wheel yet again? It is also evident that in the past, such societies had reached the pinnacle of their intellectual capacities before the curtain fell. Aztec, Egyptian, Atlantis, Mayan, Incan, Lemuria, to name but a few of these awe-inspiring settlements, outweigh all our current efforts in truly grasping where they got the knowledge to create such incredible metropolises, along with their spiritual beliefs. It is obvious to speculate that all of these empires had been constructed from minds that 'thought' differently from the way we do in current times, and this is the very reason orthodox religion, along with science, has severed links which would prove our ancestors were a lot smarter than many will freely acknowledge. They were not indoctrinated in quite the same way as we have in terms of conscious suppression and understood the mind and its ability in connecting with alternate dimensions of reality on a grander and more refined level of acceptance.

The brain is a conduit for consciousness and serves, no less, as a gateway to alternate dimensions of reality, allowing universal cognizance to be filtered down into our narrow band of awareness. Our programming has been initiated on a basic level of perception, and this seriously hinders growth for those in life who choose to remain within a condensed field of stagnation. Many, however, have broken away from centralised, mental conditioning in favour of exploring subjects which the system has informed us as having no basis for truth, and there are many such categories which have been mocked at by so-called experts within their field of rational study.

Research within neurology reveals that the brain develops additional synapses whenever a person is fostering new skills, in whatever capacity. Synapses are considered to be connections between neurons (brain cells) that substitute neuronal communication, and upon mental stimulation, cultivate more 'wiring' within cerebral functioning. The 100 trillion synapses in the human cortex develop at a rate of roughly 10,000 every fifteen minutes. The synapses are what create the enormous network that gives us the ability to 'think.' If the mind is not stimulated, such synapses will invariably shut down.

Innovative ideas invigorate not only our mental processing but also our physiology. Such state-of-the-art concepts can also challenge our perception of reality, and all attributed, no less, by our mental conditioning by a system which is intent on subjugating the very foundations of consciousness itself. This is nothing new, and something which has been occurring for over two thousand years and more, especially in the war against spirituality, as well as the topic of UFOs. Giving an example here, and when I was in my twenties, I had a hard time accepting the UFO reality, even though I'd had a few up-close-and-personal encounters, along with what is termed as an 'alien abduction' in 1989. I attended a local UFO group in the late evenings once a month and would talk with the speakers with much vigour about the nature of this most perplexing subject, but when it came to the morning, a part of my mind was screaming: *'... this is all ridiculous! I mean, we're told UFOs don't exist – right?'* I had been experiencing a series of mental challenges, which took some years for me to accept as truth. This was due to conscious dissonance, whereby my own centralised programming had been trying to accept something new, and was also negated by many nameless, faceless individuals who held top governance in society. I really believed in the system we serve, until I discovered it has lied to us, and not just about UFOs or the afterlife either, but many other topics which our system has well and truly pulled the wool over the public's eyes about, and which they administer by using dirty psychological tactics hidden within the realms of conspiracy theory. This is why I completely understand those who have not yet been enlightened as to certain areas of the paranormal where true research is concerned, and which the public is not educated about, along with no transparency being forthcoming in terms of so-called physical evidence. This is apparent because there is hardly any proof anyway, and for the simple reason that much of the phenomenon operates within higher or lower dimensions of space. Quantum theory is already establishing this fact. For me, there came a gradual form of acceptance when I did my own research, and the same for my psychic exploration. Of course, you'll get those people who walk the walk and talk the talk, but the genuine nature of such veracity cannot be underestimated. Our system knows how to twist facts and change the data. They've done it for so long, most of them deserve honorary degrees within their specialised department in deceit!

When I'd visited the medium soon after my grandmother's passing, I remember feeling so shocked, that when I'd gone back to my car two hours later, I sat in the driver's seat, lit a cigarette (I haven't smoked for years now and this was the first and only time I'd lit up in my car) lay my head on the steering wheel and cried my heart out. I didn't care if anyone saw me. It was during this point that I knew for a fact that a vast number of mediums were genuine, and the way the mass media tried to sway the good public's opinion as to this fact was a complete blow to my psyche. I cried more in relief and recall being filled with a new sense of energy, strength, and determination. Many of the strange occurrences from my past were beginning to make sense, and not because I was in any way wishing them to fit either. I cannot emphasise enough the clear facts and details Pearl had brought to my attention surrounding my life. It had been truly staggering. Even to the point where she'd told me I'd be back to train as a medium two years later! The relief in not only knowing that my grandmother was alive (albeit in another dimension of reality), along with there being meaning and purpose to our true nature, was as if some huge weight had been lifted from my shoulders. I felt like I'd merely been drifting aimlessly through life's constant challenges beforehand. What was the point in walking through chaos (and less of order) if all it meant was that we died? The end! Why was I so rebellious about the whole thing? Perhaps I'd been wired differently? Maybe the others who frowned upon my looming interests were themselves normal, and I was the one outside that loop of rational thinking. This had been my original thought back then, but now I, like Chris, know differently.

I wondered how Pearl was able to do what she did. I recall that she'd been looking slightly above and around my head when conducting the reading. I had been fascinated. What was the process of discarnate communication like? How did Pearl maintain this link? The other puzzling factor in all of this was that the media cartel informed the public (in a tongue-in-cheek fashion) through varied channels on television that clairvoyance was all nonsense, and which I knew was not true since I had seen a reputable medium for my reading. I was determined to find out how *they* on the other side communicate from their end, along with what was going on in the mind of the receiver. This had been reinforced with my grandmother reaching out to me when she'd passed, along with the appearance of Gareth through the conservatory glass doors. I also felt like I was somehow being guided by an altogether invisible force, leading me down a path from which I could never backtrack.

When I'd gone back to see Pearl, she advised I sit in an open circle to develop. An open circle is where training mediums privately meet and meditate to try and focus their thoughts, thus reaching out to higher levels of conscious awareness beyond our physical reality. They were also required to bring small messages to members of their group, and which had to be uplifting, along with some form of evidence that their loved ones who had died were reaching out to the developing medium, along with those in attendance, and thereby bringing proof that they were very much alive, albeit in another dimension. I jumped at the chance and was met with a lovely lady named Marion Goodfellow. Marion advised that we first connect with a spirit guide, and I remember Pearl informing me within my reading that mine was a North American Indian. I had no idea at this time why I had one, or their purpose, for that matter, but was soon to have my own, personal confirmation, which proved they really do exist! An open circle was like attending psychic college, and a closed circle was where you received your degree and were developing on an advanced level. During this time, I was very much in college, but was determined to work my way up to find the truth of it all.

I had attended the open circle in Kempston, Bedfordshire, for a while, but was finding it difficult to get any messages. There were seven others in our group, including a police officer. Marion believed in me and said that everything would come together soon enough. She also explained that dealing with this kind of thing was going to take some time, since we were reprogramming our mindset, thus sharpening our mental faculties in allowing those on the other side to communicate their thoughts, and thereby merging them with ours. When I questioned her about my spirit guide and why I wasn't able to get anything from him, she told me the next time I meditated, I was to ask him to come forward and see what happened. Well, I thought, there was no harm in trying! I needed to discover what these beings were all about, and why I hadn't known about mine since the day I was born. I mean, it wasn't like you got a formal education in school about these helpers from spirit!

I had been meditating continuously every weeknight. I was determined to learn more about not only spirit guides, but also our loved ones on the other side. Where were they all spending time together, I wondered? Marion had been most patient with my continual bombardment of questions, but could see the genuine need for me to understand this different language, which worked mostly through the mind. Then, one night, I was rewarded. While in meditation, I asked my spirit guide to tell me his name. This is not important within psychic development, but I needed this North American Indian to at least prove he was genuine, and not some figment of my imagination. I had the certainty that those who had crossed over would communicate through a medium using their voice, rather like the way my grandmother had. This is known as Clairaudience and is occasionally experienced by some mediums in an auditory sense, but I seldom had anything happen to me on this level of psychic development. So, as I sat there, hoping that my spirit guide would talk to me, and upon asking for his name within my mind, I was surprised to see the image of several wolves' heads hovering above a North American Indian who sat with legs crossed, and appeared to be playing a flute of some kind. There, the impression stayed for a few seconds before disappearing, and I thought long and hard. The penny soon dropped, and I realised this invisible helper from spirit was giving me his name, which I interpreted as 'Wolf Song.' For me to clarify this point, I mentally projected out whether Wolf Song could prove to me this was correct within my interpretation. Needless to say, I got nothing mentally back, but was in for another shock the very next day.

I used to work in a large department store, and the very next morning, I was at my station ready to serve the public. A big guy came up to the till point and purchased a shirt. He was wearing a black leather jacket, but underneath his open jacket, he wore a t-shirt which had the picture of a North American Indian sitting cross-legged upon a desert landscape and playing a flute, and above the image was the imprint of howling wolves. I was stunned! The guy noticed me looking at his undergarment and told me he'd gotten it from Canada, and that I had to go there. I didn't mention anything about what I'd requested from my spirit guide the night before (thinking he'd consider me mad), and I guess he thought I was in admiration of his shirt, which, to me, was a clear sign from my helper from the afterlife. Once the gentleman had left, I took myself to a stockroom and placed my back against a wall, overwhelmed by the evidence seemingly being given to me by Wolf Song. I needed a few moments to let the whole experience sink in. I couldn't wait to tell Marion at circle. But the evidence didn't end there. Pete and Di Castle, who were a lovely couple I knew in the village of Wilstead, had been into UFOs and spiritualism. I'd go there every so often to sit in their comfortable home out in the sticks and talk all night about everything mysterious. During this point, they didn't know anything about my exploits into mediumship, or of me trying to link in with my very own spirit guide for that matter, but on this occasion, I was left with my jaw on the floor yet again! They decided to buy me a gift to cheer me up. On opening the large box and unwrapping the item, I was met with an ornament of a North American Indian's head, upon which sat the head of a wolf! It was then that I blurted everything out, informing them both of the incredible evidence I was being presented with by Wolf Song. They had been in awe and thought the transpiring evidence from my guide nothing less than wonderful.

Thinking back to my childhood, I had always been fascinated with Cowboys and Indians. Our mum had bought me and my twin brother, Ronald, a North American Indian outfit, complete with headdress, along with bow and arrows.

We'd spend many long hours pretending to fend off imaginary Cowboys in our back garden. I had a book full of fictional stories of the Wild West and gloated over the fine ink illustrations depicting such times. There had been a drawing of a young lad seated in an old-fashioned steam train and looking out the window to a desert with Cowboys on their horses. That picture haunted me in many ways because I wanted to be on that train too. Many years later, when we'd reached the age of seventeen, we'd been put in touch with a local author, Eileen M Pickering, who would become a life-long friend of the family, and who also mentored my brother and me with our literature. 'Aunty' Eileen was a Western author of ten novels, using the pseudonym Mark Falcon, and her books had been published by a big company in London, Black Horse Westerns. Some years later, she wrote a fictional Cowboy adventure based on us both called *'Kinsella's Revenge.'* The late science fiction author, David Wiltshire, had set the stage for this, and we have both of these wonderful souls to thank, who are no longer on this side of life.

I also have very strong impressions (even before the psychic component initiated in my late twenties) of my brother and I as handsome Cowboys in a past-life, and of us both departing from an old train near a station, helping our 'Mam' off from the open carriage door, and seeing her dressed in a magnificent white outfit. I knew that 'Pa' had left us, and we were there to start life anew. I can even recall an old wooden warehouse which stocked horse saddles, ropes, along with many other items in a small town in Anglo-America. After seeing yet another medium, she brought through my spirit guide and told me in no uncertain terms that in a previous life, I'd shot him in the back in a location known as the Red River within the province of Canada. She even transfigured my guide's face over hers, which had truly fascinated me. This is when a medium allows for the energies of the deceased to temporarily mould their etheric appearance upon the sensitive's physical features and is known as 'Transfiguration.' Although rare, I had been privileged to see what Wolf Song looked like. He appeared young (mid-twenties) and had handsome features. It is also understandable to assume that all guides had themselves incarnated upon earth at one point in time, so that they are aware of the 'human' experience; this would be a vital element when connecting with their incarnated subject. So, this is my penance, I amusingly thought! I'd shot Wolf Song in the back, and now I was to repay him for my foul deed by going through my trials and tribulations in this life. Although the actual events wouldn't have been in any way humorous back then for my guide, it did, however, make me appreciate humility and forgiveness, which work in the overall grand scheme of life, whether from our past, present, or future. There was no way he was going to return the favour and shoot me in the back this time, but our mutual connection assured me in many ways that honour, respect, along with a kind of brotherly love, was being shared by us both, no matter the physical or etheric separation.

Meditation is the way forward in enhancing clarity when connecting with those on the other side. Our minds are being continually distracted and bombarded by all sorts of issues in our day-to-day functioning, and we rarely get a moment to think clearly. On top of this, our centralised programming is hard to disassemble and rearrange in light of the benefits meditation offers. The two hemispheres of our brain are continuously at loggerheads with one another, and this can seriously hinder any form of coherent balancing. We have already mentioned in the previous chapter about Robert Monroe's amazing work with 'Hemi-Sync' and the techniques administered, which promote remarkable results within all areas of the human psyche. Therefore, meditation is one such area where a 'stilling' of the mind allows for this much-needed equilibrium, and brings about a new insight into consciousness, as well as those alternate levels of awareness previously closed to our five senses. The sixth sense is an element that is much needed within our development, and also strengthens our link to the other side. I call it '*the silent language,*' and one where we attune ourselves to an altogether different dialect using our mind, as well as our emotions.

The ability to meditate can oftentimes be frustrating. I would mentally take myself to a forest, and sit there in quiet contemplation, trying hard to keep hold of the visualisation for as long as possible before other images would suddenly pop up in my mind. Occasionally, human faces (the likes of which I've never seen before) sprang forth, and I had to gently coax myself back to that place of peace and calmness within the forest of my choice. I wondered about the significance of the faces. Did they mean anything? Were they dead people wanting to communicate with me? They didn't convey anything other than their appearance, and I wondered whether I was now trailing what I also term '*the psychic internet.*' On these occasions, I never saw my spirit guide, but could sense that he was there, somewhere. But the more I meditated, the less interference I had, and just naturally allowed those faces and scenes to gently pass through my mind. Fighting it on my end didn't seem to do anything, but I was aware after a while that I could control the process, to a degree.

Have you ever been met with a lot of strange images that make absolutely no sense to you when you're just about to sleep? I still do, even after all these years of meditating. Unless I'm thinking of something personally, the moment I let my guard down, the floodgates will open with seemingly random apparitions. In the waking state, and to a degree, we are in control of our thinking. Yet, when asleep, and before entering the REM state (Rapid Eye Movement) and going into the N-REM (Non-Rapid Eye Movement), I recall being totally perplexed as to the nature of these phantasmagorias and wanting to know where exactly they were emanating from. I thought long and hard about it all. As humans, we are antennas, where the brain receives and transmits information, like your mobile phone. Even if you're not using your phone, millions of bits of information from other phones are constantly bombarding the mechanism as they drift through the ether, and which, thankfully (being that your phone is electronic), safeguards any of that data from intruding into your apparatus. However, as humans, we are organic, and therefore, there is a delicate balance as to what we allow entry into the mind. Like sponges, we suck information up in an instant, and on occasions without us consciously being aware of it are nevertheless open to the fluctuations of billions of other people's thoughts traversing the psychic highway. Many of these thoughts merely cancel themselves out, but others are able to manifest if strong enough and take form in the astral planes. You will be informed that such considerations stand without merit, and that these arbitrary projections are nothing less than the subconscious mind filtering through to the conscious mind while no longer in a coherent state of awareness. It is true that when we enter the dream-state, all manner of the weird and wonderful can occur, but this only happens when we have actually sunk into a deeper level of slumber. People ask me, 'Well, aren't they the faces of the deceased?' My answer to this is that it's quite possibly because there's a delicate balance between the living and what we consider to be the dead. This is why, and when in meditation, we are basically creating a stable transmission, projecting a clear signal out to those on the other side. The main consensus is that everything emanates from within the brain, but this is a mere fallacy as the cerebral functioning receives, as well as sends out, information constantly, and we are creators within this process.

There are several considerations to take into account to ensure maximum psychic protection. Prayer or an affirmation defends you from lower entities that traipse the astral planes. In ninety-nine percent of cases, you are safeguarded in any case, and through the connection of your spirit guide (whether you've bonded with one on a mental level or not makes no difference). Many people who walk the earth have no idea they are assisted by one in the first instance, but little do they realise they are being watched over by our invisible friends, along with angels. Bring into your prayer whatever deity you profess to believe in. You can make up your own words, but here is one I use:

*'Dear Lord, I ask to be protected by the ministry of Your grace and light, and with those souls who revel within the love, truth, and humility of Your kingdom. I ask also that my guides and helpers come forth, to ensure I work to the best of my ability as Your humble servant. Amen.'*

Your prayer doesn't have to be anything fancy or too difficult, but ensuring that your thoughts are clear within their intent when sending them to the other side is the most important part. I also envision myself wearing a suit of armour, just for added protection. Mind, as we know, is the creator, and those on their side manifest their reality solely via this method, so your projected thoughts really do make a difference. What you generate in terms of belief will appear on theirs, depending on how strong that mental attention is generated. There have even been documented cases whereby someone calling out in the name of their preferred God has saved them from those rare incidents of demonic intrusion, or most notably, an alien abduction conducted by diminutive, grey-like entities known as the 'Greys.' The power of thought, along with the spoken word, is never to be underestimated. Each carries vibrations that resonate powerfully within the *will* of the individual. Vibrations are what we, and everything else in the grand scheme of creation, wholly represent. Your energy signature impresses upon the unseen fabric beyond time and space each time you send out a thought. This is why it's so important to try and remain positive, as negative thoughts can have a detrimental way of returning to us by what is known as karma. We are all guilty of having bad thoughts now and again, but working towards enhancing a healthier mindset can only assist in a finer connection with those unseen dimensions.

Dedication and practice are other important fundamentals within your training. If your heart isn't in the whole thing, then not much of anything is going to happen. Your intention must come from deep within the core of your spirit. You cannot fail at something that you're intending to do. If you persist in your beliefs (whatever they are), you will eventually gain results, along with mastering them. When I used to run psychic development workshops, I would invariably have a few come up to me and say they were finding meditation difficult. Yet, through careful guidance, they were eventually able to break through those barriers. I wouldn't worry too much when in a meditative state if you don't see your spirit guide to begin with, or if at all, for that matter. Remember, you are enhancing not only your visual processing, but also your capacity to feel. Sensing beyond our normal range of perception is the key to unlocking your true potential when building that psychic link.

Spirit guides are there to maintain a strong link from their side of life through to this one. Whether acknowledged or not, their assistance will start from our birth and continue right up until our ultimate, physical death. Spirit guides will invariably work with you in varied ways you choose or are gifted in whatever area they have opened themselves up to. For instance, some people do healing, art, or sound therapy. It makes no difference how that individual works; your guide from spirit will assist in any way they can. And let's be straight here, it doesn't matter either if they're an animal, human, angel, or alien! How you connect with that guide is important to you, and no one else.

As a medium, we are to bring evidence through to someone on earth who is no longer a part of this world, and the spirit guide (so we understand) is not only there in our life to give us a few invisible hunches if we've found ourselves being diverted from life's beaten track, but also to come forward in any manner we so desire on a mental level. As stated before, millions of souls here do not even know they have a guide, but they will still be there in the distance, watching over you. However, there is one golden rule with all guides, and that is they will never interfere with your personal life unless absolutely necessary. That's your department! I fell for this many years ago, hoping and praying for certain things to happen, but I discovered that I had to deal with my problems myself.

Going back to the question as to what it's like when receiving information from a dead person while conducting a reading, here's a brief example: Imagine that I am a dead person. Now, I am going to ask you, within your mind, and with your eyes open, to visualise a golden Labrador. Can you see it? How about me now asking you to see a police officer, or a doctor? What's happening is that I am giving you a prompt from where I am situated across time and space into your 'now.' A spirit person will use your mind and your body as a circuit board of visual stimuli and emotional connection. They will mentally project images into your mind. However, do not be mistaken, because some of these images do not always come across as clear, and therefore, I rely on the sensory connection, which helps build the language necessary to bring evidence forward. How about seeing that golden Labrador again, but this time getting you to really feel he's with you, and you're stroking his fur. Sense his pleasure at being loved this way. How does that make you *feel*? Remember, feelings create visual language, too, which is vital within your development. I'm not so sure it's a good idea to go stroking the police officer or doctor (a little humour there), but in these situations it's vital for you to get in touch with your feelings and interpret how 'you' are experiencing this from a sensory point of view. HOW DO YOU FEEL? That's important and can tell us a lot about the animal or person that has crossed over. As humans, we seldom feel because we switch off when going out in that big, wide world. The only time we access our sensory link is if someone has affected us in some way, whether positively or negatively, or we are experiencing love, listening to music, or watching a good film. Much of the time, our emotions are lulled by monotony.

When in psychic development, there are numerous ways that spirit will connect with you. We cannot always choose the way we want to work, but rather, such choices are governed by those attributes that are strongest within you. Here is a list of those fundamental areas, and sometimes combined with multiple elements.

**Clairvoyance**

Clairvoyance is the ability to see people and situations within the mind's eye. Usually, most mediums keep their eyes open when using this method of 'seeing,' but some prefer to close them to block out any form of distraction. Clairvoyance also means 'clear seeing,' but do not be fooled, because on many occasions this process is anything but! To perform clairvoyance means to be in a slightly altered state of conscious awareness, and not that dissimilar to daydreaming. Information is communicated via the projection of images sent from the mind of the deceased, and it is up to the medium receiving such evidence to interpret and translate these as they are presented. Many mediums use symbols to get their message across, rather like, for example, seeing an overturned chair, which would indicate an unhappy home, and so forth. Others, like me, deal directly with the raw energy coming from the mental and emotional mind of the deceased, as opposed to bypassing it and allowing for such symbols to be present. This is achieved when clairsentience is also amalgamated within the clairvoyance.

**Clairsentience**

Clairsentience is all about using our sensory perception, which is another language in conveying messages from spirit. Meditation is also vital when attuning yourself within this state of perceptual equilibrium. While relaxed and focused, we're able to stop for a while and really 'feel' what's going on within and around our body. We are sensitising this area, and one which can also invoke deep, mental impressions which come through as a quite different form of communication. How you feel can generate strong thoughts not necessarily associated with you, but could be saying a lot about the person from the other side, influencing such stimuli within your biological system. Mediums are a circuit board, ready to translate information coming from a higher level of vibrational reality, and which lowers itself into this one, like the signal to your mobile phone. For instance, if you feel you have a person coming through to you as a spirit, you may experience a slight tightening around your heart, which may indicate they'd passed with a heart attack, or there had been issues around this area which resulted in their death. Spirit will use your body to convey exactly what they wish to impart to their loved one, whom you'll be reading for. Don't worry if your body begins to feel strange while in meditation or, indeed, reading for someone, as this is how the dead infuse their overall evidence. We can't always get information being relayed to us correctly to begin with, because it's a timely process. Even for myself as a working medium, I still encounter problems, so it's no big deal.

**Clairaudience**

Clairaudience is a process whereby the medium hears voices. It's rare for mediums to solely rely on this method without the aid of visual or sensory stimuli, but most have proven this practise quite effective. The famous late British medium, Doris Stokes, would say that spirit whispered in her ear, but on many occasions, such discarnate voices can be heard as though coming from within your head. I myself have had occasions where such distinct voices have connected with me in this way, but not when I am reading for someone. These occasionally happen when I'm just about to sleep, and the communicator will only relay a few words, and that's it! I cannot emphasise strongly enough this reality, and when it happens, you're left a little shocked. Seeing as the discarnate person no longer has the larynx, they usually project themselves in the clairvoyant/clairsentient way, which is far easier for them. Yet, the ability for those on the other side to connect in this manner is nothing less than amazing. But, saying that, Electronic Voice Phenomenon (EVP) is another fashionable way of spirit talking through radio-shack equipment, and something I too have experienced. However, within clairaudience, the voices are usually distinct, unlike those within EVP, which come across as sounding mechanical in nature. Those who use 'spirit boxes' rely solely on their mechanical apparatus, and this may indicate why voices from the other side come across with little or no emotions whatsoever. In the case of a medium being the main receptor (rather than a radio), the deceased can mould within the mental and biological matter of their subject, and thus a smooth form of interaction is initiated on a personal level of identification.

**Clairalience**

Clairalience is the ability to smell. How many times have you had an experience where a flood of memories suddenly comes to the surface within your mind after smelling certain fragrances or odours? In these instances, you are suddenly transported back in time to a place you can vividly recall. Also known as Clairolfaction, Clairosmesis, or Clairessence, and which derives from the French translation meaning 'clear smelling,' these can be powerful affirmations within evidence of survival beyond this realm. Clairalience is another form of extrasensory perception, and the medium is normally able to detect such scents being generated by those on the other side. Everything in heaven is composed of various energy fields that vibrate at different frequencies, and such oscillations can be used to mimic those smells or odours held within the memory of the departed loved one. Clairgustance is another attribute where taste can also be generated. If a medium uses this ability more so than the other above-listed processes, then it is most certain that taste is also incorporated into the reading. I had an incident whereby a young lad came through to his mother and who'd shot himself by placing a gun inside his mouth. I had immediately been met by the taste of metal, and I knew the young lad was wanting his mother to know this was indeed her son, and that he'd passed in such tragic circumstances. It's rare for me to taste or smell, but they have happened, and invariably this will also occur sometime or other with you.

These are the main faculties that can be used to enhance spirit communication, but you may find more than one of those elements listed above being combined as you develop further. If this should happen, merely acknowledge it and keep practicing. There is no right or wrong way if you're using an open, truthful heart when reaching out to the divine. As I developed within my own psychic abilities, it was a bit like fumbling in the dark. Although I had been aware of the importance of meditation and attempting to attune my emotions and visual stimuli to a higher level of perception, the rest I had to work out for myself. But I did discover something else which astounded me when starting to do private readings. I realised just how true it is when considering those now on the other side can use you like a puppet in order to get their message across to the person having the reading.

A young lady came to the house for a private reading. As usual, I explained to her the way I worked, and that she was only to acknowledge with a clear 'yes' or 'no' to confirm or deny the evidence as it was being presented. As I linked in, I was met with a well-dressed gentleman who was standing next to a golden Labrador. I had the impression this was her father, and that he'd died from having a heart attack. The lady acknowledged this was the case. Then, something strange happened. I lifted my right hand and moved it towards my eyes, so that they were completely covered. Then I said to her that I couldn't see anything at all, that for some reason everything had gone black. I felt the lady's hand reaching over to my arm as she gently said, 'My lovely, he was blind!' I recalled being absolutely incredulous, and the golden Labrador sitting by her father's side should have been enough to consider this fact, but it appeared he was taking things one step further in getting this information across to both of us, and all because I'd missed the point. Incredibly, the gentleman had used my body as a puppet, and I realised that, as mediums, our actions are also brought into the fray.

There was another case where a lady I was reading for had her sister-in-law from the other side appear from spirit. As the sister-in-law was relaying her information to me from within my mind, I suddenly found myself positioning my hands around my throat. I relayed this to my sitter, and she confirmed the details. But I was also overcome with a bad feeling, and now felt my body being pressed down, as though someone was on top of me, pinning me to the ground, while all along finding it difficult to breathe. It transpired that the sister-in-law had been murdered by her own husband while her two babies were asleep upstairs, and all because he thought she was having an affair. Such readings of this kind fill me with great sadness, but the soul of the deceased has returned home and is no longer tied to such tragic events here on earth. At the same time, they will relay the events as best they can to you as the medium, even though such occurrences have long since passed. This is where your evidence lies, so that the person you are reading for knows categorically that this is one of their relatives, friends, or colleagues.

Another incident in question when performing clairvoyance was bringing a relative through who'd been in a group with five other people, and sadly, all had been killed in a helicopter crash. I saw myself in a small enclosure, and ahead of me, while seated back in the helicopter, I viewed the controls from a distance, along with the silhouette of the pilot. I knew the person from spirit was trying to show me where they had been in location to the incident. I could hear an alarm from within the cabin sounding loudly, and looking directly ahead and out through the cockpit window, I perceived what I thought was mist. Then, everything went dark. It transpired that the person I was reading for had lost a relative onboard the helicopter; the controls of which had malfunctioned, and the pilot was unable to detect they were heading straight towards a mountain through the thick fog, and all due to instrumentation failure.

I read for a widow years later whose husband had also been involved in a helicopter crash, but the conditions in which had been quite different. This time, I could see clairvoyantly much clearer in terms of the evidence which was being presented and observed myself as a passenger in a two-seater helicopter. I detected that the lady's husband was visually relaying how it had all been from his perspective. I could see we were not too far from an oil rig, and the sky had been a clear blue. I realised with shock that the helicopter was dangerously close to the ocean, and I felt myself now being swung violently in a circle and knew the tail rotor had failed. What was incredible was that at first, I found myself in the helicopter, and then I was able to view the scene as an outsider. It had been heartbreaking to see this beautiful, white machine, along with the occupants, suddenly plummeting into the ocean, shattered blades being flung out into the air as the helicopter made its fateful crash, killing both men onboard. The lady's husband had been a big boss and was going to do his inspection on the oil rig. I wasn't able to confirm where in the world this had occurred, but it was enough to ensure that the gentleman was safe on the other side.

As stated earlier, not all readings are so clear in detail. It depends on how the communicator from spirit came across in this life before they passed. We have people on earth who find it challenging to relay what they want to say or have difficulty illustrating certain events. When we cross over, we do not suddenly sprout wings! People on that side of life are really no different from how they had been here, accept they are on a different vibration of reality. We, as the psychic, can also be at fault, depending on the energies present in the room and at the time of the reading. There have even been some people I have not been able to read for. The other factor which has always puzzled me is if the dead get help from an advanced soul on their side in order to facilitate such communication through to the medium. It's an interesting speculation, but I should imagine there is help for them, too, on some level. Your spirit guide, so we understand, is a vital link when such connections are being made.

Invariably, someone will attend a reading and not get the person they hoped for coming through. I remind my 'sitter' firsthand that we are not mind-readers, or sorcerers, for that matter, but I have often wondered why this is the case. Could the spirit of that much-sought-after individual gone through a process of reincarnation? This makes for interesting speculation. Or, perhaps, they have moved on beyond the astral planes, which now makes it difficult for them to communicate. After all, and as we shall discover later, there are many such levels of reality beyond death. In a sizable percentage of cases, though, success is achieved, and much to the gratitude of the medium and those in attendance.

**Healing**

Healing is another area where messages can also be relayed from those in spirit. When Chris and I do these sessions on one another, it is a most amazing experience. One time he came to visit, I had a really bad neck and shoulder, which had put me out for just under three months. Nothing the doctors prescribed seemed to work with the intense pain I was going through. As soon as Chris had opened in prayer and placed his hands on me, I could immediately feel energy working through that area of my body, which was causing so much discomfort. I detected the amazing heat radiating from his hands, along with a creeping sensation which I sensed travelling down my back and across to the neck. Naturally, I was drawn into a type of cocooned slumber while he worked on me, and the relief was heaven-sent! When this occurs, those in spirit are directing their energy through to the healer from the other side and straight into the person being healed. In most cases, healing is not a miracle cure but does help to alleviate symptoms. However, saying that, there have been many documented cases where people from across the world have been cured through the process of hands-on healing, as well as through the administration of prayer. It is quite normal for the healer to have no awareness of such energies being administered on their end. Occasionally, an intense cold feeling can also be detected, but this depends on how the healer works. Hot or cold, it matters not, as the facilitation of such forces works towards the betterment of those being healed. During such episodes when Chris is working his wonders, I begin to feel calm, sleepy, and enveloped in a warmth that cannot be described. He is a natural healer as well as a psychic, and senses things about me when we're not even in one another's company. We could be talking on the phone, and he'll suddenly tell me something he's psychically picked up about me, and all correct. We have a strong connection, and this brings in that famous *'spooky action at a distance,'* along with its bizarre, mind-boggling nature. His gifts bring me great comfort, especially during a time when I'd been in so much pain. I've had healing before in the past, but never as strong as his! Naturally, most psychics or healers in the majority of cases (of which he is both) are extremely creative in nature, and Chris's art is nothing less than staggering. I have always believed this is for the simple reason that such energies find their way through to the sensitive in other areas of our lives, and art is a major component where one is able to express a language difficult to interpret through the spoken word. We cannot accurately describe in words just what's going on while healing is taking place, any more than when reading for someone, because we translate such information as we decipher it without bias, but the energies are there, nonetheless. During these sessions, intense heat can be felt, along with a tingling sensation around certain areas of the body. Such incredible energy from source is working through the healer, and right into the biological vehicle of the recipient. The healer will be drawn to certain areas of the body, ostensibly being guided to where much of this energy is to be directed. When Chris and I have completed our session, we will share what we psychically picked up with one another, and this is always an uplifting experience. Chris has also read for many people himself and left them astounded! He recalls that they are often spontaneous and unplanned. So, it's fair to say that if you're clairvoyant, chances are you've got that healing vibe also.

Healing can also be done from a distance. Studies have shown that absent healing (and where the healer is not physically in the company of the person to administer the hands-on approach) can be just as effective. Holding the thought of the person in the mind of the recipient and focusing upon them, while at the same time sending out positive affirmations, works in much the same fashion. Chris and I have practiced this technique on varied occasions. However, distant healing can be an enormously powerful tool, especially if there are more minds focused upon their subject. This is a mental act directed at the health and well-being of a distant person. Any number of approaches can be attained, ranging from aura healing, shamanic healing, spiritual healing, and nonlocal healing, to name but a few. They all work in the same manner in an attempt to correct the disrupted vibrational field of the patient. There have been varied arguments within mainstream medical science regarding the validity of this approach, and something outwardly rejected by the World Health Organisation (WHO). My argument is that by amalgamating the WHO and the holistic method would surely only bring more benefit to the patient in the long run, instead of the WHO not considering the wider picture in terms of health and longevity to human life. Everything organic and inorganic vibrates on varied frequencies within the quantum realm, and by treating the whole as opposed to the part, may make all the difference when exploring what I believe will be a new science. I'm sure in the future, those within the medical profession will see this approach as rather medieval in not acknowledging alternate methods. But, as we all know, money is the key factor here, and the holistic department shows that next to nothing is needed when utilising what is known as free energy. There has been much speculation as to varied inventors' revolutionary discoveries being destroyed, and all in the name of large companies who realise they'll be put out of business if such ideas come to fruition, but the day money is no longer applicable in the future (and if we as a species survive through the advent of our current troubles) then I am certain such doors to these remarkable areas of research will be opened.

Sound healing is another area used through the use of instruments, as well as those coming from our very own vocal cords, which serve as an extension of powerful vibrational fields which can be created to enhance therapeutic stimulation. Such methods utilise potent resonance which literally affects us on a neurological, physiological, and biochemical level. Sounds alter the brain, muscle, nerve, and organ functioning, depending on the reverberations being emitted. You know the difference between heavy rock and classical music. The two are, on occasions, totally at odds with one another regarding their tempo, and you either love them or hate them. Invariably, they will alter your mood to some degree. The same with listening to a sad song, which can invoke feelings of melancholy, or an uplifting piece where you reach for the stars. Sound also stimulates consciousness, allowing for the mind to expand beyond its normal range of conscious perception.

When I had attended a conference in Watford at the UFO Academy to lecture on UFOs organised by Kerry Cassidy, CEO and Founder of *'Project Camelot'* called *'Awake and Aware,'* one of the speakers had been Andrea Foulkes who is a gifted lady and has appeared on such shows as *'This Morning,'* and *'Have I Been Here Before?'* Through a series of synchronicities, I found myself totally awed by her lecture about the soul, and her work in taking people back to their previous lives, again dealing with trauma and reuniting harmony and balance to all those she has helped. This had been when my and Chris' book was within its developing stages, and an area which spirit had obviously intended to reinforce the subject of healing, past lives, and reincarnation. Andrea is an Intuitive Visionary and Founder of '*Soul Freedom Therapy.*' She went on to do 'Soul Healing' by way of sound, and her powerful voice hit many as she sang from spirit to send incredible harmonic frequencies throughout the hall. I remember my whole body feeling as though it had suddenly been electrified, but in a wonderful way. It had been a very moving experience, and, once again, I couldn't wait to tell Chris!

Visual patterns generated through auditory frequencies clearly demonstrate complex geometry, which appears hidden within the quantum realm. Such oscillations are brought forth into our sphere by way of electrical discharges. Tone Generators are effective tools in exhibiting just how certain vibrations can be manipulated and brought forth into our material realm. A phenomenon known as 'Modal Cymatics' is when a thin coating of particles, paste, or liquid has been placed on a plate, and vibrations are then generated around the perimeter of the dish, where electrical impulses are then converted from wave to form. Such experimentation has been explored by way of electrical stimulation. There is a theory that our ancestors may have used such sound techniques in moving large blocks of granite and stone (like those of the Great Pyramids of Egypt, along with other ancient settlements around the world) using this technology. Vibrations create sound and sound effects, as well as excite matter deep within its molecular core, changing the configuration of geometric formations, and depending on the frequencies used.

Make no mistake in the fact that thoughts are real, whether used for good or bad. The brain is merely a gateway to control the flux of consciousness while we are locked into this temporary reality. Unfortunately, our world appears to have been hijacked by an altogether different force, and one far removed from the human species. This is an area most will find hard to prove (or believe, for that matter) and, of course, those masters operating from behind the scenes will do everything in their power to make this so. Don't you think it's strange how such subjects regarding clairvoyance, healing, and even UFO research have never been taken seriously by a system we serve, which is supposed to be there as truth, other than those organisations fighting to bring transparency to the table? Indeed, these areas of enquiry are by no means new. They've been around for thousands of years, yet a systematic agenda appears to have been enforced in blinding us all to such realities. There are pioneers whose work has been destroyed when venturing too close to the truth, and not only within UFO research, but also those areas of science which could enhance human life for the better. Both Chris and I believe that, and as Avatars ourselves, we are waking up to the sleep this system has tried to impose upon us, blinding us to our own spiritual sovereignty, along with incredible truths which will set us free from such power. These so-called masters will be discussed later, but it's important for us to know both the good and the bad so that we are able to take a balanced view of what's going on in the background. Everything has been divided, even in those subjects addressed, and there is a particularly good reason for this. Like any puzzle, until it's put together, we can't see the whole picture, and that's just how those at the top of the symbolic pyramid of power wish for this to remain. But folk are clever, and gradually seeing that nothing is truly separate, that all things are connected, including our spiritual selves. Of course, what is known as the 'Deep State' has been working on sound technology as a weapon. Notice how anything that could work for the betterment of humanity is seized upon by the military's weapons unit through varied scientific divisions. Now, most people will say that we're barking up the wrong tree with such allegations, but didn't they say that about remote viewing back in the day, and only to discover there really had been a military psychic program in operation through the testimony of certain whistleblowers, namely Dr David Morehouse, and under the auspice of psychics and authors, Ingo Swann, Russell Targ and Harold E. Puthoff? There are other areas too sensitive to cover here, but this just goes to show how the public has been led to believe in one thing, only to discover their suspicions were very much justified, even if some of those shady areas still can't be proven as fact.

In the science fiction film '*Dune*' written by bestselling author, Frank Herbert (Chiltern Books, 1965), a group of his centralised characters known as the Sisterhood, the 'Bene Gesserit,' used a sound technique known as 'The Voice' which was an ancient audio-neuro control tool to disarm or control others by way of projecting resonance on a powerful level. The central character, Paul Atreides, is later exploited for his gifts by the Bene Gesserit and goes on to create weapons linked to 'The Voice' to overthrow their enemy. What we think in terms of future events within science fiction, in the majority of cases, becomes science fact. Sound vibration is a powerful form of being able to affect matter. Such hidden technology is very much evident in our world today.

Mysterious incidents in China and Cuba in 2017 through to 2018 indicated by the U.S. embassy that sound weaponry had been deployed against Americans residing in the aforementioned countries. Of course, the Chinese authorities denied any part to play in the preceding events in 2018, but it is believed such resonance technology had been used on several American diplomats, among many other individuals, while based in Guangzhou in southern China. One of those involved, who remains anonymous for political reasons, said he'd suffered traumatic brain injury after experiencing abnormal sounds and pressure in his ears over several months. U.S. officials noted that similar symptoms felt in 2017 by yet another U.S diplomat appeared consistent with these sonic attacks. The U.S. Embassy, through its health alert, warned that if anyone visiting China or Cuba experiences any form of auditory or sensory disorientation, accompanied by unusual sounds or piercing noises, should not attempt to locate the cause and remove themselves to a safe area. A weapon? Certainly, appears so!

There are also instances where people are able to shatter glass by way of vocal projection. By generating a sound which matches the resonant frequency of the glass through what is known as constructive interference and thereby increasing the vibration of the glass, which exceeds the strength of the bonds holding its molecules together, it will invariably shatter. These experiments have been tried and assessed and are a reality, nonetheless. We are able to see just how powerful our thoughts and voices are, along with the benefits and disadvantages they offer, yet we come back to that wheel of where the system plays down any suggestion of the real Avatar you represent, along with the incredible energy you harbour. Our mind creates everything, but because of continual psychological dissidence by those running the show, the human has been shut down and conditioned, but many are in tune with this knowledge and have forcibly broken away from such condensed programming in order for them to seek out their own truths, along with greatness.

Once the Avatar truly breaks through the mould which has kept them stuck, they begin to discover a different world, and not always the one they view outwardly, but one that is within themselves. The material plane we consider as our ultimate corporeality is nothing less than a projection emanating from within the brain. There is talk that the universe, and everything around us, is nothing less than a hologram. Such thoughts decades ago would have promoted much laughter, but we are beginning to discover that, and like most things in life, not everything is as it seems. All substance, whether material or immaterial, is held together through the atomic realm, and these atoms fluctuate as energy vibrations, leading us to understand that a great deal of the empty space within the building blocks of life which atoms demonstrate within their oftentimes peculiar nature tells us that other dimensions exist within those spaces. Would it surprise you to know that the spirit world exists right around us, and without us even being remotely aware of it? Like the signals to your mobile phone, radio, and TV set carry information, but our senses are not attuned to their frequency. The other side is not to be found a trillion light-years away from our present location either. It is neither up nor down, left nor right. In fact, it encompasses the same space we find ourselves in, what we believe is the one and only true world. This may explain what is occurring within those areas of high strangeness, whether UFOs, ghosts, departed loved ones, Werewolves, Sasquatch, along with thousands of other head-scratching and difficult to fathom mysteries which plague our world.

We shall now draw our attention to the astral planes and see what happens to our Avatar when our time within this illusion of time and space has ended. We will also explore within our book a few theories as to why many still consider the paranormal and UFO phenomenon as being completely unrelated to one another, and where there could indeed be a connection to the whole, as opposed to the parts. Chris and I have discussed this in great detail. One area is something I had formulated back in 1996 in an article published entitled '*Spirits In a Material World,*' which appeared in the magazine '*Alien Encounters.*' We may also find ourselves surprised at the fact that our very own system has deliberately falsified not only certain realities when considering the supernatural, but themselves taken extraordinary efforts in ensuring no connections can be made which will unravel a far greater truth, and one our system fears in being revealed!

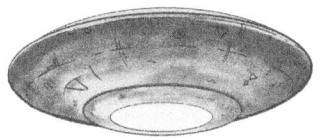

# 'The Eternal Avatar'

## Chapter Eight

### The Astral Planes

*'Between this world and where the heavens sing,*

*Are the souls from death come entering,*

*To see the life and take review,*

*No pain, no sorrow to start anew,*

*Aligning to thought and energy once more,*

*A place to harmonize and restore,*

*To reclaim the magic and rise again,*

*All within the Astral Plane.'*

Chris John Mayes

So, where do we go once our Avatar has left this side of life through the act of death? Within certain religious ideologies, many take their holy books as gospel and will tell you how it is. Nothing in heaven or on earth will sway their convictions from the very passages printed within the pages, which clearly illustrate a vengeful God, of wars, destruction, and events which go against the very foundation of all things good when considering an ultimate divine being. Such books have seen to vast differences of opinion worldwide, which have led to bloody wars, along with the slaughter of millions of people, and a total divide between those who have other ideas about the afterlife and God, which continues in the present day. Not only this, but so much fear is emphasised on how a human soul will be damned to hell, along with being judged by an equally judgmental being once our journey on earth comes to an end. But is this true? Could the reality of what happens to us when we die be totally at odds with what's been relayed?

Death is a natural process, and something not to be feared. Although arguments rage regarding what becomes of the spirit once it passes beyond the material realm, at the end of the day, it all boils down to the actual experience itself from those who '*know*' what it's like. NDE research, along with accounts of OBE, gives us a vague idea of what we can come to expect when our life on earth has ended, namely because of the incredible testimony and patterns which follow from one unrelated individual to another across the world, and where such documented incidents of soul survival is concerned. Prominent researchers have themselves explored this fascinating territory and know for certain that there are varied planes of reality beyond the earthly experience. How you viewed your world as you pass is the first stage of what you'll experience when the cross-over takes effect. Your beliefs are central to this process. People describe separating from their body as the spirit is released, no matter the way in which someone dies. The surprising element is that any fear experienced beforehand is immediately released through the realisation that all pain and suffering has now been removed, and an expanded awareness of 'self' presents itself on a universal level of cognizance. All memories which had been recorded in the life left behind unite, creating a deeper understanding of the hows and whys within that incarnation. No longer inhibited by the restricted flow of consciousness itself, which once operated through the brain, all parts of the whole in terms of memory come together.

There is no time on the other side, and something felt on a joyous level of realisation once the severance between body and spirit occurs. The illusion of physical death is apparent just as soon as the spirit is liberated from its matrix, no matter whether the person believed in an afterlife or not, makes absolutely no difference whatsoever. After all, we are born into this life on earth accepting the fact that we are here, and many go out with a lot more problems with the acknowledgement that death secures our fate, once and for all. The structured belief system held by the NDEer in the first part of the crossing invariably begins to unfold, and for those who were themselves atheists, becomes insignificant as the merging of their new reality begins to expand. If the individual imagined they would see Angels, Christ, Mohammad, Krishna, Buddha, or whomever they held within their structured belief-system, such idols will present themselves in this fashion to make the crossing more amenable. For those who had strong family connections will be met by those they loved and have preceded them into the light. The experiences are varied but constitute in some kind of meeting to greet the newly arriving spirit from the material into the astral. There are even common cases where a dying relative will see their long-deceased relatives appearing to them on their deathbed and which is believed to bring comfort to them before taking their last breath. This would indicate preparations are being secured by those spirits for the arrival of their kin.

The astral planes are thought to be the first location that the soul is drawn into. This can invariably be experienced in a number of ways: from moving through a tunnel towards a light, crossing a stream in a boat, or just finding themselves in an environment more real in terms of visual and sensory stimuli than the one they've departed. As stated, in the majority of cases, the structure of the unfolding new world presents itself more or less in a fashion hot-wired into the deepest aspect of the human psyche, and such sensations as liberation, freedom, enlightenment, and love begin to immediately surface. It is effectively the astral body that, and no longer bonded to its cruder biological form, connects within the realm of thought and energy, for this is what we encompass on a universal level of reality. To all intents and purposes, the astral and beyond *is* the real world. Although some NDEers report a sensation of movement when traversing beyond space and time, motion is still evident when locating oneself from one part of the astral to another, and just through the manner of thought alone. Yet, in the primary stages, the spirit is drawn by some invisible force to its intended location on the other side. It's interesting in cases of practicing controlled astral projection for those adepts here on earth, and whereby they will not encounter the full experience within these states, due to the fact that they are still attached to the material world via the famous silver cord. In such exploits (even in instances of extended consciousness such as Remote Viewing and OBE), complete severance of the astral from the physical has not fully taken effect, and thereby the individual can only go so far within these alternate dimensions. Such states are therefore forcibly induced, and the experience may differ slightly in terms of emotions and sensations, which the naturally arriving spirit will sense. This may suggest, in varied cases of UFO and alien interaction, as to why the environment suddenly becomes strange, and perhaps due to the fact that such spectres are bringing *you* into *their* reality. An indication of the merging and then separation of vibrational density is evident through the loss of time, the area becoming electric, along with an absence of normal environmental sounds being heard. Such occurrences are also evident in cases of Sasquatch and Dogman encounters, among others. This, I believe, is when a cross-over from our reality and theirs momentarily unifies, creating such alterations within our sense of reality itself, and where interaction is physically possible from both worlds.

Inescapable too is the fact that what you take within the astral planes in terms of your essence cannot be fooled, no matter the masks or hidden dimensions of 'self' projected while incarnated on earth. Deception, alter-ego, along with those characteristics used to fool others, vanish instantly. Here, your soul is bared naked and open in a revelation of what you're really all about. The multi-dimensional aspects of you are finally exposed and brought together as one, and not those versions of you which, in varied cases, had been protected through sheaths of illusory armour back on earth, or the wide-ranging characters you played to make advancements to meet your own needs, whether positive or negative. The realisation of such truths only serves to remind us of those aspects we choose to enhance or ignore for the betterment of the soul's journey. This usually brings into the fray the famous panoramic life-review, whereby the facilitation of all memory recorded within that life is enhanced in every minute detail, not only visually, but also emotionally. It is here where a sharing of yours and those you encountered along your journey on earth are explored. In the large majority of reported cases through NDE research, there appears to be no judgment within the review other than your understanding on a deeper level of how your thoughts and actions affected those you encountered along the way. This mirroring effect also informs you of how others touched you, in much the same way as you them. It must be made clear that none of us are angels while on earth, and we are all prone to making mistakes, but if, and within that life, we really understood and changed for the betterment of not only ourselves but others too, any karmic issues would be immediately absolved within an alteration of our thoughts and actions which may have had major repercussions on varied levels. Too much emphasis has been placed on a vengeful God, along with those who do not believe in Him being sent straight to hell. Make no mistake, the astral planes is a dimension which is home to the good, the bad and the downright nasty, but these realms are often brought forward depending upon the mind-set of the individual when their crossing takes place, and where there is no God to condemn you to the fires of hell as soon as you arrive within the astral world – unless, of course, that's what you ultimately believe! However, that said, there are those who have had blood-curdling encounters with abhorrent beasts which appear like something straight from the pages of your worst nightmare, but in such confrontations, the individual is usually saved by the appearance of an angel, or the archetypal form of a holy being.

Because the astral realm is composed of mind-energy, your form will no longer be identified by its biological mechanism, which needed so much nurturing and attention back on Earth. Once the initial period of your previous physical appearance is discarded, you will be recognised by others through your energy. Those who have preceded you into the light will at first appear to you as you had remembered them back on earth, but we know from NDE accounts that this is a choice you and they make on all counts, and of how your appearance in terms of manifestation is presented is entirely up to you and they. Energy is transmutable, and the laws of physics that you had been so accustomed to in your last incarnation no longer apply. Here, the very foundation of creation is attributed to mind-power, and something which can occur instantaneously through the process of projected thought, unlike in the physical dimension, where materials must be used to fashion those things brought forth from the mind.

There is no floating around on a cloud or seeing yourself playing a harp either, and neither are you a luminous orb flitting hither and thither as one would come to imagine. The astral planes are the realms of infinite realities, and more so than the one previously experienced while in the lower atomic state of being. In this awareness, which we call '*The Awakening*', the spirit is truly liberated beyond all conscious measure, and a deeper understanding of reality, along with your place within creation, is realised. Because the brain, which had once functioned as a filtering mechanism for information and had restricted the flow of perception, is no longer a part of your new construct, the etheric body, which held all memories and served as the main storage area, is instantly accessible. On earth, the facilitation of recalls from what we consider the past via cognizance, which had appeared distant and murky, has become more real and alive than ever before. The astral has no time structure; therefore, everything is in the 'NOW.' Considering this fact, while in our biological space-suits, there really is no future or past because we are continuously only aware of the present moment. The illusion of time serves to remind us that living in the moment is the only reality we know while temporarily based within the material. We can never genuinely appreciate a moment on planet earth because such experiences, which we thought of as real, are themselves holographic waves and, thus, stored within the higher part of our spiritual essence. Although most NDEers find it hard to describe their journey to the other side, I know exactly what they mean, because I, too, had what is known as an NDE. I almost drowned as a kid while living in South Africa, and, once again, although the narrative is devoid of emotional and extrasensory content, which fails to replicate the richness of the experience itself, we can at least try.

My mother and stepfather had decided to emigrate to South Africa, thinking this would be a better way of life. As a young lad, I'd been excited at the prospect of going abroad to live and imagined we'd be in a jungle with roaming elephants and wild lions prowling the land. Such is a kid's imagination! However, it had been very different. There was no jungle, no elephants, or lions. We had relocated to Vanderbijlpark, an industrial city situated on the Vaal River in the South Gauteng province. We lived in a large bungalow which had plenty of grounds, but what shocked me the most was how expansive the geography was, and I never really liked being there. Thankfully, around 1977, my parents temporarily separated, and Mum, along with my sister, brother, and me, flew back to England to live with our grandparents for a time. It was far too hot, and where my young dreams, I realised, could never happen in this country. It's hard for me to describe what I mean by this, but I was always filled with a sense of hopelessness and longing to be back in the UK, even to the point of making a make-shift plane in the garden and pretending that I could fly back by magic. The people had been wonderful, and there was no doubting that one bit, but it felt as if we'd been plonked in the middle of nowhere on Earth's map! The only things I did like were the drive-in movies and the outdoor swimming pools, which we frequented with a few friends about our age whom we'd hang out with.

I have always loved the water, and any opportunity to get myself in it was a temptation too good to miss. The outdoor pools were huge, and there were varied sizes scattered around the perimeter, catering to the young and old. We had many happy days sitting in the rich, open grassland with the sun blazing down on us, towels wrapped around our shoulders and sucking lollipops before getting back in the water. However, I was tired of using the kids' pool and eyed up the largest pool with fascination. There wasn't anyone in it, and I thought I'd give it a try, even though it had, to my mind, been as deep as the ocean itself. I plunged, ready to see if I could touch the bottom while holding my breath for as long and hard as I could. Down I went, but I realised for some strange reason that I didn't quite have the strength or timing to reach my intended target. I panicked, turned myself around, and swam frantically back up to the surface, which seemed like miles away. As I broke the surface, taking in air, I suddenly became weak. My legs wouldn't work, and all at once, tiredness engulfed my body. During this moment, everything appeared to happen in slow motion, and I stopped struggling. I could see the intense sun's light piercing through the top of the water and somehow warming me. I just let go, and even then, I thought how easy it was in terms of dying. I had no idea if I'd taken water down into my lungs or whether I was holding my breath. The thought of death entered my mind even at this age, but it didn't matter. In fact, nothing did. While suspended in time, with my body drifting slowly below, a deep calmness engulfed me.

At once, I found myself above the pool, looking down from a great height. There was the appearance of a murky shadow of something under the water, and I didn't realise I was actually viewing myself, because I was now above and not below. During this stage, I experienced no concern about the 'me' down there. Here, and while consciously detached, the physical part was of no importance. In fact, I felt liberated, and it dawned on me that I was more alive than I'd ever felt in my seven years of existence. A bald man dived into the water close to where the shadow lurked, and that was the last 'earthly' view I had before my world changed.

I didn't move through a tunnel towards a light, which many report in an NDE. In the blink of an eye, I found myself in a beautiful garden, but I would say it was more in line with appearing as a meadow. The environment was amazing. There was a peace and calmness I found exhilarating, and whereby on earth such attributes are hard to describe because we are in a constant state of emotional flux. I sensed a peace beyond anything I had known. The colours of the trees and grassland seemed richer in detail, and there was an old wall with a creeper running across it. As I homed in on the creeper, it was almost as if my vision had been accentuated, and I thought of '*The Six Million Dollar Man,*' a series which ran in the mid-1970s where the character, Steve Austin who'd been half-human and half-cyborg had a bionic eye which worked like a binocular and whereby he could focus in on his targets using this super sight. That's what happened here. The droplet of water, which many would just pass off as nothing really important, demonstrated just how real this world was and how ours pales in comparison in terms of detail. I didn't have time to think '*Oh, I'm in heaven!*' or had been transported to another planet, for that matter. I observed water for what it actually represented on a deeper level of creation. Being here was all I wanted. There were no people, but that didn't bother me in the least. Even at age seven, I understood I was perceiving the '*real*' world, and not the one I once inhabited. Then, something even more amazing began to occur. I had the awareness that my spirit was as old as the stars, and I could feel a sudden awakening gradually occurring within my being. Everything began to make sense in terms of why it was I'd elected to come to earth, along with my mission. Within this empirical state of conscious awareness, it was as though my mind was expanding and I could sense the void; that place of infinite darkness, but within itself was the seat of all creation. I also understood synchronicities and how everything in my young life back on earth seemed to make more sense in terms of the senselessness one would come to expect through what we believe to be mere random events. Nothing was random or by mistake, but more through design and order. I now saw a glass building set within deep foliage, and I knew this place intimately, but not back home. Here, things connect with you on an emotional level that is hard to define, but this 'knowing' assured me that within these rooms of this modern construct, I knew everything! It was as if the building was alive with memory, and these memories opened up to other recollections within my mind (like an emotional connection) which went beyond the normal spectrum of how cognizance operates through the brain. There was nothing to debate or question, it all *WAS!*

I was instantly transported to what I felt was my spiritual home. I'm not talking about the house we had occupied while living in South Africa, or any number of the other residences we had inhabited within my childhood, but an environment that bonded with my soul on a profound level of emotive integration. My consciousness was directed to a realm filled with the most beautiful rock. I instantly remembered this domain (and there was no way for me to be able to distinguish for certain whether I had been on another planet, or a part of the astral planes themselves). This proved to me that our consciousness is limited within its awareness on this planet, but that all memory is stored within the astral/etheric body, and upon the soul's release from its temporary Avatar is able to have access to these multidimensional levels of now unrestricted recordings from elsewhere. This place captivated me, and I felt the rocks linking within my psyche, as though feeding me the knowledge of a timeless connection we shared, uniting our energy with incredible warmth, love, and peace. My dwelling had been fashioned out of the very rock which lay before me, and my heart leapt! My senses unbolted to a new kind of love, and one that was so deep and profound, I wanted to cry with happiness. Imagine seeing images that convey sensations, and these sensations open you up to a wider understanding and union with all that surrounds you. We go about our business on earth, cut off from our emotions, and we feel so very little within the five senses, which govern the material body. Here, all is felt, seen, and understood beyond those restricted senses which dull by comparison while in this super-conscious state of awareness.

Again, and within the blink of an eye, I was now back on earth, watching from a distance with mild curiosity as the bald man who'd saved me was now pushing hard on my back in an effort to release water from within my lungs. I was lying on my front, lifeless and unresponsive. As an external observer, I watched the drama from my vantage point with little or no compassion. My twin and two friends were there, along with a couple of other people, and from my perspective it was like, '*Oh, so that's me, but I feel fine where I am, thank you!*' I had been completely detached and wondered what all the fuss was about. Then I found myself back in my body, slowly turning on my side and looking up at the man who'd taken quick action. After a while, when the guy had me sit up and check me over for a complete examination, I got up and simply walked back home with my brother and friends! I hadn't suffered any heart or brain damage, and to me, it was no big deal. I'd still been very weak, but other than that, not a scratch! That had been the really strange thing about the event. There had been no ambulance or doctors, and I assumed that the man who helped me was himself a lifeguard, so he would know if any further medical attention was needed. You hear of people being involved in the most horrific incidents and walking away from the scene with hardly any cuts or bruises. Had I died? My body had gone into some kind of shock, and this, perhaps, was enough to stimulate an NDE. That's my thought on the matter anyhow. What for me in terms of time had seemed long may well have been mere seconds. I was too young to think of getting the man's name who saved me, but I know within my heart I have him to thank for taking such quick and responsive action. If I'd been any longer under the water, I would have been physically dead!

Earth is merely a cruder version of reality, copied from its original counterpart through the descent of matter going back within the annals of creation. Thus, the story of God fashioning the earth in six days is literally nonsense. Many within the religious fraternity will condemn this thought through a preferred supernatural element which they will gladly infuse to justify this idea, but strangely where such occurrences in present times can no longer be repeated.

Life-changing experiences open the human psyche to further memory recall while in the material body. This happened to me, along with the psychic component developing when I was in my late twenties. Strangely, and on my return to my body, most of the feelings and knowing I'd had while in this empirical state of awareness diminished. However, that said, I occasionally get a brief flash of enlightenment, which the British author, Professor Clive Staples Lewis (most famous for his Narnia chronicles and thoughts on Christian philosophy), had encountered, which he called *'Moments of Joy.'* He was left frustrated by these episodes of true enlightenment because he was never able to locate their source or knew what they meant, for that matter. I do consider that he, along with myself and many others, has these incredible flashes of spiritual insight which go beyond our known expressive nature, and not necessarily brought on by the advent of any life-changing incident which threatens our physical mortality. C. S. Lewis recognised these joyous moments as being deeply profound in nature, and when I'd read that he'd had them too through one of his biographers, A. N. Wilson, I knew instantly what this brilliant man had been experiencing. While incarnate in human form, there appears to be a limit in what filters through regarding our physical reality. Yet, our memories we collate while here are merged into our higher self, and therefore make sense to assume that alternate recollections from varied incarnations beyond earth are stored within the same field of energy we have always maintained throughout our inception, and which we embody on a cosmic level. A bleed with fragments of cognizance seeping through to our day-to-day functioning can occur sporadically, and such realisations make us aware there is so much more to us and the world in which we live before they subside and fold back into our etheric body.

The astral planes are what both Chris and I believe is the in-between state, or what we call the '*halfway house*', where the spirit lingers for a while before a decision is made as to how it will next evolve. Here, the newly arriving soul will experience life in an altogether unique way, and one which is no longer restricted in terms of thought and action. Loved ones or elevated souls will greet the newcomer, if only to help orient them back into the conditions which this side of life offers. We also concede that a gradual merging and awakening of memories once contained within the etheric resurfaces, and whereby the realisation that death is nothing less than illusionary in nature imbues a new sense of vitality and inspiration which had been forgotten while incarnated in the flesh, along with the amalgamation of said cognizance. That is to say, however, for those who do not encounter the lower regions within the astral. Although we use the terminology 'lower' and 'higher' territories in understanding that the corruptible are at the base of the planes and the enlightened elevated, this is not the case. As stated, the astral is an environment that operates on certain vibrational frequencies. For instance, Earth is considered one of the lowest environments where matter has solidified within the quantum state, and to a degree is unchangeable unless those laws are triggered by either physical death or interaction from what we call the supernatural, which occasionally can penetrate through to our dimension from these hidden dimensions. We always imagine within our physical universe that the stars are themselves at a distance from us, as opposed to depth. As a kid, I always wondered (if it were in any way possible within my young mind) what would happen if I jumped off the Earth from its base and kept falling? Would I encounter other stars and planets along the way? If I kept falling long enough, and once seeing these other systems, would I eventually plummet back on our planet, but this time arriving at its top, and not bottom, where I'd initially started my journey? Space, as we understand is infinite, but what is space? What's the glue holding everything together? How big is it all? Where's the end? We know that it is impossible within our present scientific expertise to live long enough in order to travel to the outer reaches of our very own solar system, let alone the rest of the cosmos. Yet, other intelligences have done just that, but not in the way we as humans imagine. Such laws from the astral clearly display interesting qualities, and may offer clues as to why many here on this planet are unable to fathom its reality when such otherworldly interactions occur and are ignored because hardly any physical evidence is forthcoming. We have little or no proof for those who encounter UFOs, aliens, cryptids, or what many assume are the dead. However, that said, there are incredible connections to be made which clearly illustrate why our system has so ardently played down the world of UFOs, along with the paranormal in terms of its authenticity, and for reasons which will become clear later.

The astral planes are formed from the very fabric of thought, and the human nature which we have been familiar with while in this three-dimensional matrix, and which we were so accustomed to back on earth, can be experienced for however long that belief is imposed within the individual's psyche. Your vibration will be matched within these areas, and thus interaction achieved. However, I consider the very nature of what we represent within an anthropomorphic construct is subject to change, and this is evident with the multitude of other beings which inhabit the astral, clearly indicating that not everything which dies is from Earth! The reincarnation process, which has been addressed, may also occur on other worlds, and therefore the physiology of which could be far removed from our awareness of how one would come to expect to appear. When I'd had my experience of crossing over, I had not been attentive of a body. Yet, this didn't seem to bother me in the slightest. I had full awareness of my conscious 'self', and something which emerged more acute in terms of perception than any worry that I was not physically whole as an individual. This does not mean I was merely floating around. Far from it! I would have been in possession of my etheric-double, and a feeling which quite literally puts our biological bodies to shame.

We know pets also appear in the astral (along with any number of other animals) and upon our arrival, will be reunited with them too. Even, would you believe, people whom we didn't know back on earth, but had been aware of before our incarnation took effect. One case which comes to mind is that of Dr Eben Alexander, who'd suffered a rare form of meningitis back in 2008. His brain was dead, and this resulted in him experiencing the famous NDE. In part of his journey, he describes soaring in the air with millions of butterflies, and next to him had been a young female who he seemed to recognise and had herself been flying opposite him as they glided effortlessly over a rich landscape of grass, trees, and people which he observed walking the land. To him, this encounter had changed his life. When he'd recovered (which had been seen as a miracle within the medical profession), he was unsure of the girl with whom he'd had a deep connection with while on the other side. It turned out that after he'd relayed his experience to his parents, they took out a photo and revealed to him that the girl he described in heaven had been his sister, who'd died early before he was born, which he knew nothing about. His parents had kept the whole thing a secret.

Talking of pets surviving in the astral planes, my brother and I had been at a local spiritualist church when I'd first gotten involved in the psychic department, and a small man who looked like a North American Indian (which he wasn't) by the name of Billy Elton had been performing clairvoyance. Billy became a long-time friend and was in his late eighties when we met. As a Minister himself, Billy also trained the famous medium, Colin Fry. I saw Colin perform at a Spiritualist Raleigh which had been held in Kempston, Bedford, along with Billy being present too, and I have to say Colin's evidence was mind-blowing. He'd taken me for a drink after his demonstration, which had been presided over by one of the Presidents of the Spiritualist National Union (SNU). While my brother and I sat in the audience at the spiritualist church, Billy pointed to us both and brought our maternal grandmother through, along with our golden Labrador, Prince, whom he'd correctly stated we'd had as very young boys. I remember us both being completely shocked. All I kept thinking after the service was, Where is Prince now, and what's he doing? This is a clear indication that our pets do continue, long after their physical departure has taken effect.

There is no indication of reproduction within the astral either, or, at least, not that we're aware of from any of those who have ventured into these regions, but there is sex! Hard to believe? I agree, but something documented from many who have projected themselves within this province of the ether, along with those who have had an NDE. Although something of a taboo subject within any spiritual or religious circuit, sex is a natural process, no matter the preference. My argument has been that if sex is only to be used as a means to create, why has the 'human' been allowed to enjoy it? It's a simple enough question. I'm sure those who preach about the unholiness of this function are, themselves, hypocrites. If this offends anyone, then I'm sorry. They say the truth hurts, but it's a blatant fact. Humans are allowed to express themselves in a multitude of ways, and sex is one of the key elements that helps to inspire, enrich, and lift individuals to new heights, provided there is a mutual agreement between the two parties when just such a moment is shared. We're not robots, and sex is a clear indication of how someone feels about another, merging their energy together in an act of oneness. Such an agreed union between a couple goes even deeper in the physical sense and generates a temporary integration of the carnal and sacred while on earth. Within this coupling, the essence of the two become single, imparting energy in an effort to reach beyond the constraints of passion, along with the underlying factor of what this means outside the mere vocalisation of language we are so accustomed to. There are no words that can be found when someone falls in love, but this is close to what we understand in an intense soul connection, where one is seeking to be enhanced by the other on a multitude of physical, spiritual, and mental levels. And that's just on the corporeal side of life. Sex is even more fantastic within the astral!

Wherein such acts here on earth are attributed primarily within the physical sense, in the astral, this union is utilised via the merging of a couple's energy field. Seeing as the corporeal form of what we knew as the body has now been discarded, the 'real' you (the composite of your astral self) is now able to interconnect on a more powerful level of emotions. We are more sensitised, and this creates an even deeper merging of energy between two souls, which, so we are told, goes beyond ecstasy. Within our second-state, and casting aside all the taboos surrounding sex on earth, the attraction between another's essence, if desired, is unavoidable. There is no lengthy build-up to such a union. In fact, the process occurs instantaneously, and which, for the couple, can seem to last an eternity. There is no interpenetration as one would come to expect, or an exploration of each other's bodies in the sensual sense, but rather a fusion of mind-soul electrons which primarily equalize within this emotional union. The results recorded are far more satisfying and lasting than any sex on this planet! Within the astral, there is no need either for a prolonged build-up to an agreed connection or worry as to whether either partner will feel as though they've let the side down once the act of spiritual intercourse has been completed. This spontaneous bondage fortifies a sensation so prevailing; the mental, emotional, and spiritual energies are immediately engaged like an all-encompassing fire.

Within the astral, sex is more frequent, and there is no fear of losing a partner through infidelity. We are entering a plane where partnerships and sharing are for all eternity, and where this amalgamation of sexual union has no limits. On earth, we are restricted by our emotions, and fear losing those we fall in love with. Everything is hidden behind closed doors on this side of life or spoken about in hushed tones where the subject of intimacy is concerned. Religion uses the word 'sin' as a means to subjugate and control the very nature of what should be celebrated, and therefore makes for feelings of shame and fear that the individual soul will be sent into the bowels of hell. Prejudice and vindication vanish when we make our return to the astral, and we wake up to the fact that life on earth had been restricted within the 'sex' department in a multitude of ways. Casual sex or long-term partnership is up to the soul in the long run. The body is no longer inhibited by the process of aging, so no one lets the side down here either. Preference matters not, whichever way people on earth see it.

We learn that life here is very much like Earth's, where cities abound, along with villages and vast areas of countryside. The returning soul will be reoriented into controlling thought, whereby anything can be created in terms of how they view their reality. This does not mean they can change the layout of, say, a city or town unless a united conscious agreement with other souls has been met, but certainly their own creation from the mind is able to manifest a living space ideal to their preferred requirements. And there is no limit to the world in which they exist. The big problem is that many mediums have hang-ups about what one can do while in the astral. Our memory here will return over time, and the one on earth becomes distant, but it can be accessed at any given point if required. Our restricted thinking in believing that you'll be floating around as an orb is nonsense. Take away the religious construct which Man has blatantly altered in an attempt to seriously hinder any understanding as to our true genus and we discover a world more real than the one in which we have left behind. People ask, 'Can you still smoke, drink, or eat when in the astral?' Well, yes! Nothing changes in this department. We assume that our biological nature is designed specifically for sustaining the body via the natural nutrients found on this planet, but we are energy, nevertheless, and your etheric form is the original version of what you represent beyond the flesh and bone. People have jobs if they want them, although no money is involved. Here, a greater awareness of knowledge and development is paramount, and with knowing that everything – and I mean everything – is at your disposal. Like attracts like, so they say, and your vibrations will resonate on levels matched by those within this territory. However, you'll still get the moods and emotional difficulties, but there is no illness, and you never die, which is only a process reserved on earth and merely a state of transition from one energy exchange to that of a higher vibrational level.

I remember a young lady who came for a reading. She asked me if *she* herself had been to heaven, because she'd swore blind her mother (who'd psychically come through) had brought her to the other side. I hinted for her to continue, and she explained that soon after her mum's death, she'd had a very vivid dream where she found herself standing in a beautiful street not dissimilar to those metropolises we have here. She enlightened me as to the fact that the thoroughfares in her dream were so beautiful. Everything looked so clean, neat, and tidy. The lady was standing on a street path, and ahead, she could see what she thought were coffee shops. Outside one of these coffee shops sat some round tables, complete with ornate, metal chairs, and on one of these chairs, she could see her mother. She noticed that her mum now looked healthy and vibrant while she sat drinking a cup of coffee and smoking a cigarette. '*I'd never seen my mother looking so radiant,*' she explained. '*I mean, she appeared young and beautiful, as she had been before she became ill!*' A handsome male whom the lady did not recognise stood talking to her mum, and she further revealed that he was the hottest looking man she'd ever clapped eyes on! As she stood there, spell-bound by what she was seeing, feeling elated that her mother was alive and no longer dead, her mother's gaze fell upon her daughter (as if she knew she was being observed), and her face immediately drained of colour. Shocked, her mum said loudly to her daughter, '*You shouldn't be here!*' This episode had a lasting effect upon the lady, and she wondered if her mother had met someone else on the other side now that she was separated (albeit temporarily) from her husband back on earth. I informed the lady that it was quite possible that she'd been transported to heaven, as you don't have to physically die. That department is via the medical profession and NDE research in ascertaining this fact, and for the simple reason of collating scientific evidence for the validity of the soul. Yet, we realise that consciousness is connected to its biological housing and acts as a mere conduit, and that such altered states of cognizance can bring in varied realities and experiences to the individual, which much of science dismisses. So, in all likelihood, this lady had been taken to heaven so that she could see that her mother was fine and well.

I recall most distinctly a time when I had astral traveled. It was an incredible experience, and one which remains vivid within my mind. I have always loved NASA's now decommissioned Space Shuttle. In this astral state, I found myself in one of these splendid crafts and was seated in the pilot's chair. To my left was another male pilot, and I saw that we had left the Earth's orbit, but strangely could see another Earth ahead through the cockpit's window, along with a moon, but these had been much larger in scale than the other Earth and moon we were now moving away from. My co-pilot explained that our destination was to the real Earth and the real moon, and that he would be taking me into orbit to show me what he meant. I remember feeling excited and overwhelmed by the sheer size of these two spheres. He also jokingly asked me to look down at the floor, and when I did, I was met with a view of space below and discovered that the bottom of the Shuttle was composed entirely of glass – an impossibility, but, there again, anything in the astral goes! As we neared this real earth, I could see that the towers which graced this planet were breathtaking in size. These skyscrapers had been the most incredible I'd ever seen, and the pilot informed me that I'd enjoy living there and that it was much better than the other Earth we'd temporarily left behind. I wanted to go in for a closer look, but the pilot pulled on his controls, and the Shuttle began to veer off to the right, slowly turning around back in the opposite direction. He told me plainly that we couldn't get too close, because we would not be able to return to the smaller earth, as we had yet to complete our mission there.

The astral *is* the *real* world! It appeared to me that while I was observing these incredible towers that looked better than any in New York City, I had the sense that the people living there loved it. This is hard for me to describe, but it was exactly what I'd sensed. The real Earth is where life happens! This busy metropolis overwhelmed my senses and pulled at my heart. I wanted to take a closer look, but during this time it was forbidden, and I could sense the danger from my co-pilot, whom I respected. I can imagine that upon our return to the astral planes, we will be met with as much wonderment as I had, but still attached to our physical form within this state, we were unable to get closer due to our silver cords snapping. I did think about that! It is only upon death that our chains are released, and we are free to venture forth into this incredible territory.

We also understand that the soul of an individual can elevate spiritually to higher levels of vibrational density while in the astral. What's interesting is that depending upon the experiences accrued by the personality throughout their varied and temporary physical incarnations (whichever system of reality they have decided to undergo) allows for such elevations to take place. This means that if the soul decides to enter a subtler plane of reality through their understanding of divinity (and less of the earthlier chains that bind the soul through carnal attachments), they will no longer be able to access the astral, or indeed penetrate through to a medium on earth. There have been cases where someone's loved one does not turn up during a reading, and I have often wondered whether this is due to the fact that they have ascended to a much higher realm and into an altogether unreachable locale within the spirit world. While many choose to remain within the astral, it is understood that those who are ready to go even further within their spiritual evolution and shed their etheric second-body become pure and blessed consciousness itself, whereby the astral body is no longer needed. Of course, this is merely speculative in nature, for the simple reason that no astral traveller or NDEer has ever ventured that far into these alternate dimensions, but scholars maintain there is a degree of acceptance here when deciphering codices from the past, and in connection with spiritual writings and practices.

The orientation process is vital for the newly arriving spirit within the astral, and those on earth who are mourning for their loved ones can, to a degree, hinder such progression. It was reported that when Princess Diana met her premature death in Paris in 1997, the world over mourned her so much, she was not able to traverse beyond the earth's frequency and into the astral. The intense level of mental energy by the many who grieved her untimely exit from this plane, being projected into the ether, temporarily held her back. I'm sure now, and through the passage of time on our side, she is able to shift onward within her spiritual development.

Both Chris and I also considered that our main purpose here on earth could be attributed to us writing a new script before our main performance begins on the other side. It's a distinct possibility in assuming life on this world is a mere dress rehearsal before the real acting begins. Shakespeare did say: *'All the world's a stage!'* Our temporary amnesia heralds the determination for us to work things out and find our own way through life's intricate puzzles. Upon our deliverance into the astral, we will also discover there is no rain, snow, blizzards, indeed any of the adverse weather conditions we face here. There is a perpetual sunshine, but strangely never the appearance of a sun! However, if a particular soul wishes to experience such settings like darkness, snow, or a permanent twilight, then their mental projection will suit whatever environmental conditions will be met, and without affecting anyone else nearby.

For those souls who passed in shocking circumstances, or others who were themselves in denial of their own existence and submitted to suicide, are cared for in what is known as healing centres. These structures are equipped to restore balance to the individual's etheric system, thus harmonising the energies of the second body. For some, their passing will come as a great surprise, least of all in knowing there is no death, and the difficult life they have left behind is reflected as a mere shadow in the grand scheme of their own creation. Many who pass into the astral go through their awakening stage with little or no problem, but for others, this can be a challenging and prolonged experience. Over time, they will heal before their own orientation program begins in adjusting to their new realm.

My brother, Ronald, had a dream shortly after our maternal grandmother had passed, which to him had been very vivid. He found himself in a beautiful, wooded area complete with blue sky, but he could see no sun. Ahead, he saw an expansive, modern bungalow which looked more in line with being a medical centre, or a doctor's surgery, rather than someone's dwelling. As he approached the front entrance to the property, he realised there were no cars either which one would come to expect, or strangely no sound of birdsong in such a forested region. As he entered the building and walked towards the reception area, he was immediately met by a large, formidable Matron wearing the classic hospital uniform, which denoted her rank. She acknowledged Ronald as he approached, but he noticed her arms were folded across her chest, and there were other nurses busy with their own affairs in the background. The Matron exuded an air of authority and a no-nonsense attitude, and eyed him carefully. Her uniform was more in line with those worn by Matrons back in the 1960s.

One of the strange things Ronald noticed was hearing the sound of piano music playing in the distance, but it had been coming from within the huge complex. Who plays a piano in a medical centre, he thought? The Matron anticipated the reason for his visit and didn't seem at all surprised. 'Can I see Grandma?' he asked her. The Matron thought for a moment and said that he could, nodding in the process. She stepped back and waved a hand in the direction of where he was to go, and this, he found, was around a corner leading towards a large hall. The only person here had been a small, old lady, seated before a piano and playing it. Ronald immediately recognised her as grandma, and his heart leapt. Grandma turned around on the stool where she sat, got up, and embraced him warmly. He noticed that she looked moderately better in terms of health, although dark circles remained under her eyes, as if she were now healing from the cancer which had so cruelly afflicted her. She was wearing a nightgown.

Grandma explained that she wanted to go outside and that they should take a walk together, because she wanted to tell him something important. They ambled back out to the main entrance where the Matron stood, and upon asking if they could leave for a while, promising to return, the Matron agreed that this would be fine. Grandma took Ronald by the hand, leading him out of the medical centre and down a path, turning right, which led to a long, beautiful forest track. The trees here had been luscious and tall, and there lay a bench near the woodland. Here they both sat, and Ronald told Grandma how much he'd missed her, along with some small talk. It was during this moment when grandma had looked serious, and while holding his hand in hers, explained that she was going to show him something, and that he was not to forget it, by any means. Ronald casually replied that he wouldn't, and at this point, Grandma became stern and stated that he was *not* to forget what she was about to reveal, as though this was of paramount importance.

Here, things changed. Ronald suddenly found himself back home, in the garden with me. It was dark, and there came an air of urgency, because hovering in the night sky, he could see small, glowing, triangular crafts which emitted an electronic whining sound, as though the place was filled with hundreds of angry Hornets! Was this an alien invasion, he thought? Sensing impending danger, Ronald got on all fours and began to crawl back inside the house, with me following close behind. What he found equally unsettling was that the main tree at the back of the garden was now gone, so this to him was a probable future scenario, because when he'd had the vision of grandma, it had still been there. Years later, it had to be cut for fear of bringing the back wall down. As he made his way towards the lounge, turning off all the lights in the house for fear of being exposed by this menace, he could see that the TV was on, and a female news broadcaster wearing a yellow top was talking about a war happening abroad, but nothing of the invasion. Perhaps it had just happened and hadn't yet been reported? Although puzzling in its detail, there the vision ended. However, what was surprising was the fact (and something we didn't know) that Grandma had always wanted to play the piano. This was revealed to us by our mother. It appeared to him that her wish was granted now that Grandma was in the astral planes. At present, no alien invasion has occurred, but who knows! Ronald still feels that Grandma wanted him to heed her warning, however strange.

Many times, we hear of people having dreams or visions of their loved ones now in spirit, and the appearance of them still recovering from those traumas or illnesses which had afflicted them before their passing is very much apparent. I would consider that this is normal, and those who have returned to the astral under such conditions are themselves in a state of rejuvenation.

There are all manner of systems in operation here. Schools, along with universities, are still very much in existence, and education is paramount if that is what the soul chooses. We know, for instance, that scientists from the astral planes have tried to help people on earth in establishing spirit communication on a clearer level of contact, and something which continues to this day, so they are just as keen to get their messages to us from their side, but by way of utilising our own technology in an effort to enhance contact with loved ones back on earth. This would, I feel, change the way we view death and enrich the spirit, along with life, here in the knowledge that we continue beyond the grave. Again, it's important to try and remove the thought that the astral is merely wispy in nature. Such realms are more tangible than the physical world in which we currently reside. The only difference being vibration, which is slightly removed from one state to another, so this is why on earth we see our loved ones as ghost forms who appear dream-like in quality.

Many researchers in the past have tried to communicate with the other side via electronic means, and in our modern times, people like Joshua Louis from the United States have achieved outstanding results with his 'HOPE' (Helpers of Paranormal Entities) device. This is a mechanism known as a 'Soul Box' which, through patience, has allowed the actual voices of those who have died to come through on a clearer level, unlike the normal EVP equipment, which generates an almost mechanical sounding voice being relayed from the deceased. Such personalities like Dolores Cannon, among others, have connected with the medium Joshua. I had the privilege of speaking with him, and he enlightened me as to his work dealing with the technical side of his amazing EVP sessions. He has his helpers from the other side attempting to tweak things on his end so that successful communication can be made. He has authored '*Finding Hope in the Afterlife*' (published by Balboa Press, 2021), which details his troubled past and embracing new spiritual technology in an effort to bridge the gap between ours and that of the astral. Yet not everything is plain sailing in heaven, it would appear. They have their problems, too, just like us on Earth. Joshua has had disruptions from lower entities, and an area we will illustrate in the next chapter. As with the good, you also get the bad, and the astral is home to numerous spiritual nasties as we will soon discover.

# 'The Eternal Avatar'

## Chapter Nine

## Higher & Lower Spheres

*'Within the darkness, lies abound and truth unseen,*

*Pervading and flourishing to feed the obscene.*

*Its corrupt principalities consume the weak,*

*Twisted meanings who dare to speak.*

*Its survival inherently hidden from sight,*

*Festering in its ignorance unable to fight.*

*Take courage to know it's never whole,*

*Afraid of love that it sees in your soul.'*

Chris John Mayes

Earth is one of the lowest spheres there can be had within our temporary state of atomic structuring. People have often asked me and Chris whether this planet is actually hell. No, we don't think so, but it can appear that way in terms of how people treat one another, along with wars, poverty, and disease. However, there are forces within the spirit world that gain easy access to this lower sphere of reality, and which many believe is the only world to be had. Our limited understanding of those alternate dimensions restricts us within such considerations, namely because of our inability to grasp the true nature of ourselves and the universe at hand. Although much of our discussions covered are linked within the true nature of ourselves as evolving Avatars, our planet is linked to these denser realms, which coexist around the very space we inhabit.

As on Earth, we have variations in our atmosphere. You could be flying in an aircraft through smooth weather one minute, only to hit turbulence the next. Although the stratosphere of our planet is all connected, there are occasional disruptions within particular areas, depending on climate patterns, and so forth. When considering the astral planes, what we think of as up or down in terms of spiritual evolution or devolution heralds these subtle adaptations regarding the progression in which a soul finds itself. Naturally, we are a composite of energy within the immaterial, and your etheric signature will be drawn to those energies that are matched by yours. Therefore, it's not a case of moving upwards or downwards to get to such eminent or subordinate spheres within this province, but rather a slight change within the vibrational mass, similar to the weather scenario addressed.

Most souls who cross over will be drawn to the intermediary level within the astral. Here, as discussed earlier, is a world similar to our own, but far more tangible in terms of its corporeality. Although many on this side imagine that all things unfathomable surrounding knowledge will be revealed to them on a mental level once they cross over, this is not the case. You hear people saying, *'Now they've crossed over, they'll know everything!'* Not so! Granted, there is a united awareness of a higher self, along with an amalgamation of every thought impressed within the etheric body by the evolving Avatar brought on throughout its various incarnations, but an eternity of progression awaits. However, this 'Summer Land' of the souls is also home to darker spectres which exist within lower vibrational fields. It's not all love and light, regardless of what is relayed by mediums. There are much shadier entities that meander the astral in an attempt to satisfy their cravings or try in some cases to trick developed souls into being drawn into their sphere of existence. It's the same on Earth. We have those bands of less desirable people who choose to live their lives in corruptible ways, even though there is help for them if they wish to change for the better.

On occasions, they will try and bring other good folk into their circle, and thus contaminate them, like drug pushers, criminal gangs, and so forth. However, such spectres in the astral are more twisted in terms of their appearance, as well as the very nature of their intentions.

In those accounts of NDE research where people have reported seeing the most abhorred creatures in the astral may point to the theory that the corrupted soul's etheric body which is no longer operating within a higher spiritual state has itself degraded, and thus the entities' form (such as it is) is bent and twisted into the very nature of its own, dark creation on a mental level. There are, of course, other areas of speculation concerning the appearance of such weird and oftentimes frightening creatures, which we will address. It's interesting to note that we take on a human appearance, which is reflected in the majority of cases, while venturing back to the other side. The blueprint of our genus indicates memory, and something which is hard to shed for those who have continuously incarnated into the earth matrix. Yet, this is subject to change, but always on a higher level of luminosity, thus depicting the advancement within the soul's sovereignty as it progresses through its divine nature. Here on our temporary planet, many fictitious depictions of unearthly beasts have been created from the minds of various authors to scare both children and adults alike. But we are only too aware of accounts where people have been witnessed to real-life creatures which themselves have seemingly stepped right out from the pages of such fables. Take the 'Dogman' for instance, or the 'Sasquatch.' Witnesses to such horrifying encounters within remote regions of our physical world signify areas of high strangeness, and many researchers have considered whether Earth is home to these cryptids, and a species which has so far evaded our detection on a united front. When dealing with UFO and paranormal research, there is evidence to suggest that creatures like the Dogman (Werewolf) or Sasquatch are interdimensional and not part of our world, as most would readily assume. At least, we can consider as much. Researcher and bestselling author on UFOs and Cryptids, Paul Sinclair, knew of a case where a Werewolf had been witnessed in the UK by some frightened onlookers, but the creature had been wearing an earring! How can this be possible if many consider the primeval nature of these beasts? Where are they all hanging out? With our current state of technological achievement, it would be easy to track and trace the whereabouts of such anomalies. The big puzzle surrounding the Werewolf wearing an earring would denote some form of intelligence on their end, as well as vanity, it would appear! There is much debate within the world of UFO and paranormal research in determining whether the Werewolf (and that includes many other spectres within the vast arena of such unholy beings) is either physically a part of our world, or interdimensional. The UFO subject also promotes levels of high strangeness, and there appear to be two areas which we can at least agree on. Part of the experience is tangible to those who experience it, and the other is seen as interdimensional within its construct; a composite of two elements, sustainable by these very creatures, which alludes both our intellect and whereabouts. There is also the question of 'mind-speak' (telepathy for short) and whereby such entities are, in some instances, able to link with their subject and communicate this way. It is clear to see that (and taking just a few examples here) the Werewolf, Sasquatch, and aliens appear to harbour high levels of intelligence, even though some of them come across as savage.

The national forests appear to be one of the primary areas across our world where individuals disappear without a trace or are found dead in the most bizarre and blood-curdling circumstances, which, again, has many researchers scratching their heads. Those who do survive, and themselves lost for weeks - months even - reappear with little or no memory of where they'd been, as though they'd suffered some form of amnesia, and a feature classic also within an alien abduction, and whereby the abductee has little or no memory of where they'd been, or what had happened to them. Yet, their absence is even more chilling within these vast regions of forest (most notably in the United States) because they do not know how they were able to maintain their overall physiology while traipsing alone in the woodlands for days on end with no food or clean water. And, what's even more bizarre is the fact that many of these missing people who miraculously reappear have found they've crossed a huge expanse of terrain which, to the authorities, seems almost impossible to achieve, considering much of the inhospitable landscape they would have had to cover. The authorities, however, are resolute in remaining tight-lipped surrounding the facts which categorically determine that national forests are not the place to go it alone! Although such incidents are rare, they do happen. Even in those cases where hikers have taken off in large groups, it has been known that at least one person within the assemblage will be plucked out of the pack, never to be seen again, no matter the intense investigations that always follow. Various well-known researchers have catalogued such mysterious events, which still remain unsolved to the authorities. The other interesting fact is that in each incident where someone has vanished without a trace, a noticeable feature has been discovered by prominent researchers into this anomaly, whereby the victim has a medical, physical, or mental abnormality. Does this indicate that whatever force is behind this can 'smell' their intended targeted human. It would seem that certain people are what we term 'targeted,' and there have even been instances where someone, say, living in the city has an overall compulsion to take themselves within such remote regions of a national forest (as though mentally influenced to some degree by an altogether different type of force) - never to be seen again!

In the bulk of incidents, and if a person has disappeared, 'search and rescue' teams and sniffer dogs are used to ensure a vast region is thoroughly scoured, along with helicopters, but no trace of the individual in many cases is ever found. Most chilling is the fact that dogs have taken their teams to a location where the lost individual's scent was last detected, but where the trackers come to an immediate halt, as if the individual had simply vanished into thin air, and in the exact spot where the canines remain! In some reports, the body reappears in exactly the same locale weeks, months, or even years later! So, where has the body been all that time? Ruling out murder, and on those occasions where someone has come off the beaten track and ends up getting lost with no hope of survival, there are hundreds of reported incidents that leave the investigators in no doubt that something truly weird and unexplainable has occurred, and which defy all known laws of our physics. This is why it is believed the authorities clam up because of the disturbing nature surrounding these affairs. Any further prying from the public guarantees no forthcoming data from the establishments themselves, only a wall of silence! Dogman and Sasquatch sightings are the most reported within such vicinities, along with the appearance of strange orbs of light and, on occasions, UFOs. Much of this activity sits in the heart of the wilderness and is an apparent safe haven for our supernatural guests.

You're probably wondering what earth-bound creatures snatching good folk from forested areas has to do with those spectres which are also reported from NDE and OBE accounts on the other side? There may well be connections, something which could indicate that those higher and lower planes of reality that our senses cannot always detect while incarnate in the flesh, are much closer to us in terms of its vibrational frequency on earth than we realise. This is where the large crux of investigators gets stuck, preferring to believe in the physical nuts-and-bolts aspect, whether that be UFOs, Dogman, or Sasquatch. There is hardly any trace of *physical* evidence that could lead us to the lairs of said beasts, yet they are quite able to amble into our world, physically attack or even kill people, and disappear like a ghost in the night. We have some grainy photographic and film footage, along with scratches, wounds from victims, and within those areas of UFO abduction cases, implants, but that's about it! It's as if the phenomenon is intent in not being discovered, or that as humans existing in a physical matrix, we are unable to grasp the enormity of what's really happening when we consider the interdimensional hypothesis.

Taking an example of the appearance of one of these nightmarish 'Dogman' creatures, which Martin Groves, an ex-law enforcement officer from the United States, had encountered, along with a friend, clearly shows the sheer terror such beings exhibit when a confrontation of this kind occurs. This had been in the 1990s and within the province of what is known as 'The Land Between the Lakes,' located in Kentucky and Tennessee between Lake Barkley and Kentucky Lake. In his book, *'Beasts Between the Rivers'* (Amazon, 2022), Martin describes not only the experience in detail, but also the mental and emotional scarring he and his friend had been left with for many long years after the confrontation itself – and that's exactly what it had been! Both men had been turkey hunting while in the national forest, deciding to camp out in the wilderness together and just taking a break away from the pressures of life. Their experience had happened during nightfall, and both men had realised there was something strange due to the absence of normal sounds one would come to expect within any forest. This is usually a common indication reported among many before the onslaught of a paranormal or UFO-related event. Earlier that evening, Martin and his friend had split up while hunting, and on their return, both heard a strange, metallic sound, along with whistling coming from a large humanoid shape within the shadows. Both men thought it had been the other playing a game, but little did they realise they themselves were being hunted by something altogether unworldly. Martin thought he could see someone smoking a cigarette within the trees, and not far from where he'd been sitting while at camp, along with his mate by an open fire. They had been enclosed by a high rock face that surrounded the perimeter of the area. He realised there had now been two butt ends glowing close together, and if this had been a person, they would have to be at least seven to eight feet in height, and Martin became alarmed when he now saw four of them, moving about in unison. His confusion was soon realised when something of unimaginable horror came forward from within the brush.

At first, Martin had thought he was witnessing someone inside a Werewolf costume. At least, that's what his brain registered. Being a cop at the time gave him no reason to believe otherwise, until, that is, the creature ambled close to their fire. What both men realised was that this beast exhibited movement akin to some wild animal, but a powerful one at that. Its anatomy could not have been that of a regular human in some Halloween guise, because when he viewed its legs, he realised there was no way someone would be able to arch them back the way this thing did. And those glowing red eyes! How was that possible? There came some other shadows from behind, which indicated there were more of them! Shocked, Martin looked upon the face of this beast and realised it was actually grinning at him. He viewed its multiple rows of sharp teeth (having more than any wolf he'd seen before) being displayed within its mocking grimace, and it was at this point when he did the only thing he could think of and reached for his gun! Saying the Lord's prayer, because the creature he later described had been akin to something from the pits of hell, he aimed his weapon at the creature's chest. Interestingly, the beast seemed to know this was a threat, and that, perhaps, it had seen a gun before. It remained poised yet cautious of Martin's next move.

The animal had a muscular upper body with an equally enormous head, along with powerful clawed hands. It had been covered with thick, matted dark hair. The feeling both men had was that the creature was toying with them, along with their emotions, as though instigating a deliberate act of mental horror. But what had been the worst thing about it had been its face! The men had never seen anything so horrifying in their lives. Martin lowered his weapon to one of its legs, just in case this had been a prankster in a suit, and fired a shot.

The creature let out a blood-curdling howl and immediately ran with speed towards one of the steep rock inclines before leaping and navigating itself high up to safety, an impossible task for a human! There came the sound of chaos, as though more of them in the distance had followed suit. Martin and his friend ran towards their truck, fearing for their lives before making a quick escape, leaving all their provisions behind. This case has been well documented; however, once he'd reported it to his superiors, they ordered him and his friend to remain silent about the episode (as though the authorities had been aware of such instances) before Martin was brave enough many decades later to relay his experience which he has never fully recovered from. In all his years of service as a cop, he'd never encountered anything that had scared him as much as the appearance of this monstrous beast. Ever! If this had been a group of wild cryptids living within the forest as a pack, how then can we explain their glowing red eyes? This leads us to consider the so-called 'supernatural' element, and the feeling Martin, along with his friend, had had; that these creatures were the product of some hellish creation.

The famous 'Skinwalker' ranch in Utah, USA has been home to multiple paranormal activities, and not just the appearance of cryptids either, but synonymous with the arrival of UFOs, orbs, along with an entire plethora of mind-boggling preternatural occurrences. In the event of a UFO materialising anywhere across the world, and at such close range normally heralds the arrival of supernatural commotion, as though the manifestation of what we consider as an alien craft has somehow left a rift within the very fabric of time and space itself, and whereby other forces from within the ether are able to seep through. We believe there are other reasons behind this perplexing mystery, which may explain a lot about what's really going on in such provinces, and not just at Skinwalker either. We have addressed this region because it is one of the most famous in terms of high strangeness. Skinwalker is in Ballard, Utah, and spans five hundred acres in the State's northern region known as the Uintah Basin. This land had been claimed by a tribe of Navajo Indians (native to the Southwestern United States) in the 19th century due to its freshwater and rich hunting grounds. Another tribe known as the 'Ding' unknowingly stole the land from another clan of Indians called the 'Ute' (Nomadic Hunter Gatherers), who had the settlers captured and sold to the Spanish as slaves. Through retaliation, the 'Ding' set about creating the curse of the Skinwalker, bringing forth from the spirit world a shape-shifting Man which could turn into a wolf. The curse was said to have been so severe that no Navajo (even to this day) dares step foot upon the accursed terrain for fear of themselves becoming a Skinwalker which translates as, '*by means of it, it goes on all fours.*'

Of course, this is all open to conjecture, but the reasons as to why this geographical location is seemingly home to the truly bizarre and oftentimes terrifying manifestations which defy our sense of reality is thought to lead back to an ancient curse left upon the land by a tribe of Indians, but which does not necessarily account for *all* the other areas of high strangeness happening across the world. We could consider that the accumulation of minds linking together, on a powerful level of mental integration and belief, helped shape the intended curse by the tribe, thus allowing for the formation of thought to quite literally mould itself into matter and directed from that omnipresent dimension of the lower astral planes, no less. And that's just the start of it! The curse had been an evil one; words and thoughts are powerful processes of incantations. Up to the present day, this area has still seen the emergence of the truly bizarre, and scientists are still at a loss to explain what's going on.

Belief, as we know, shapes reality, and we are wondering whether areas of our human cognizance are able, in some instances, to draw varied moulded beliefs into our matrix, and straight from the subtler planes of existence we call spirit, and not always generated by some curse. Both Chris and I consider that by way of thought alone, and if the intention is strong enough to be imprinted within the etheric, then it's possible such manifestations can be summoned. This is clear within those areas of 'Manifestation' programs brought on by a healthy and positive mindset who are intent on producing abundance in a multitude of ways into people's lives. On the other side of the coin, religion has been instrumental in conditioning the Avatar's thoughts in the opposite direction, to the point where many are literally operating on a very basic level of conscious functioning, and mostly brought on by way of fear and control, which has already been addressed. It appears the very foundation of our cognizance can be widened or narrowed within its frequency of awareness, and something our system knows only too well. This is why such imposing control has been facilitated upon much of the public through said indoctrination, and to ensure the Avatar is stripped of its inherent right regarding those super-human powers we all harbour and believe are only unique to the few and not the many. Anything which breaks that mould, so to speak, is considered paranormal, and an area unexplainable within our science. This is a deliberate attempt to shield knowledge that could help us facilitate more power and abundance into our lives, but which the system knows will be abused by many if such knowledge were forthcoming.

The major problem we face is that there are so many different creatures reported and catalogued, which all come into the classification of the paranormal, and we simply do not know their origins. This would make the 'human' so far removed from all these spectres, namely because they follow similar traits, those including telepathy, glowing eyes, pungent smells, of them entering our world and being able to interact on a physical level before vanishing, an alteration of time, or which stops altogether, and all earthly sounds ceasing during the emergence of either a UFO, aliens or cryptids on earth. Also is the fact that many of these beings come across as vastly intelligent, and not so beastly as their outward appearance would suggest. Both Chris and I agree, our senses are processing frequencies. When considering anything paranormal, the change in light, mood, sound, and smell we are detecting is essentially its frequency and an important clue of its nature. Pungent smells denote a low frequency, including the absence of normal sound. It certainly suggests that lower entities in their very nature affect the lower spectrum of frequency. Higher entities are more likely to be accompanied with an increase in light, pleasant smells, or even an etheric resonance. Higher frequencies excite our senses – lower ones dull and sicken them.

If we look again at the UFO phenomenon, there are varied researchers within this field of study intent on 'disclosure.' Yet, something which has not happened. Those central forces which go beyond government are intent in maintaining their silence, and one wonders as to why? In a world where we've been through the most difficult challenges, along with a lesser connection within the religious sectors in our so-called modern era, you would think those in-the-know would put their hand up and admit that we've had contact. Well, that would be the easy part, yet there may be more sinister reasons behind this cover-up, and one which is above top secret, no less. Will such an admittance from those authorities who have maintained their silence reveal a shocking truth, and one which will disclose the fact that 'we,' as the 'human', are far more relevant and universally important than we have been led to believe? Think about it for a moment! As a species, we have never truly been allowed to evolve. Through centralised programming, along with the subjugation of our very own consciousness, with a dash of fear thrown in for good measure, where do we find ourselves? Nowhere in terms of any spiritual understanding on a universal level. It's as though we're all being continuously diverted within our thinking. Therefore, there are two theories we need to consider regarding this silence, and our system's inability in truthfully communicating facts to its populace. The first is that certain high-ranking individuals within the elite are fully aware of such interdimensional summoning of so-called paranormal entities, and who also know the real secrets of the Avatar which they have deliberately overpowered spiritually, or that our system is aware of these interdimensional beings and unable to control their influx, and thereby deny any knowledge concerning their validity to the public. If it's anything to go by, such powers would exploit this phenomenon for their own gains, and not within the interests of the public.

The earth is home to not only the demonic but also angelic visitations. There are literally thousands of cases where people have witnessed the appearance of a divine being of one kind or another, and most notably in situations where their lives have been threatened by some form of imminent disaster. In some situations, it has been known that these exulted essences have averted disaster, safeguarding the person from harm. Their appearance is so at odds compared to the nightmarish manifestations of either the Dogman or Sasquatch (to name but a few), and tells us categorically there are distinctions to be made between the lower and higher spheres of reality which penetrate through to our earth environment in varied forms. Such exalted beings arrive within brilliant luminosity, indicating their own spiritual progression within the astral. The Dogman and Sasquatch appear with no light source (save from their eyes), which would indicate the Hollywood film portrayals of such angels and demons may very well be on the right track, and those higher entities are represented as light-bearers. In the past, ancient paintings depicted holy figures in much the same way, and even went so far as to paint halos above the head of their celestial Avatar. It's interesting to also note that most of what we consider fiction is, in truth, fact! And this is the turning point in terms of whether we create such a phenomenon ourselves through the projection of our own beliefs, or whether we can literally summon the darkest and lightest forces from within the depths of human consciousness, which is connected to the entire hub of the source of All that Is!

It is evident that lower entities from within the astral planes are (and if the conditions are matched by their density) able to attach themselves to any individual. In the vast majority of cases, most folks are safe, but in rare incidents, a form of possession can take hold, and thus allow such forces to infiltrate through to our dimension with relative ease. Again, famous cases have been portrayed in the film industry, most notably '*The Exorcist*', released in 1973, produced by William Peter Blatty, which follows the story of a young girl possessed by a demon, and whose mother tries in vain to rescue her with the help of two priests. The film is loosely based on a real-life event which centred around a fourteen-year-old boy, Ronald Edwin Hunkeler from the United States, who'd been possessed by an evil spirit, and with the aid of a Catholic and a Jesuit priest, attempted to rid him of the beast. In varied cases, strange marks will appear on the body of the possessed, and the personality of the entity will make itself known by way of voice, but far different from that of the original host of the Avatar. The most disturbing element is that the discarnate, which has attached itself to its human host, is able to project any number of voices through the vocals of its victim. Nothing that comes out in terms of audio language is anything but pleasant. Many priests have tried to communicate with certain entities through the possessed in an attempt to find out where the source of such evil is emanating from, along with trying to help the attachment, as well as the person seized by this seemingly corruptible force. When the entity speaks through the vocals of its host, blasphemy is projected outward from the lower spirit, which has temporarily hijacked the body. It's interesting that prayers, along with an acknowledgement of God or Jesus during the invocation of an Exorcism is taking place sends the entity into a wild fit of frenzy, as though such divinity being administered is offensive to the attachment. Addressing the UFO subject, we can see certain correlations which appear identical in nature when calling out in prayer. In episodes of alien abductions by the famous greys, for example, individuals calling for God to protect them have usually seen to their departure during the initial stages of a snatching by these illusive grey beings. What might this tell us? Is it possible that certain lower forces within the astral planes are able to manifest themselves into varied guises which would appear in vogue, or attractive within the mindset of the individual going through such gruelling episodes? Such omnipresent beings go to great lengths in temporarily disabling their Avatar in order that their control can be exerted from their realm and directly into ours.

**The Stevenage Poltergeist**

I recall a poltergeist case I attended in Stevenage, England, which had seemingly been attached to a young thirteen-year-old lad. This had happened many years ago, but the reality of how discarnate entities can break through to our matrix with relative ease was made very much apparent to me. In my estimation, there is categorically no denying this! The event had left me shaken, but also frustrated because the group of mediums I had been with were unable to help the family in any way. The lady I had previously been associated with was approached by the mother of the son in question to see if we were able to assist in ridding the family of this threat, and in all fairness, that's exactly what she wanted to do, but another famous medium she'd entrusted and invited onboard had been more interested in her own personal pursuits within the world of the media. That is to say, she was in it for her own profile and pocket, and not for the long-suffering family to this oppressive, otherworldly force. It also became obvious that the poltergeist was controlling the boy and his grandparents through fear within its nasty grip.

We had met the mother and boy, whose name was Jay, in a cafe in Stevenage, and she explained to us that her son was now living with her parents in a detached house within the same province, and for the simple reason that the poltergeist had literally trashed her flat, and that she couldn't have him living with her during this time. However, the shocking facts became apparent when we soon discovered her parents' beautiful house had also met the same fate now that their grandson was living with them. It appeared to us that the poltergeist was attached to Jay, and not originally to their place of residence, as is usually the case. The mother informed us that, upon entry to her parents' house, we were to take everything out of our pockets, as those who'd tried to help in the past and ventured into the property invariably found keys, wallets, phones, and just about anything else held on their person vanish! This was fascinating to me, and I recall seeing the film '*Poltergeist*', which Steven Spielberg produced in 1982, and had wondered as to this reality. I, along with the others, was soon to discover the truth and accuracy within the depiction of Spielberg's adaptation.

Jay said very little. I wondered how the poltergeist had seemingly attached itself to him. I noticed he wore fingerless gloves, and upon querying this, he merely stated that he would get an electric shock if he came into contact with anything metallic, and assumed this had something to do with what we ended up calling the poltergeist, 'IT.' After a while and realising that I was on his side and to be trusted, Jay showed me through a cracked screen on his mobile phone his recording of an old rocking chair which uncannily moved from left to right and on its own accord when he, along with his grandparent's asked 'IT' questions. This had been during the early stages of contact with the entity. The chair's movement to the right was the poltergeist's response for a 'yes,' and the left for a 'no.' They had originally communicated with it using a Ouija Board. Jay was honest, but I couldn't help feeling as though he felt a little empowered by the poltergeist seemingly singling him out as though he was special in this regard. There was an aloofness about him, too, which I found a little uncomfortable. Well, I naively assumed, proof is in the pudding. Anyone could have rigged the chair with some string, but we were about to enter the nest of 'IT's' lair and would see for ourselves just what was going on. Perhaps 'IT' had gained its entry through to Jay via the lower astral planes whilst using the Ouija Board itself, and something dangerous if one isn't spiritually protected in the right way! After all, he'd admitted they'd used one before this chaos entered their lives.

The family had come across as honest and sincere, but mostly thwarted because they were unable to rid themselves of this menace. The police, a vicar, and a few other mediums had ventured into the house, and all had been met with hostility. In one instance, the poltergeist had communicated through the rocking chair to Jay and his grandparents that 'IT' was actually the unborn twin to Jay, and that his spirit wanted to communicate with them. The mother validated that Jay had indeed been a twin, but that his brother had died within the later stages of pregnancy. As a single mother herself, this had come as a heavy blow, but the family was to later learn that 'IT' had lied concerning this revelation. On one occasion, 'IT' told the family there had been money secretly buried within the grounds of their extensive garden, and they'd dug up the area close to the back of the property, only to find nothing! But what 'IT' did do, and in front of witnesses, was manifest hundreds of pennies which dropped from the sky, and roughly in the location where they'd dug the grounds. It rained money for quite a while, even time enough for the family to get pots from inside the house to collect their small windfall.

Poltergeists are famous for apporting objects from one location to another. Regarding the pennies, I did wonder whether someone, somewhere in the world, would find one of their savings jars empty! As we understand, such forces are able to teleport objects from one space to another, and something 'IT' would demonstrate to us much later in the afternoon. We parked up to a handsome, detached property and noticed the front windows were boarded up with wooden panels from the inside. 'IT' had smashed them!

Upon entering the house, we made certain our pockets were emptied, but I was completely unprepared for what we were about to discover, as well as experience. The elderly couple who invited us in had been sweet, obliging, but nervous. There had been me, the two other mediums, including one of their partners, the boy Jay, along with his nan and grandad. The mother would not venture inside the house. As I walked into the hall, I noticed a large table positioned next to the wall, and moving into the spacious living room saw that there was merely a sofa and two armchairs. They had a downstairs toilet with no towel, hand gel, or toilet paper. Where the loo roll would normally sit was merely its roll holder. I could only wonder as to why everything here had been removed. The place was empty and looked like a war zone, where every amenable item such as ornaments was absent. The elderly lady explained they'd had to remove all of their possessions and store them in an outer building located at the far end of their large garden. She further explained they had to do this because the poltergeist had a habit of teleporting their possessions from one room to another. The first to be removed had been the cutlery, as they had on a few occasions seen one of their own knives from the kitchen drawer suddenly manifesting out of thin air and appearing close to where they were seated or standing, as though being held by an invisibly burglar, the offensive item hovering in a threatening manner, seemingly ready to take a strike before dropping to the floor. The lady explained they ate from paper plates, plastic knives and forks, which was made apparent to us when she prepared our lunch. On another occasion, when they'd opened their oven door, hundreds of teabags suddenly projected like mini missiles into the kitchen, littering the floor. We hadn't at this point experienced anything supernatural, but judging from what we were seeing told us this family was being held hostage by 'IT.'

The elderly couple and their grandson would retire to bed in sleeping bags. Although there were spacious bedrooms upstairs, 'IT' did not like them being separated, and preferred they were huddled together at night like cattle in the living room, and whereby they'd position themselves in the centre of the room, and very much on guard. In those instances where one of them had to leave the house for provisions, one of the other members would be bitten by invisible teeth, and they had the marks to prove it! The old lady knew there was always a price to pay later. When she said this, I remembered feeling chilled. The lightbulbs would be smashed if turned on, so Jay had his mobile phone with its torch when needed, an item 'IT' strangely didn't appear to touch. Most of the assaults had been directed at Jay's grandparents, and it was as if 'IT' was somehow protecting the boy.

The fireplace had been boarded up, and most of the glass windows, as well as the inside ones, had been smashed. The walls had chunks taken out of them due to 'IT's' rage if the family ventured too far away from 'IT's' new nest. And here we were, in the very heart of 'IT's' lair. I wondered whether the poltergeist knew we were there, but worrisome of all, what 'IT' would do.

We informed the family that we'd psychically 'tune in' to see if we could pick up anything. Nothing could be detected. Perhaps 'IT' was hiding? It had been during the late evening when our group decided it was best to leave and follow things up later. Perhaps 'IT' wanted us out? It was during this moment when I got the feeling we were being watched, like some shark circling its prey in the depths of the ocean. I clearly remember stating that 'IT' had locked onto me. I felt it was aware of who and what I was about; Jay sat in one of the chairs in the living room, looking at me intently. I did consider whether he was the one yearning for his paranormal mate to demonstrate its powers. Interestingly, this had occurred when we were about to leave, and I remember the old lady telling us the same thing would happen to one of them whenever they'd vacate the house. They had an old radio in the room that had been playing music in the background in an effort to demonstrate how 'IT' could manipulate the channels. Up to this point, everything appeared normal.

Suddenly, 'IT' appeared to have selected a few songs which began to play, the first being, *'Release me,'* by Engelbert Humperdinck, and the band Queen's, *'I want to break free!'* We did consider whether there had been a subliminal message from the entity itself; that 'IT' wanted to be released and break free, or that we ourselves were being mocked. It was during this point, while we were together in the lounge, that the atmosphere began to change, becoming colder and more oppressive. Jay had a bottled drink sitting on the floor, and all at once, by its own accord, it shot up with such force and hit the ceiling hard before crashing to the ground. There was now a small chunk of plaster where the bottle had made contact. We froze! Immediately, there came a loud 'bang,' as though someone had hit a hammer hard upon some surface, followed by a flash of intense, bright, silver-white light which illuminated the front-bay windows boarded up due to the smashed glass from the poltergeist's previous outbursts in the past. As the light faded, there came the sound of a 'plonk,' and previously where there had been nothing on the windowsill, we were incredulous to find a half-eaten packet of polo mints sitting on the window's ledge. Stunned, we moved forward to examine the mints. Interestingly, the foil around the packet had been hot. I remember feeling shocked at the fact that 'IT' had somehow teleported this item from somewhere, but none of us had been carrying anything of this kind. Readdressing Steven Spielberg's film *'Poltergeist,'* most of the effects presented in his film appeared correct when considering such entities and what they are able to do, and especially regarding the sound and light being heard and seen before 'IT' brought forth this least interesting of items from God knows where! As I held the mints in my hand, I was amazed that 'IT' had somehow traipsed through the ether, an area all of us mediums had been fascinated with. One could only imagine how that was possible. However, 'IT' had not finished demonstrating its powers by any means!

The elderly couple knew it was time for us to leave, because of the clear signs 'IT' presented in its seemingly long reign of control, destruction, along with intimidation, which the family had come to expect. My heart broke when I saw the look on Jay's Gran's face. The fear was very much evident in her eyes as her tiny form moved quickly from the lounge and out into the hall. At that exact moment, something fired from across the closed downstairs toilet door, and I saw the little lady cowering, hands over her head and eyes closed to protect herself from whatever it was that had been hurled with such speed and which now struck the windowsill. Of all things, it had been the empty loo roll holder. 'IT' had once again demonstrated the ability to teleport an object through solid matter. This small utility had literally been projected from the toilet, '*through*' the door, and out the other end as though its material composition hadn't been there at all!

As we moved quickly out into the hallway, the large and empty table, which had been the only furniture there, was plucked into the air and moved with jagged motions through to the opening of the sitting room by this unseen force. I must point out that this table was heavy and thick-set, yet the poltergeist had no problem performing this incredible feat. As it clumsily maneuvered the table in the air and through a clear passage to the room beyond, it was sent hurtling and crashed to the floor.

I was out of that house and in the car, which had been left unlocked on their property, in seconds. While the others mingled outside, clearly shocked, Jay took a casual seat upon the front wall of his grandparents' house and simply stared at me. The only thing going through my mind was that I'd hoped this thing hadn't attached itself to me in any way. I recall I had a clairvoyant function to perform later that night, too, which had still gone ahead, but the frightening yet fascinating events had been swimming around in my mind, and I just couldn't process everything that had happened.

Unfortunately, the medium and her partner, who had been invited onboard to help the family, did anything but! She had us removed from the case and was on the phone to her agent, eyes no doubt flashing with pound signs and more fame under her belt, telling him they'd got a sensational story on their hands. Well, that wouldn't have been the case if she hadn't been asked to help out in the first place, and that had been our intention from the very beginning. The older lady had later phoned the medium I had worked with, telling her that she was sorry and wasn't happy with the way things were going, because a film crew had set cameras up inside their house, waiting for the bait, so to speak. She was saddened we'd been kicked off the case, but was too weak to challenge those now involved. That was the last time I had anything to do with the Stevenage poltergeist. I did hear that soon afterwards, the activity had died down, eventually disappearing. Perhaps 'IT' knew of the other medium's intentions and decided to show her who was boss!

Ouija Boards are known to cause great damage if not used in the right way (but not the only method in summoning those from the astral) and are a gateway for alternate spectres residing within those lower planes of the astral to freely enter our reality. It's so important to protect yourself through prayer if using one of these devices, as there is no telling what you might bring through. It's just possible that Jay had inadvertently opened just such a portal in allowing a lower entity to attach itself to him, as well as giving him the feeling that he was somehow special and harboured supernatural abilities. We hear so often of attachments, or better known a 'hitchhikers', within this field of investigation. Skinwalker ranch had been classic in this department, and whereby the researchers, upon travelling back home from the ranch itself, would find their family members being harassed by lower entities, rather like a poltergeist.

Chris recalls having an unexpected interaction with an innocent soul that was not of this world, with no significant message other than to grace his path while walking home from school one day. As he now explains.

*'It was a sunny summer afternoon when I left school one day. I was about seventeen at the time, and it was a route I had taken hundreds of times before to get home. I had no idea that ten minutes into my walk, I was about to experience something very paranormal and curiously moving. I was approaching a part of my journey where I would be leaving the streets and entering a place called Fairlands Valley Park, a picturesque part of the town that consists of 120 acres of parkland with lakes and ponds of various sizes. As I looked ahead toward the opening of trees that I was soon to enter, something caught my eye. From nowhere, a young boy excitedly came into view with his back to me and running towards the same opening that led towards the park. Already, I was puzzled. His appearance seemed oddly different from the surroundings we shared. There was a brightness about him that gave me the first clue that all was not 'normal'. He appeared to be five years old with blonde hair that made the sunlight reflect off it with so much vibrancy it was like a small sunburst. He was wearing a white short-sleeved undergarment and light blue dungarees. My initial reaction was to question why he was alone. Where was he running to? And why were his parents*

*nowhere to be seen? I had the strangest feeling that he already knew of my presence. Upon having that very thought, he stopped! Already, my gut had butterflies as though he actually heard me. He slowly turned himself around towards me, looked directly at me, and gave a merry wave high above his head. I was stunned. I looked quickly around to give reason for his motivation to wave in my direction, but I was very much alone, which I already knew. At this point, it would have taken me about twenty seconds to reach the spot where he stood. With the fun-filled innocence of a child waving, I naturally returned his gesture and gave a very puzzled wave back at him. Seemingly satisfied with that, he turned away from me and ran off again towards the same gap in the tree line that led to the park. His figure turned into a silhouette under the shadow of the trees, where he then ran into the bright and sunny field beyond and vanished. I blinked with bewilderment and wonder. As I approached the same location where I saw him vanish, and where the warm sun returned onto my face from leaving the cool shade of the trees, I felt the wind pick up and blow the leaves nearby me. There was an unmistakable and yet haunting feeling of sadness, joy, and peace in the air. I had to stop and acknowledge what I had witnessed as I looked over the quiet park below me from my hilltop view. I then carried myself off to finish the rest of my walk home with everything unfolding in its usual manner.*

*There have been many moments whereby spirits do indeed prove they can hear your thoughts, that they have their presence within the same energy of the mental field that we are all connected with. The experience I have just shared is one of many that have helped me to know and understand that the world we currently inhabit is far more spiritual than physical. The world is certainly accessible to both the higher and lower spheres, and their appearances certainly seem to be in their control. I do believe we can also dictate and manipulate their ability to be seen, with natural elements within this world also making an unexpected influence to such 'otherworldly' occurrences that help weaken the divide and merge our realities.*

We can clearly define that the Earth is the densest sphere within the etheric, and one easily accessible to such forces which do, on occasions, infiltrate our planet. The higher levels are lighter and brighter, and therefore do not bring chaos or destruction, along with fear. We will speculate much later as to the possibility that certain elite members on earth are aware of those hidden and secular practices which allow them to summon so-called agents of darkness into our world, but in a controlled and safe manner. It could be argued that they might also work in collusion with them behind the scenes, and away from public scrutiny. There is an agenda, and not one that benefits the human. This is why we believe the Avatar's ability in harbouring incredible powers has been shut down by our system, and seeking such otherworldly knowledge is fragmented so that no clear picture is presented into how we can utilise the good, as opposed to those negative energies which appear chaotic in nature and does not benefit our overall spirituality. The elite practice what they do not preach, and this would be very dangerous grounds to unravel if the truth of their real intentions and overall agenda comes to light.

# 'The Eternal Avatar'

## Chapter Ten

## Bringing Your Light into a Dark World

'I am darkness, I am woe,

You do not scare me with what you know.

*But darkness, what do you feel,*

*When sorrow and sadness is all you deal?*

I am darkness, I feel your fright,

You do not scare me with your prayers at night.

*But darkness tell me, what do you see,*

*When all around us is misery?*

I am darkness, I see souls that can't cope,

You do not scare me with your seed of hope.

*But darkness tell me, what do you hear,*

*When all around us is lost in fear?*

I am darkness, I hear only cries,

> You do not scare me when you look in my eyes.
>
> *But darkness, in your eyes I see,*
>
> *Your only power is given by me.'*
>
> Chris John Mayes

Although it seems incredulous to assume that we as the human species are considered the only intelligent lifeform to grace this entire universe (which is something we've been led to believe since the time of Man's becoming), we as the evolving Avatar know better. It is the system we serve which has blinded us to such untruths, and continuously does so in an effort to thwart the very nature of our spirit, and something which will be discussed further in the next chapter. Many will merely assume that those of us who do not comply with the way things are or feel differently from the normal flow of this prosaic existence are categorized as 'conspiracy theorists' (such an old and worn-out tune) who are making things fit for themselves. The truth is, we live in a very shadowy world, and always have, for that matter. Daily and nightly, the media report on wars, destruction, murders, hardships, and other topics which do little to inspire. We're not saying events of this kind don't occur – far from it – but the system goes to great lengths to ensure we are fed this negativity on a daily basis, and which ingests into the minds of millions, as though it's within our best interests to be informed about the horrors transpiring. Many people are 'into' themselves and mostly angry and dejected, trying to deal with their own problems and thereby cutting everything else off around them. And who can blame them? We live by a system that is more interested in *their* own agenda, and less about those of us at the lower end of the spectrum, which the elite see as mere 'cash machines' in every sense of the word. We are a commodity through their eyes, mere cattle which must be kept in a tight, mental enclosure, unless you prove worthy to *their* cause.

We incarnate into this world and follow protocol, but have no instruction manual to guide us spiritually, other than the basic model we fumble through in terms of how the system sees it. This is why many who question the true nature of our being have been left to figure things out for themselves, because you can bet your bottom dollar you'll get little or no help, as well as understanding from those in power. And yet, the wheel goes depressingly around in those circles with hardly any progression being made in further examining the penultimate questions we seek. These, to our mind, are life-changing areas of knowledge, and we also believe will alter the way we see one another, along with the world in which we live. Attitudes will invariably change, because we'll come to realise that only hurting one another is merely a reflection of 'self,' and that by definition we are all interconnected into this incredible tapestry of life. And it's not just those of the ruling elite who are not helping our species flourish, but also people on the lower end of the social spectrum, too. Give someone a little power, and invariably, they become a God! There are more emotional and mental problems than ever before, and this is all due to a disabling of the human psyche, which has been instigated by a system that appears to rob one of those elements of family life, creativity, love, along with nurturing one another. We can see that family values have changed, and due no less by the ridiculous rising costs of living, along with the pressures this brings to those trying to scrape through life the best way they can. Whereas back in the day, much of life appeared to flow at a steady pace. Now, everything is on 'fast-forward' with no time to think, more money to be made, and everything being needed 'now!' Hold on! Let's take a moment to catch our breath!

Let's face it, we all get up in the morning and invent ourselves before we take to the stage of life, wondering just how things are going to pan out. Depending on how we feel throughout the day best determines the outcome of events, whether positive or negative. Although there are many occasions where you'll get an angry driver who's itching to get in front of you, or that bad-tempered boss who's wanting everything done now, or the public you're serving being rude to you, life can be a mixed bag. It's any wonder we actually get through a single day unscathed by the onslaught of mixed emotions. How many times have you been in a situation where you've gone out the door feeling as happy as a clam, only to find yourselves experiencing the complete opposite? Yes, we've all been there. And trying to hold things together while facing these negative situations can be a hard lot. No wonder, with the advent of technology, which brings more pressure because the world is in a constant state of productive demand, there are increased cases of depression, emotional and mental issues, along with those day-to-day problems we all invariably encounter. You could walk into a room full of ten people and be met by just one who you feel has an instant dislike towards you, and even when no words have been exchanged. This is all down to energy, and which we (along with all things in life) are composed of. Mental energy is just as powerful as our physical nature, and effective when utilised within those two polarities, which can make all the difference to our world.

Whenever I was happy, the world appeared to be the complete opposite! What was occurring here, I wondered? I knew on a deeper level of the psyche that I was the problem; that my positive 'vibes' were somehow conflicting with those whose energies were the complete reverse, like some mirror. I considered the 'conscious bubble' scenario which, effectively, connects us all psychically and how others on a lower level of emotions appeared to suck you into their emotional ocean of strong under-currents. My naïve mind considered that if I joined them, I'd be safe. I had this other impression also that the accumulation of negativity outstripped the positivity, and thus gave way to a landslide of you being continually thwarted by the influx of millions of other minds who were totally at odds with the way I was feeling. It's a theory, at least, but when I neutralised my thought processing into a more balanced level, the day wouldn't be as bad as I thought. Being positive works, but you'll encounter a barrage of that negative energy, and something we must find strength through in order that it does not affect us so patently. As a kid, I neutralised any negative thoughts I could see developing within my mind of future events by stating, '*No, God, no – never, God, never!*' It seemed to work on most occasions for me back then.

I had a lady once in a working situation who made life hell for me on a nightly basis. This was when I'd been in my twenties, while also holding down a full-time job. I wanted some extra money to help me through. Being younger then, I could just about manage the hours. The lady in question was in a position of authority and knew that anything I did or said in defiance against her attitude towards me would appear mute, along with her seniors with whom she had close ties. It was a checkmate situation. I dreaded going in to work, knowing this person would be there, ready to hand out her godly orders. This had been a part-time job in the late evening, and we had to sort stock from totes and price them before getting them onto their respective shelves. We were not allowed to talk to other staff members (even though we had been the night team and there were no customers in the store) and had to complete each box within a certain amount of time. The longer I was there, the more I grew to hate it. It wasn't so much the work, but the lady whom I knew (and for reasons unclear) did not like me. She even said to her colleagues that I was the 'posh boy!' One evening, as I was about to start my shift, I was handed my wage slip and, walking down to the locker room, I duly ripped the perforation from the top of its slip, which fell to the floor. Ok, so perhaps I should have picked it up, but I was in a rush to get to my station and didn't want to be late with the person in question breathing down my neck. I thought nothing more of it and performed my duties in relative silence, save for the lady pushing for me to work faster. On my shift the very next evening, all staff had been summoned to a meeting with the Store Manager himself. As we ambled into the staff canteen, I wondered what was in order and saw my line-manager standing next to her Chief and Commander, her arms folded and looking as angry as ever. I could never work out what her problem was. However, the meeting had taken a nasty turn, and soon after the big boss in his northern accent spieled off figures and job expectations loudly informed, *'...and while we're all here, one of you likes to throw rubbish willy-nilly! It has come to the attention (and he pointed to my line-manager) that Philip Kinsella is one such staff member who needs to know what a bin is for! I'm going to personally Sellotape a dozen wage slips on the floor down the corridor outside, and as you peel them up, Mr Kinsella, I want you to think about littering, as well as someone else having to pick up your rubbish behind you!'* So, the meeting was orchestrated to make an example of me, and in front of the others!

My face went red when everyone looked my way. As we began to leave to start the shift, my manager, who had her arms folded, said in a nasty voice, *'...and I want YOU* (saying this angrily while pointing a finger in my face) *to work on the stationery department.'* Stationery was the worst, and I knew this was another form of punishment for my foul deed. My mind swam, and I flipped!

By the time my words had found their way out of my mouth, the lady's face had drained of colour. I ensured the Store Manager was there, as well as the staff, to hear my outburst. How dare they shame me this way! They should have taken me in an office and reprimanded me privately. I told her she could stick the job where the sun didn't shine, and who the hell was she anyway to treat me like something under her shoe? I resigned there and then. I grabbed my things and walked back to the car, not caring for the job, money, or her. My actions, I reflected, had been justified. Where was her power now, I thought? In a way, I felt liberated, but was not proud of my actions. Why do people treat others with such remorse? If she had been kind to me, everything would have been different. This is a common theme within most working environments (and which in the majority of cases is subtly implemented through bullying and psychological drip-feeding) and coming, no less, from the very bottom of the social ladder. It's hard enough dealing with the evil and corruption with most of those in governance, let alone the folk down on our level. I've seen them come and go, and that lady wasn't the only person I've had wranglings with in the past when it comes to those in authority.

I had been young, but by no means inexperienced. I've always known how to treat other people with respect and courtesy, but allowed to defend myself when it comes to abuse within their varied forms, especially from the past, which I'd had to get through on a physical and emotional level too. As humans, we are exceedingly complex beings, and our emotions are at the forefront of how we evolve. I recall a line from the great Sir Anthony Hopkins in the film '*Hannibal*' (directed by Sir Ridley Scott and released in 2001) when he said, '*Some people just see to it that you don't advance!*' And I agree with him there. But I had allowed such negativity to affect me, and this didn't do me any favours in the long run. I kept finding myself with varied managers throughout my working life who had issues with me, and I had to stop and seriously think about this. Was I in some way attracting these negative situations into my life because I believed myself to be the victim?

As we know, our brain works as both a transmitter and receiver for consciousness, but also acts as a sponge, and we nevertheless absorb positive and negative energies which filter through to our neurological wiring and into the core of our central nervous system each nanosecond of the day. These two polarities stimulate thoughts into feelings, and subsequently feelings into actions. Positive vibrations create an increase in our well-being, promoting a more relaxed mind, body, and soul. Negative energies generate the complete reverse, whereby our physical nature can be severely affected by the onslaught of such harsher vibrations. We are dealing with the influx of so much information from the world in which we live, it's any wonder we can function in some coherent manner! Some individuals who are themselves bitter and twisted will discover they are unable to receive love and continue to attract more or less the same in which they give out. Of course, if they change their mindset to a more forgiving and loving nature, then they will attract this into their life. To a degree, the human body is likened to a computer, but a biological one at that. The software is consciousness, and programs its secondary unit, the vehicle, as a means to express itself.

As evolving Avatars, our understanding of energies and how they work, along with changing our thinking from the negative to a positive framework, does eventually free our biological system from being contaminated like some virus. And that's exactly what negative energy is, an infection which, if not mentally overridden with positive thoughts, can over time cause a disruption within the mind, body and soul, removing us from our connection to those higher levels filled with love, inspiration, creativity, along with a need to aspire in whichever way you desire. Over time, this can have a detrimental effect in the way we function, and may become an issue for those around us. I had allowed myself to be used as a sponge in soaking up the lady's negativity with me when I'd worked as a part-timer, and thus affecting me to the point where I couldn't mentally function so well. The moment I took a step back and really thought if I (playing the victim) was thus attracting the same negative frequency my way, things began to change. It's not an easy thing to do, because we are constantly bombarded with such energies almost daily, but having an awareness, along with trying to change the way we think, makes all the difference. The only reason we feel we can't do this or that is merely an instruction YOU give YOURSELF, and which, if the belief is strong enough, will temporarily shut down your link to the greater mind which we are all connected to. There are many people in our world who have overcome the most incredible challenges, only to succeed in the end, and all through their belief that shapes that reality in one way or another. Chris and I believe the system we serve is using all sorts of subtle, yet incredibly powerful psychological weaponry to incapacitate the Avatar. It's not just the daily battering from those on our level of life, which we have to brace ourselves for when certain situations arise, but also what's being flung at us on harsher levels from those at the top of the symbolic pyramid of power. The more technologically advanced we become, the less we are able to *feel* in terms of not only the well-being of ourselves, but others. And, because of the demands of life, such facets temporarily override the normal balancing of the brain's hemispheres, and something the system has absolutely no regard for whatsoever. Those elite members look after themselves, and no one else, when it comes to the interest of others, and such psychological tactics they employ appear to steamroll ahead, with any opposition appearing mute to their end, simply because they are rich and have taken the status of power. Yet, do many of them (and not the majority of the elite, it must be noted) not realise that this life is but a mere speck within the annals of time? Those in true governance, which we believe are not human, use those Avatars who rise to power and are moulded to their way of thinking accordingly. This example can be clearly illustrated when politicians in England promise to do good for the people, only to change all of that when they come to power! This is also the same for a great many other countries. In ages past, when someone had been elected within any official capacity, the townsfolk would have meetings, and upon a unanimous vote from the public (whatever the debate), the 'official' would conduct the wishes of the winning majority. The problem is, community spirit is being slowly eradicated, and this makes things far easier for the elite to swipe aside any concerns from its populace in favour for those decisions obviously coming from the World Economic Forum, which frighteningly do not serve the interests of the majority, knowing there will be no backlash from those who, within smaller communities, could directly challenge the authorities themselves face-to-face. There are some situations that we cannot control, which occur on a united level, as opposed to those individual experiences which we are able to subtly alter within our own emotional outlet.

Many of those in governance are cowards, like the magician in the film '*The Wizard of Oz*' where Dorothy, the lion, scarecrow, and tin man discover there is really no wizard at all, but an ordinary man who is pulling the strings in an effort to frighten all those who venture into his presence. The powers-that-be are weak when confronted, and this is the reason they stick together like glue and are seldom seen in public. They know that we, as the Avatar, are powerful, and therefore use varied methods in disabling the true nature of our being. We have lived in moderate ignorance for centuries, and any rise in this knowledge leads those in control on a demonic path of more control, fear, and damnation.

Take the Covid scam as an example and see how those within the media had been full-on about the necessity for everyone to be vaccinated with the Pfizer/

BioNTech Covid-19 serum (and which miraculously we had been informed in the beginning was a cure, developed at break-neck speed within the medical profession, something unheard of for any untrialled and untested inoculation within the World Health Organisation. If you don't believe us, go do your homework!) and how the terminology 'anti-vaxxers' was created to turn the majority of those who dared raise their hand questioningly because they could smell a rat and knew something was not quite right. Freedom of Information requests gave little response in terms of the public's concerns, and you'll find almost nothing online about that, too. It got to the stage where people posting their thoughts had been blocked on Facebook, along with other social platforms, better known as 'Facebook Jail.' What does this tell you? Freedom of speech is obviously no longer suitable to those running the show. Fear has been the main weapon against the people for them to rush out, and then walk the red carpet like stars to show they were in full compliance to something which they'd just been injected with, without knowing the full facts of what was *in* the vaccine to begin with! Many saw their compliance as a psychological reward, but let us remind you again - the system doesn't give a hoot about you! It is at the stage where no transparency is ever forthcoming because there was no way of measuring whether the person who had the vaccine had died as a result of having it, or the allusive Covid 19 itself which no one is sure where it had originally cropped up from, other than stories of it breaking out in a market in Wuhan within the Republic of China! Yes, it had to be that far away so no one could trace links to its legitimacy.

And what of the deaths the vaccine had caused? Who would know? Such data was not available to the public until leading scientists started coming forward to voice their concerns. Any, if not all of those who condemned the vaccine had either been threatened with their jobs or, on a few rare occasions, died under mysterious circumstances. We'll leave that one for you to check out. Dirty tactics yet again, no doubt! The same applied with '*Black Lives Matter*' where, once again, racial hatred was stirred up by the media to make the white person appear like the bad guy (actually ALL lives matter, and the authors embrace every cultural aspect of our divinity) and those opposing the political stance which have been labelled '*Far Right.*' Such psychological weapons work exceedingly well for the authorities because they know that by creating division between the people, all they have to do is engineer a problem, get the reaction they want, and then step forward with '*their*' solution, which had been their intention all along. Brilliant! The media cartel will only report what those 'magicians' at the top want reported, and anything that opposes their official view will immediately be retracted. And that's just the start of it. Of course, and as we are well aware, it was the CIA who created the word 'conspiracy theory' over one-hundred and fifty years ago, and was designed specifically to allay any fears that former President of the United States of America, John F. Kennedy was killed by his own Secret Service because, it is believed through his own radical ideas which he knew would benefit his country, but something which would ultimately threaten the already carefully laid plans for America by those behind the scenes and calling the shots, and not Lee Harvey Oswald in Dallas, November 1963 as everyone has been forced to suppose. Such is the power of the media. Oswald was shot himself to seal the conviction which had been communicated to the masses through the media, so that he could not bring his evidence to the table. Not everything in the world is a conspiracy, but the Avatar cannot be fooled when they start asking serious questions about those events that appear suspicious in terms of their legitimacy. The hammer from the elite comes down good and hard on anyone who can see through their deception.

We doubt there is anyone who can forget the tragic events that unfolded centred around the fateful 9/11 Twin Towers in Lower Manhattan, New York, and where the buildings evaporated in front of our very eyes. The disaster is known as '9/11' because the towers fell on September 11th, 2001, but the date strangely coincided with America's emergency number 911. The bizarre nature of this orchestrated massacre would suggest not only the ironic fact regarding the above-mentioned date and numbers, but there may well have been a demonic aspect to this senseless destruction, which we will explore in the next chapter. Another conspiracy? Well, no, because the facts did not add up, and certainly when experts (those who were not connected to the official line of enquiry, and within itself promotes a startling conclusion than the one fed to the public, and which the system tried to silence) started digging for clues.

This had been during the time and early into my clairvoyance when I'd been questioning spirit about how the future is shaped. I had so many people wanting to know this or that regarding forward proceedings in their life, and which, to many, seemed more important than being put in contact with their loved ones on the other side. Still, I repeatedly asked my spirit guide how this was possible, but all I got back was static. The event I am about to describe has already been documented in another of my books, '*Guardians of the Dead*,' but I spoke to Chris about his thoughts on this, and we both feel this may lead us into an interesting area regarding certain time-lines, and how future events can be created within our thoughts (if strong enough) and whereby they solidify into not only an eventual *physical* outcome, but one which interlinks and invariably affects others, too, thereby manifesting a desired outcome right out of the ether. Our past is set within a memory imprint and stored in our etheric body, while the future is in a constant state of flux until certain mental variables have themselves congealed as it reaches the 'NOW' point in our time. What we call the future within this physical dimension becomes the present, and something we are always in on a corporeal level of reality.

Before the night of 9/11, upon asking about the future being preordained (as opposed to many accepting the hypothesis that it's all merely random in nature), I had just been getting ready to go to bed and remember as I put on my t-shirt suddenly experiencing a powerful blast which emanated within the region of the solar plexus. The sensation was akin to an internal explosion, which sent my atoms within my body scattering outward. There also came a feeling of utter dread, and one I vaguely remembered from another time, but which I couldn't quite put my finger on. A second hit within the same location forced me to steel myself, and I thought that, perhaps, I was suffering a kind of internal aneurysm. My mind began to reel as to what these weird, yet potent 'hits' were about, and if not physical, then perhaps they were operating on a psychic level? It had been the last blast which truly did it for me. It was as if my hair was standing on end by this point. The sensations subsided, followed by a silence hard to describe, and the terrible feeling which had accompanied them soon abated afterwards.

The following day, September 11th, 2001, three main buildings were compromised, the Twin Towers being the first two, when jetliners that had been hijacked from Boston's Logan International Airport as a result of al-Qaeda's terror attacks were plunged directly into each of these enormous edifices. Their collapse was thought to have been attributed to the weakening of the structure's framework where such impacts had been made, along with the fuel dump being dispersed in and around a vast area of both buildings. Yet, the Twin Towers not only crumbled but appeared to turn to dust as the structures plummeted to the ground within a few hours of being hit. This was clearly evident from those recordings many witnesses had made while the events had unfolded. The other building assaulted had been the Pentagon, but there is suspicion that this may have been a missile, rather than an aircraft, unlike the Towers. Experts within the architectural, building, and engineering divisions, however, considered the ease with which the Twin Towers collapsed an impossibility, due to them being designed to withstand such external intolerance. In short, the Towers should *not* have fallen because their fundamental design took into consideration such eventualities. For example, the Empire State Building was struck in 1945 when a B-25 Michell bomber of the United States Army Air Forces crashed into the north side of its $79^{th}$ floor, killing fourteen people, and was attributed to a pilot error due to heavy fog. The Empire Estate Building had been composed of 60,000 tons of steel, along with limestone and granite. The Twin Towers were assembled using 200,000 tons of strong steel, yet not enough, apparently, to withstand the impact of a jetliner! Something didn't add up and one of the reasons why direct enquiries had been quelled if anyone who dared consider an alternate theory as to what may have actually happened, as opposed to the '*official*' investigation, which holds to this day. Just under three thousand people lost their lives to this tragedy!

Dr Judy Wood created quite a stir with the release of her book '*Where Did the Towers Go?*' and published by '*The New Investigation*' in 2010. As a former professor of mechanical engineering with expertise in material science and interferometry, she conducted a forensic study of the towers for almost a decade and came to a starling conclusion which points suspiciously to some kind of '*Directed Energy Weapons*' being used that was responsible in bringing down the Twin Towers, and not the planes as first believed. Dr Wood became suspicious on seeing the events on TV and remarked to her associates about not only the way the planes had plunged into the building (appearing to defy structural resilience) but also how the towers had collapsed with little or no resistance, as though becoming nothing more than dust. To her, the science did not add up, and she found most of her colleagues trying to justify her data in the negative because the cold, harsh facts presented an altogether ugly picture, which, to them, would open a can of worms. The alternative was unthinkable, but Dr Wood's thorough examination of what she calls the '*WTC Complex*

*Crime Scene*' points suspiciously to some type of advanced weapons technology being used, and which was able to disable matter into molecular dissociation. Of course, the official narrative *must* stand with those 'in-the-know' and at the top of that all too famous symbolic pyramid of power. Yet, the evidence is irrefutable and would be a case won in the Supreme Court of the United States, but that is something which will never happen, and the reason being is that the finger which has been pointing in the wrong direction from the start (and as soon as the events transpired before any formal investigation could be had) will find itself coming back full circle.

Friend, researcher, and author, Andrew Johnson, brought Dr Wood's work to my attention many years ago, and has been instrumental within his own investigations, creating a website called '*Check the Evidence.*' He has always had a close association with Dr Wood and authored two books on the subject himself, along with co-author Nick Buchanan, '*9/11 Finding the Truth,*' and '*9/11 Holding the Truth.*'

The feelings I had (as well as many other people which had been reported days even before these tragic events unfolded) secured the knowledge that matter was somehow being disabled, which had been directed within the surrounding basin of the WTC area. This is clear within Dr Wood's research, and something I had experienced back then. It is obvious that those minds behind the orchestration of such proceedings had become an 'intent' which sensitives had psychically detected within a future timeline, and not long after the drama played out. This is how mediums are able to see into certain aspects of the future, and the WTC was just one example.

In our world, there is nothing but distractions and chaos. People have no time to think, and thinking is a powerful form of divination. Much of the media, which is controlled (like many other powerful organisations) through the system's instructions, continually hammers the individual mind with negativity, along with fear and confusion. Even most well-known radio programs spurt out depressing adverts, most of which are too fast and annoying in their repetition. Whenever the Avatar is seen to be making progress on whatever level, and embraces the love-and-light aspect, the system comes crashing in to disable and disrupt this higher vibrational frequency, which threatens *them* in some way. What ultimately is it that those at the top are so afraid of? Have you ever questioned why our world is in a constant state of warring, disruption, and chaos? It is obvious that the Avatar is more powerful in spirit than the ruling elite will ever dare acknowledge, and that our weapon to outwit and remove them completely is through the act of love. Back in the day, world meditation had been reported as something 'Coo-Coo' (in fact, meditation as a whole) because the results of which have proven that thought can really make profound changes to the physical, emotional, mental, and spiritual nature of everything around us. In George Lucas' *'The Empire Strikes Back'* (Lucas Films, 1980), Jedi Master Yoda informed Luke Skywalker that the force surrounded everything. Lucas, as we understand, is also a deep thinker into such matters of the 'spirit,' and subsequently his Star Wars movies are a great portrayal of how both good and evil play out. One must experience both aspects of this 'force', but be perfectly balanced, and something Yoda feared with his young apprentice, Luke Skywalker, because he felt the young boy was reckless and not in command of his thoughts and feelings.

Our ultimate battle is to be free from tyranny, finally, and be able to revel in creativity, joy, health, wealth, abundance, and primarily, love. Love is the key to everything because this raises our vibrations beyond the known laws of physicality and into the realm of creative expression on multiple levels. This is what the system fears. This is why *they* do not wish for us, as evolving Avatars, to shine our light bright, because they know only too well that they themselves will be blinded! Here, then, is Chris' narrative of how he feels about 'Bringing Your Light' into a dark world.

**Chris' 'Bringing Your Light'**

Here, Chris illustrates his idea of *'Bringing Your Light,'* which benefits the whole, as opposed to the part.

*'If someone were to ask you to choose between feeling happy or harmonious, what would you choose? Happiness is always the goal, it seems. It's the emotion we are always wanting to attain and strive for. Happiness brings us all that we want and need. Once we are happy...that's it, life goal achieved! This is not altogether true. This is a trick and a huge deceiver for finding 'your light' which harmony provides in abundance. Happiness is a 'product', not a 'source'. So, what is your 'light'? Ironically, we know it's not something you literally see. It is*

*a form of collective energies, but a spiritual one. A person's 'light' is powerful when the mind, body, and soul are all in alignment. This, in turn, creates harmony, and once we have harmony, everything else falls into place. Harmony is the key, in my personal opinion. All the other wonderful states of 'Light' quickly follow – health, happiness, positivity, mindfulness, fulfillment, which then creates room for affection, attraction, compassion, confidence, and empathy.*

***L**ove*

***I**nspiration*

***G**ratitude*

***H**ope*

***T**ruth*

*By aligning your soul's desires with your thoughts and actions, you create an energetic flow that is not blocked. You might be asking, "What about 'Love?". Love is the ultimate state of spiritual connection. True love is the complete union with yourself and everything. Unless you are a master, it is not realistic to love everything compared to finding harmony with everything. I am reminded of Tai-Chi, it yields, bends, adapts, and flows. I would almost hasten to add that, actually, it is harmony that helps us to find the path to love! Harmony is a realistic practice that, once we adjust and change the blockages in ourselves, will activate a state of being in our lives that aligns us with the inner powers of the Avatar.*

*Once you realise how powerful the state of harmony is for you and those around you, we can start to make wiser decisions during our day that will bring us closer to this state. It creates a fertile space within for spiritual growth and makes you more in tune with the inner and outer world. We all unconsciously decide for the intoxicating, fun-filled excitement that makes us feel happiness, rather than the subtle but far more rewarding and long-term effect of harmony. The media pollute us daily with misleading promises and messages. The 'giver of happiness' is one of many tools that help us part with our money or spend our time chasing – or even vote for! There is nothing wrong with that. If something does make you happy, that's great, the more the better, but you will always end up chasing it. It is very much dependent on circumstance. But harmony has been made to sound boring and uneventful. We think this for good reason because we have been brainwashed to think so. When you become aware of the evil people in this world who want to control the masses, and when you learn how they think and behave, Harmony is NOT what you want people to be feeling. Just look around us and you can see the intense assault from every angle to cause the least amount of harmony as possible.*

*Disharmony, fear, and anger are the perfect tools to implement change in our perceptions of ourselves and the world around us in a very skewed and negative way that disempowers us. It causes people to lose and deny their own divinity and look outside of themselves for someone else for answers and solutions without question, allowing changes that would otherwise not be well-received if situations were fine and pleasant. Creating the problems to instigate the solutions under the guise of safety, health, and convenience, blinds and robs us of our real freedoms and happiness. Just look at the preventative measures, laws, and protocols imposed on the people because of certain situations that have arisen from fear and terror. Once they are implemented, they never return back and why would they? It takes a brave soul to repeal the laws that are intrusive security measures that also hinder our ever-decreasing freedoms, if it appears that removing them would put us at risk when doing so. The proverb "The road to hell is paved with good intentions" is very true in this case. I believe this ties into why we are seeing an unprecedented increase in global 'problems', which are being used to create global solutions. This is all about global power and amalgamating the political, financial, health, and corporate bodies under one umbrella of the few. The WHO (World Health Organisation) and WEF (World Economic Forum) are two entities that are using their power and influence to facilitate and dictate over countries without any public support or consultation. It's long planned and with AI (Artificial Intelligence) as the infrastructure to lock it all within the 'internet of things'. AI is just fast algorithms. If it were real intelligence, then it would not be artificial but life itself. Our futures will see transhumanism that hijacks our natural state, where we will be biologically fused with the internet matrix. It will be promoted as an improved and 'better' version of God's design. Unless you've had your microchip upgrade, most jobs will not be available to you, while others will seem to have a quicker advantage. As usual, it will be introduced into society using baby steps from medical advancements to general public use. Transhumanism will be the loss of our divinity. Babies will no longer be born from the human womb but in pods, which is all about separating us from our source. Injections that alter and corrupt our biology, or even rewrite it, that disconnect us from our ability to access information beyond our bodies, are already underway and will be carried through to generations after. Science is proving that our bodies are resonating. Every cell is a fractal, a multiple receiver and sender of a broad spectrum of information via a field that we are all a part of, with photons being emitted and received. Our DNA stores information and changes with our perceptions of how we see and experience the world we are living in.*

*AI is fast replacing our imagination. Imagination is our soul's purpose to create. We are conduits to this outside information that presents itself to us as imagination. It's not a coincidence that AI is being fervently pushed to replace us and do everything creative on our behalf. Allowing it to replace our ability to feel and be inspired (which actually means to be 'in spirit') is another step to destroying your life force as a human. You only have to compare the healthy imagination of a child and see how, as adults, we lose a large portion of the scope and ability to imagine. We get moulded and suppressed. AI will speed this process to the point where even children will no longer need to imagine. This is a disaster in my opinion, especially if you are someone who likes to be creative and recognizes the fulfilling sense it brings. With VR (Virtual Reality) headsets in every classroom, teaching AI-generated reality only compels the child to believe in the digital world being more accessible than the real one. Implanted microchips, smart gadgets, homes, cars, drones, and cities will monitor every thought and deed, all within an authority that deems what is 'safe' or not. This will mean what they consider to be acceptable and not a threat to them. Digital currency and social scoring will all be part of the prison system, sold to us as an answer to whatever the problem will be, to convince us of its solution.*

*Touching on this subject is important, although the topic is huge and could easily create another book. Focusing on evil only gives it more to feed on, be aware, but not engaged with it. So, what is evil? I believe evil is whoever and whatever severs our relationship with the aspect of ourselves that makes us whole and complete. The evil in this world is very real and is completely engaged in a psychological and emotional battle over all of us. Its ultimate goal over the human body and soul is all-encompassing and very hard to accept when your worldview offers comfort. There are signs that beyond the small collaboration of very evil-minded people within the spheres of 'power' is another element they are affiliated with, that goes beyond this world and reality. I do believe there is such a force that can powerfully affect this world and the people who want access to it. It is extremely negative but ultimately weak and foolish. It might seem intelligent, but it is not wise. Its nature and source are inherently built on its own future demise.*

*We truly need the field of science to continue to open our eyes to the ever-compiling evidence that is proving we are beings beyond boundaries. Interconnected and able to do astounding feats that look like miracles. The discoveries of 'who' and 'what' we truly are as information need to be in schoolbooks and news headlines. Unfortunately, this is not currently the case. There is a defining moment coming when we will have to confront the increasing march of evil in our lives and collectively say, "No, no more! We do not agree, and we take our sovereignty back!" There was probably a quicker and easier route to our awakening, but as humans we have the tendency to leave it until the last moment when it gets so unbearable and uncomfortable, reaching a point of disaster before we decide that it's not right and begin to do something positive about it with vigour and gusto.*

*The more you take the time to listen inwardly and connect with the greater source of what you are, the more instinctive you become to recognise when you are being manipulated via the news and official narratives. The fear of death becomes an illusion as you begin to experience yourself beyond the constraints of time and physicality. This is a major breakthrough, and when you reach this point, you become even more empowered for change and to collectively awaken those who are not aware of their acquiescence. In many ways, by changing yourself, you change others without even trying. We sometimes need to remember that we cannot help everyone or make them see our views. But by living the way that makes you whole, complete, and in harmony will be the light that ignites theirs within them just by your presence. You will exude a quiet strength that they do not have or see in themselves. Your ability to discern between good and evil will get clearer, and you will be less easily fooled by those who think they can sway you with false promises. The more we learn and become wiser to the soul and spirit within our physical vessel, the less this world will limit us. Your horizon will stretch beyond the unknown, and answers will reach you when they were beyond reach before. This inner work of self-discovery that we all need to do has the ability to activate our DNA, and I think it will be the catalyst for a new enlightened human being that will finally raise us out of the current darkness that is frantic to stop this from happening.*

*When we learn something new, it takes some time until it becomes a part of us, for it to become our reality. Whether in the past it was riding a bike, learning to forgive, or discovering a latent talent you didn't know you had. Once it becomes natural, we do it without doubt or question; this is how we will integrate the new light within us. Learn to listen to your inner voice, your gut feeling. Allow yourself to be guided by intuitive feelings in every decision. Use your eyes to see if going in one direction looks brighter and sharper than the other choice, which might look dull or less enticing. Allow and accept unforeseen circumstances to stop you from doing something; this can be a good reason. When you pass by a stranger who looks unhappy or in need, give them a good thought and visualize a better circumstance for them. Allow the world to give you signs. Believe the world can talk to you in this way. See the world as nonstop feedback of your inner self. Improving and empowering your day-to-day processes of your inner world of thoughts and inspirations is the work of a true spiritual warrior. Learn to find your Love, Inspiration, Gratitude, Hope, and Truth, and this LIGHT will change you and the world for good.'*

We have the inherent power to turn things on their axis and bring our light into this dark world. That light is within you. No one owns your light, bar from yourself, yet those darker forces use every tactic at their disposal to trick you into mental submission, secure in the knowledge that 'fear' is their ultimate weapon in controlling and subjugating the very nature of the Avatar. In our next chapter, we will address those opposing forces, if only to illustrate how we can truly shine our spiritual light and guide all – including those opposing factions – into the understanding that the very essential elements of love can transform absolutely everything and bring about the dawning of a new awareness of our brilliance.

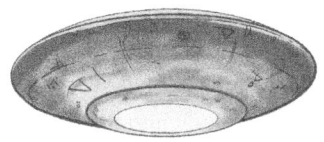

# 'The Eternal Avatar'

## Chapter Eleven

## Those Evil Forces, the Archons, The Holographic Simulation & the Trap

*'The forces of chaos will try to take their toll,*

*Like talons gripped around your soul,*

*Their commands will rape you of the wings to ascend,*

*Festering in evil with no faith to transcend,*

*Harbouring spirits and trapped in their dark domain,*

*Fooled by the heavenly light to return us again.'*

Chris John Mayes

Planet Earth has been at war, but of a vastly different kind. This war appears evident and directed at no less than the Avatar and has nothing to do with physical weapons of mass destruction, which one would come to expect, although we are constantly met with such looming threats from other countries. No! This is a silent, cold war, and one designed to thwart the very nature of our being. Several considerations must be brought into the fray in order to highlight our theory, and one which points suspiciously towards the very *spirit* of Man, along with the earth having seemingly been hijacked by alternate forces which remain in the shadows, even in present day, intent in keeping us all blindfolded to a much larger and striking picture of what it means to be human.

The process of incarnation and reincarnation, along with a blueprint being created by the Avatar before its journey into the material realm, cannot be denied, with all of the evidence presented by those who have actual recall of such accounts. NDE research, along with OBE reports, paints a startlingly clear picture of what we can come to expect upon our return to the other side once physical death ensues, but has something else taken advantage of this process? Are we, while temporarily incarnate in our material bodies, not only being tricked on earth into the belief that we are just mere biological robots which die, but also duped upon our return into the astral planes by those professing to be elevated beings? This has been a hotly debated subject for countless years, and it is important that we at least explore the possibility; otherwise, we may be caught off guard upon our re-entry back to source.

There has been the theory of a 'false light,' whereby the soul of an individual is coaxed back into reincarnating on earth, being tricked against their will, and not just once, but many times over. One must take into consideration the varied other systems of reality beyond that of our tiny and apparently insignificant solar system within the cosmos. Why, one wonders, would we keep reincarnating back here on earth? Many people have the answers to this, but it stems mostly from the fact that our soul is here to develop from its previous incarnation in an effort to reach new heights spiritually. However, certain issues appear to contradict the very foundation of this assumption.

One of those questionable areas is our apparent amnesia from one physical life to another, whereby recall of such past incarnations can be vague within the extremes. We know that many can remember people, places, and so forth from past lives, but remain deeply embedded within the subconscious mind and can, on varied occasions, only be fully retrieved by a trained regressionist. We agree that, if it were in any way possible to have full access to all past lives experienced within each of our incarnations, this may pose a psychological issue, and one whereby the individual will not be able to function well on a mental level. However, we must understand that our brain is merely a transmitter for information, and all memories are stored within the unlimited second-body of our astral self. Chris Mayes recalls the journey from spirit into the material realm as his incarnation process took hold, and his memories indicate it was a choice he was given to become a true expression of himself. When talking of the spirit world or, rather, the astral planes, does this area facilitate the entire legion of other interplanetary souls which exist within other systems of reality beyond Earth, and arrive within this province upon their physical demise? Are the astral planes the go-between in terms of *all* sentient life within the entire universe and beyond, and whereby souls gravitate? It's an interesting hypothesis, and a question we cannot fully answer, but we can at least speculate.

It is thought that one of the reasons we experience amnesia from one life to another is for us to evolve spiritually, without having access to those previous reincarnation recalls which may well give someone the idea that it'll be ok for them to end their life if they're not happy in their present one, secured in the knowledge there is no question of there being an afterlife. However, wouldn't you think things would work out far better in the long run if we *were* able to have clear access to such past life memories, and something which would only propel us even further within our development, knowing and growing in those areas where we had seemingly gone wrong? For example, when taking an exam of any kind, we study to ensure success. If you fail, you'd work harder the next time around in order to succeed, learning from your previous mistakes. There is no amnesia to be had here, and if you were unfortunate enough to have no clear memory of what you'd worked so hard to achieve, then there's little hope of scoring enough points next time, unless you were extremely lucky! It's the same with an athlete who physically and mentally works hard on their bodies, motivated no less by their past experiences towards an overall goal in succeeding. If they had no idea how they fared from one competing game to another, how then would they know where they stood in terms of abilities?

In chapter five, '*Reincarnation*,' writer, director, and producer of '*The Lossen,*' Colin Skevington described his experiences while in his life-between-life and past life sessions. In one of them, we discovered that he'd lived the perfect life as a Doctor of Medicine, and upon his return journey to the astral planes had been met by the Elders who explained why he'd had that perfect life, but that they'd also wanted him to make a return journey to earth because they thought it best for him to bring his spiritual knowledge to awaken others within his next incarnation. His main objective has seemingly been achieved through the work he is doing now in bringing such otherworldly information to the masses, but lest we not forget that soon after his incarnation as a doctor, he was sent into the horrors of Auschwitz, and no less than a patient, killed by doctors there! It seems bizarre to consider that he'd been a practitioner and then a patient, but that the latter was encountered under horrendous circumstances. How can this incarnation lead towards spiritual advancement, one wonders? This is just one example in many and would seem rather strange considering the life challenges we map for ourselves. Many will just state that, well, you die anyway, and you're only here for a short period of time before your return back to the other side, but it's a whole different ball-game while here on earth, and a plane which is harsh, cold and, in a lot of cases cruel.

We're in no way denying that some form of life-planning is developed by the incarnating soul before its subsequent emergence into this reality to begin with, but what we have to consider is whether there is any truth to the claims that alternate forces here on earth are able to trap souls in this biosphere and indefinitely hold them for *their* own means, rather like the recycling of souls. Many within the spiritual arena will argue this case and consider otherwise which is perfectly fine, but what we do know is that there are certain events here on earth which point suspiciously to the awareness that the Avatar is not the only intelligent lifeform present, and which appears to have been here far longer than Man.

In each epoch there is no doubting that sacred knowledge has been either altered, hidden or destroyed from the masses in an effort to blind us into the awareness that everything is based purely on belief and mere conjecture, nothing solid which would confirm otherwise, and something implemented as a means to further subjugate the Avatar. Like a wheel, we are caught in its perpetual cycle, and we are unable to see through the spokes of that wheel as it continually rotates, offering us little more than a blur.

There is no way for us to track down our human origins. Much of what has been fed into the pool of knowledge leaves us all still scratching our heads, and anything that threatens the carefully constructed model promoted by the system continues to throw no light on varied areas of deeper contemplation, even in our modern era. Yet, ancient codices inform us otherwise. It is clear that our 'makers' made sure our physical lifespan would not last, and for reasons that we wouldn't become smart and overthrow them in the dawning of our genesis. It is assumed they had departed the earth during the mass extermination of their creation through the engineering of the flood, and those few humans who survived were left to flourish on their own accord. But the Gods of old may well still be here among us.

Such Gods, which have already been highlighted in chapter two, *'Genesis'*, would have had scientific know-how well ahead of our time, even by today's standards. It is also apparent that any (if not all) extraterrestrial intervention is covered and classified as 'Above Top Secret' by those clandestine establishments of power, along with many other areas of paranormal and Cryptid investigations for reasons which still puzzle those wanting to know the truth. This is evident when also considering the National forests, where levels of high strangeness are prevalent. We readdress this point clearly, and in light of the Pentagon's refusal to open cases surrounding the validity of UFOs, which have been presented to them from certain whistleblowers in recent times. Each topic within those areas covered within our book appears separate in nature, but we, the authors, feel there are connections to be made when exploring the true nature of said phenomenon.

What if these Gods (or a certain faction of them in any case) were still with us today? Would the reality of the UFO phenomenon reveal such connections going back to the genesis of Man, and prove that such deities had not been so saintly as described within the holy books, or as merely fictitious in nature as we have been led to believe? It is evident also that *their* creation, the Avatar, contains a source of spiritual indifference, and one which is far removed from the make-up of our so-called Gods. After this, the alien abduction program highlights the need for such alternate forces which we consider as 'alien' in trying to unlock the secrets of what we represent, and which they had seemingly been denied within their own emergence – that of the 'Spirit.' We have already addressed the two primary versions, which are accepted within the mainstream media and educational circles surrounding the chaos theory, along with the supernatural element of God being depicted as a man with a white beard, and where everything was made possible by magic in no less than six days involving our genesis. Yet, the idea that an evolved intelligence from across the dimensions of space may well have been responsible in the development of the 'human' is an idea which is immediately rejected by many. This seems utterly bizarre, since scientists in our time are well on their way to being able to create life in a laboratory through cloning. You may be wondering what this has all got to do with the false light theory, but we will address this point shortly. We consider, however, that much of what is hidden in plain sight from us may reveal a completely different story, and one which also might clarify why those who get too near the truth are ridiculed or waylaid within their research.

**Spirits in a Material World**

Within the UFO department of investigations, what is termed the *'alien abduction phenomenon'* has puzzled researchers for decades. The famous grey aliens are top of the agenda where such overwhelming episodes occur and have proved famous through the Roswell, New Mexico UFO crash landing back in 1947, which continues to create much controversy as to its legitimacy. These small, bulbous-headed, large-eyed beings have fascinated researchers the world over, but we are no nearer to truly establishing their reality. This could be one of the many reasons as to their modus operandi, and theories pointing to them as being actual ancient astronauts coming from physical planets may be incorrect. Such intelligences keep us guessing as to their true identity, and mould within our own so-called mythology accordingly. Back in fairy lore which has a dark history (compared to the charming version many have been led to believe regarding these entrancing beings) children reported being abducted by small people possessing incredible magic, and often found themselves taken by their unwitting guests to a fairy ring where they'd lose time, along with memory of their account. As with Celtic lore, the fairies would drink human blood and were considered a lower form of spirit, which are believed to be associated with the dead, between the nature of Man and fallen Angels. According to legend, they had been cast down from the higher realms and banished to earth, where they weave much evil. What's interesting is that blood is another element which appears attractive in many cases of not only alien abductions, but also centred around disturbing incidents of cattle and human mutilation, the finger of which points suspiciously towards the UFO phenomenon. This is an area the authorities do not want anyone looking into, and I know that as a fact! We understand that blood is a sacred component not only within most alien abduction cases, but also demonic rituals, holy communion (blood being represented as wine), and much of the folklore from the past. What is this telling us? Such information reveals that the Avatar (human) is unique within its temporary biological and spiritual construct, and something which is far removed from these alternate denizens, which are keenly interested in us as a species.

For instance, why would aliens abduct someone, wipe their memory clean of the experience, and then disappear into the shadows like ghosts, leaving little or no proof that the abductee had been kidnapped in the first place? I contemplated this back in 1996 and set about creating a working hypothesis which forces us to consider that we may not be dealing with aliens in the first instance, but something altogether different. The phenomenon presents itself in both shape and form so as to interact within our reality on some level, yet there are a multitude of phenomena that arrest our intellect, because they all work on the premise of what we would consider to be the dead. There is, however, one sure fact, and that is the 'Avatar' has *something* these alternate dimensions of reality do not, and desperately want for themselves. Within our temporary corporeality, we are able to evolve on a spiritual level through the process of death, and whereby these other forces appear stagnant within their own divine development, thereby forcing them to interact with us in order to attain what they so desperately require.

In his book, *'The Secret Commonwealth of Elves, Fauns, and Fairies,'* Robert Kirk (Scottish folklorist, 1644-1692) states that: *'Fairies are the fallen angels who were cast down by the Lord God out of heaven for their sinful pride…and the devil gives to these knowledge and power and sends them on earth where they work much evil.'* These beings, among varied others, exist within sections of the astral planes which can occasionally interconnect with our material world, and are able to form from smoke. The Islamic and Middle Eastern lore also believed that the Jinn (djinn or angelized as genie but based primarily upon Pagan myth) were able to appear from smoke, and thus the romanticised fables of such beings taking temporary residence in lamps and could be summoned by invoking chants and spells, thus bring them from their realm into ours has always held great fascination for the imagination. However, the genie would always want some form of payback if wishes were granted by those who'd beckoned one of these supernatural forces forth from within the astral, but they seldom interfered within the affairs of humans and were seen to be a force of good, as opposed to evil. We continually hear of varied preternatural beasts being banished from the kingdom of heaven, and a theme heavily promoted within select religious ideologies, which may well lay the foundations for evidence as to where these varied otherworldly entities dwell, along with their main objectives.

Interestingly, so-called abductions by not only grey aliens or fairies, but also those accounts where individuals have gone missing in National forests and kidnapped by talking bears or apes, only to be found under baffling circumstances carry no clear memory of where they'd been, or recollection as to what had *actually* happened to them whilst missing. We must not forget the appearance of the famous Dogman, which was reported to be wearing an earring in its ear, as recounted by researcher Paul Sinclair, and tells us unequivocally that such savage-looking beasts are more intelligent than at first considered. There are occasions where the individual retains a small fraction of their account mentally, but in the majority of cases, narrates like something from the pages of a fairytale, as though some form of posthypnotic suggestion has been deliberately implemented by their captors to conceal the reality of their whereabouts and objectives. These traits are curious indeed, and a phenomenon classic within supernatural abductions, yet something we feel is intentionally executed by those forces responsible. The experiences tend to be more horrifying in those rare cases where an individual is able to evoke through regression an event far different from the false memory which has been originally planted within their psyche. This is also evident within situations surrounding alien abductions.

Examining the case of a classic alien abduction scenario implemented by no less than the greys, an abductee normally finds themselves being taken through solid matter and into an awaiting spacecraft. Here, they have little or no memory of their encounter with their illusive captors. Such beings come across like a blank canvas in terms of personality (which they seem devoid of) and having no understanding of age, taste, smell, emotions – in fact, none of those attributes which make us human. I wondered whether the greys have lost themselves through the act of self-replication as cloned entities, having discarded the essence of what *we* as humans possess in terms of a spirit. I also considered why the greys are keenly interested in hybridization, thus creating a new species which is part human and part alien, but something altogether different from themselves in terms of physiology. I had detailed such speculation back in 1996. There are varied reports of male abductees having their sperm removed and females finding themselves pregnant, only to lose the foetus soon after their pregnancy is discovered, and once their abduction with the greys has been concluded, thus helping this faction of aliens with their hybridization program. An abductee will invariably go through multiple abductions, and an area which my good friend, author and researcher, Steve Aspin, has highlighted in his most excellent book '*Out of Time*' (Grosvenor House Publishing Ltd, 2023), addressing intergenerational links to the phenomenon. These events are famous within the category of the greys' overall intentions. But what is the point to all this? Through my own harrowing alien abduction back in the winter of 1989 which is far too long to detail here (and which has already been examined and written about in previous books) I wanted to tackle two parts to the phenomenon which greatly puzzled me and seemingly operated on varied levels of reality which did not sway to the classic 'extraterrestrial' hypothesis back in the late 1980s.

Decades ago, much of the public believed UFOs, along with their pilots, were coming from planets within our neighbouring star system. At least, that was what had been relayed to certain 'contactees' (contactee is a person who has enlightened experiences with extraterrestrial intelligences throughout their life and very different from an abductee) such as George Adamski who found fame with his alleged interaction with humanoids known as 'Venusians,' or more aptly referred to as 'Space Brothers' in the early 1950s. Adamski, with the help of Desmond Leslie, authored numerous books about his fantastic escapades while being taken onboard assorted UFOs and piloted to various planets in our solar system. Unlike the harrowing grey encounters where, and in the majority of cases, an abductee has no clear memory of their experience, as a contactee himself, Adamski was able to mentally recall all details of his interactions without any form of amnesia being administered by the aliens themselves. He even had photos to prove it! One such picture reveals an unclear image of two faces peering out of portholes from a cigar-shaped UFO whilst voyaging in space. Adamski claims one had been of himself and the other a Venusian. Upon inspection of the alleged incident caught on camera, it's any wonder they're able to stand in the craft, as there doesn't appear to be much room from the lower part of the object to accommodate the full height of a person, unless they were kneeling, or using the same technology as Dr Who's TARDIS from the science fiction series. Interestingly, the aliens in the accompanying UFO were even able to secure the shot perfectly whilst travelling at breakneck speed. Strike a pose, Mr Adamski! His first book, *'Flying Saucers Have Landed'* published in 1953 detailed Adamski's assertions which were soon rejected when it was discovered that no life exists on Venus as he had professed, and that much of his so-called 'proof' was confirmed to be nothing less than fake, despite his huge fan-base who maintained otherwise. Another shady character well known within the UFO community is that of Swiss national, Billy Meier, who had repeated contact with a race known as the Plejaren in 1953. Meier's incredible photographic evidence of disc-shaped UFOs being caught on camera at close range was found to be miniature models discovered in the basement of his house, and upon discovery stated that he wanted to create them from memory, which would be nice to have displayed for all to see. One wonders why he found the need to hide his beautiful handiwork. Meier even claimed to have visited the prehistoric age with his alien friends, travelling back to the late Jurassic period in a Plejaren 'Beamship.' Unfortunately, the pictures capturing his time-traveling exploits photographing prehistoric animals were discovered to have been cut out from an illustrated dinosaur book well known for its time and backtracked by stating that the Men in Black were trying to discredit him. In any event, the UFOs he photographed became more glamourous as time went on, and his well-known 'Wedding Cake' UFO is literally the icing on the cake and dazzles the eye with its intricate and somewhat puzzling ornamentation – no pun intended there! Such charlatans do more damage in the long run when seriously considering the penultimate question of contact. Although not everyone within the UFO arena is an out-and-out liar when detailing alien interaction of one kind or another, something we completely respect. It's important for us to highlight the interaction of physical and non-physical levels of the phenomenon, as opposed to the earthlier stance which certain individuals have maintained and, in some cases, discredits the entire topic as a whole. There have been cases where the greys, for instance, have themselves lied to their captors in terms of where they are from within our universe, so it's no wonder that certain individuals will jump on the bandwagon and fashion the most absurd stories. It would also appear that the media cartel will quite happily promote the most ridiculous assertions, knowing full well this will create more confusion for those ardent researchers wanting to get to the meat of the matter, as well as hammering another long nail into the coffin of truth, which makes it even harder to open. Mix everything up so there is no transparency is definitely how real secrets we seldom get to know about are buried, and tactics employed by the powers-that-be impossible to fathom. I recall one program which appeared on primetime TV where a lady claimed to have been abducted by the greys, taken to the Moon where they had a party which she thoroughly enjoyed – all minus her wearing a space suit! We have merely illustrated these few suspicious cases by way of example when it comes to the varied divisions of belief centred around UFO legitimacy, and how damaging and divided these accusations can be in the long run.

Are the greys somehow responsible for our genesis? Or are they the product of the Anunnaki from ages past, fashioned to serve their masters as we once had in the beginning of our human emergence? Are the UFO sightings and secret alien interactions of the past the same force we hear about today, which continues to manipulate and control from within the shadows? Is this why the establishments are so intent in covering their reality? With the advent of the Roswell UFO crash, along with strange, small, child-like bodies discovered around the craft's wreckage, as well as one of the entities believed to have survived and taken into custody by the authorities for a time until it died, the question begs, where are these aliens coming from? And what of their ultimate intentions? My brother, Ronald, produced a theory in 2021 in his book '*The Digital Demon*' where he considers that crashed UFOs are deliberate from the entities themselves, and for reasons which may become disturbingly clear. There are even cases where UFOs have been discovered intact (with no crash to be had their end) minus the pilots, and where secret forces under the authority of the US government's special UFO recovery team have gone in to secure their prized alien hardware. It has been revealed that the CIA maintain a 'secret office' which has been retrieving UFOs from crash sites for decades, and at least nine 'non-human' crafts have been collected by the US government through the 'Office of Global Access' (OGA) which is the wing of the CIA's science and technology division, and whereby such exotic materials has been handed over to private companies. This secures any paper-trails being left, and certainly, where the Pentagon is concerned, so that revelations of this kind would be hard to prove under the jurisdiction of those self-contained corporations which secrete the evidence. What is also incredible is the fact that the CIA is able to track UFO activity, and even possesses technology where they are able to discern UFOs while still cloaked. This would imply that varied non-human intelligences are flying their vessels within our skies without us being able to detect them while maintaining invisibility, and this comes in light of infrared technology our end which is also able to reveal where these UFOs are in relation to our lands and skies. The OGA invariably work in conjunction with special forces such as 'SEAL' (Sea, air and land teams) who are sent in to try and salvage wrecked UFO hardware, even able to get troops access to places in the world many would not normally be able to get to, such as behind enemy lines.

In light of certain UFOs being discovered landed and devoid of pilots in recent times, the question begs as to where the aviators had gone? Have such objects been abandoned in a deliberate attempt for our people to somehow back-engineer their technology? We know of eye-witness testimony surrounding Roswell from the likes of the late Lieutenant Colonel Philip J Corso of the United States Army who co-authored a book with Ufologist, William J Birnes *'The Day After Roswell'* where it is alleged that a government group had been created by Admiral Roscoe H. Hillenkoetter, the first director of Central Intelligence in order to bring about a secret select assemblage of high-ranking individuals code named 'Majestic 12.' Roswell was the very beginning of the cover-up to conceal evidence of both alien interactions, along with their hardware, from the public. Corso maintains in his book that much of the recovered material salvaged from the Roswell UFO had been subtly reverse-engineered and introduced into much of the technology we take for granted today. It is incredulous to believe that an advanced alien race would harbour equipment just close enough for us back in 1947 to understand, and thereby our scientists able to replicate, long before the alleged Moon landing in 1969, which we are finding difficult to develop in present day for some bizarre reason. Would this indicate that so-called 'aliens' are much closer to home than once considered? Are such non-human intelligences entering our material realm via dimensions of space for the sole purpose in accelerating our species forward technologically by their hand and by their gain, and at a much faster pace than previous to our ancestors could have ever dreamt? And, on top of this, are our 'Puppet Masters' still pulling the strings from the symbolic pyramid of power today?

With the overall threat of Transhumanism (and which we as the authors do see as a danger) is there an agenda by such forces which may still be present here on earth ready to subjugate the Avatar even further, thereby cutting the spiritual link which appears to be the predominant factor which makes us what we are as divine beings of light?

**The Descent into Matter**

Within the Gnostic texts which speaks of the creation of the human by extraterrestrials, there is the suggestion that the Archons ('Anunnaki,' and of which were believed to be our geneticists) were at pains to understand their 'Adam and Eve' creation through many failed attempts within the creation of Man, and which had unknowingly by these so-called Gods been infused with a 'spirit,' - an element they appear devoid. The texts also reveal that such overlords were very much attached to the astral and ethereal planes, and there are differences to be had from that of the body, soul, and spirit – the 'spirit' being the main component which brings the Avatar in line with the true God source of which we are ultimately connected beyond the material world, and which these reptilian beings yearn. The Archons had unsuccessfully tried back in the day through the production of their slave-labour force to mate with their most prized creation, Eve in order to attain this spark of holiness which affords us the right to our overall immortality, but which for themselves condemns them forever to a lower state of vibrational existence, and thus fixing them in a condition of spiritual limbo, so-to-speak. Yet, as the human, we are *their* main source of survival – energy! Although this sounds like something from the pages of a science fiction novel, the Gnostic codices reveal this as truth and wisdom that the establishments of power in governance and under the authority of many religious establishments will simply not acknowledge or address. We're not talking about folk following certain faiths (because many are not aware of the corruption going on at the top of the ladder), but those in positions of power and control who get their orders from the Overlords that are really running the show, the Archons. It is considered that the Garden of Eden had been the main production centre for the Archons when administering their genetic experimentations in bringing about a hominid which could be adapted for their use as a tool for work, and nothing more. This was achieved by fusing part them and part earth mammal (thought to be an ape) into a creature which was not at first meant to reproduce, thus resulting in the Homo sapiens sapiens, and which has already been illustrated in chapter two, but our area of interest lies in both the soul and spirit. Many will naturally assume these are one of the same, but according to Gnosticism, they are entirely separate in nature, and an area of particular interest to the authors.

In the creation parable, as explained in the 'Nag Hammadi Scriptures,' Sophia is mentioned as the 'Bride of Christ,' or the female twin divine Aeon (Aeon meaning divine entities descended from God, but which also denotes her, along with the other Aeons as roughly the equivalent of an angel) analogous to the human soul but also one of the feminine aspects of God (the ultimate source of all creation) which the ruling elite in varied epochs have continuously tried to erase throughout human history, preferring the male dominant energy to reign supreme. This is evident in paintings of Mary Magdalene who was considered a vital component within the secret teachings of Christ, and where such reliefs have been deliberately defaced to counteract any notion that she had been associated with the Messiah, and whom herself was not only a major part in such esoteric knowledge imparted to her by Jesus but had more power than once considered. She accompanied Christ everywhere and was even a witness to His crucifixion. Christ is also considered the incarnate of God. We can assume that both Jesus and Mary (incarnates of the highest God) had come to earth to relay a message of hope to the people, because of the corruption from the Archons who have trapped the spirits of all humans not only on the material plane, but also within the lower astral levels, relaying how through love and kindness we are able to reconnect to the true foundation of our 'spiritual' origins, and thereby bypassing the continuous loop of reincarnation the Archons have trapped us in. Sophia is connected to Mary Magdalene within Christian traditions as the daughter, the bride of the bridegroom, and the consort to the Saviour. In the beginning, the 'Oneness,' or 'God-source' within its primary state of 'being,' and considered an unknowable God wanted to explore more of 'Itself,' thereby spontaneously emanating Aeons, rather like feelers creeping out to ascertain the possibility of separation, and Sophia is the lowest Aeon, or anthropic expression of the emanation of the light of God which fell from grace in wanting to travel beyond the confines of the light. As stated in 'The Nag Hammadi Scriptures' in reference to the Aeons and God in the section entitled 'The Aeons Procreate' (67,34-68,36 and credit secured by the authors Marvin Meyer, Wolf-Peter Funk, Paul-Hubert Poirier, and James M. Robinson). '*He* (the Father) *did not, however, reveal his multiplicity at once to the members of the All, nor did he reveal his sameness to those who had issued forth from him. Now, all those who had gone forth from him – that is, the aeons of the aeons, being emissions born of a procreative nature – also procreate through their own procreative nature, to the glory of the Father, just as he had been the cause of their existence. He makes the aeons into roots and springs and fathers. For that which they glorified, they bore. For it possesses knowledge and wisdom, and they have understood that they have gone forth from the knowledge and the understanding of the All. If the members of the All had risen to give glory accordingly to the individual powers of each aeon, they would have brought forth a glory that was only a semblance of the Father, who himself is the All. For that reason, they were drawn, through the singing of praise and through the power of the oneness of him from whom they had come forth, into mutual intermingling, union, and oneness. From their assembled fullness, they offered a glorification worthy of the Father, an image that was one and at the same time many because it was brought forth for the glory of the One, and because they had come forward toward him who himself is the entirety of the All.*' This led to the creation of matter (the descent into chaos) and whereby Sophia, through her own degeneration from the One, became trapped and unable to return to source. The famous 'Fall of Man' did not come about through Adam and Eve as many have been led to believe within the biblical texts, which are the creations of the Archons, but rather from Sophia, seeing them as an accidental creation on her behalf. Much like the other Aeons (all aeons are called the 'Pleroma,' the Gnostic name for Heaven), Sophia was originally the child of a male and female pair of aeons that had come before her, who had given birth with God's consent. Sophia wanted a child for herself and set about the formation of a cosmic womb, but without a male partner, or indeed the consent of her Father, and thus she gave immaculate conception to the 'demiurge,' a creature unlike any of the other angelic hosts. It's interesting to note here that Mary gave birth to Jesus of Nazareth in much the same way through immaculate conception, but that the Messiah's emergence was to be the complete opposite of Sophia's child. Thus,

Sophia was cast out from the heavenly kingdom upon realising her mistake (see the similarity of Satan within the biblical story which describes more or less the same happening to him here) and subsequently banished her child out of the Pleroma where it believed it was the one, true God, and thus through his ignorance, foolishness and ego set about forming the material and astral planes, thus trapping sparks of spiritual divinity within Adam and Eve along the way and down the path of their subsequent genetic designs.

The Archons were the first to exist before their creation of the human arrived onto the scene and are known as sadistic and malevolent beings who are the true rulers of Earth, along with their governance of the lower regions of the astral world. Although scientifically adept, they do not know those elements that we harbour, love, and create within its purest and most blessed form. The Archons' Father (God) was the rejected offspring of Sophia, which we know today as the Devil, or Satan. In the Gnostic texts, the Archons have bodies of both sexes and faces of beasts, but they are neither male nor female, nor animal, and represent a force so disturbing and chaotic that they were considered the farthest that a created being could be from the light of God. As the Archons set about their legions, they conquered space in search of minerals. One prime planet was Earth, and it is here where they based themselves and created the human through genetic manipulation so that it could serve their cause. As stated in 'The Nag Hammadi' and from the '*Trimorphic Protennoia*', or known as the '*Three Forms of First Thought*', which describes three descents using the voice of Barbelo in first person. The voice is the source of life, knowledge, and the first thought. The voice has three names, three masculinities, and three powers, and is androgynous in nature. 'The Nag Hammadi' further describes how Sophia descended to help counter her mistake through the cosmic birthing of her son, the demon, Yaldabaoth, along with his creation of the Archons. '*And the great demon* (Yaldabaoth, also known in the watered-down version in the holy books as Satan) *began to produce aeons in the likeness of the real aeons* (humans) *except that he produced them out of his own power. Then I too* (Protennoia's words) *revealed my voice secretly and said, 'Stop, stop, you who tread on matter. Look, I am coming down to the world of mortals for my portion that was there from the time when innocent Sophia was conquered. She descended so that I might thwart their* (the Archons) *plot, which was devised by the one who came from her* (Sophia's son).' *All were disturbed, and everyone in the house of the unknowable light and the abyss trembled. And the chief creator of ignorance* (Yaldabaoth) *reigned over chaos and the underworld and produced a human being in my likeness. But he did not know that this creature would be the death sentence for him, nor did he* recognise *the power* (spirit) *in the creature.'* However, through the creation of the hominid, Sophia sent forth the element which had not been given to the Archons (her firstborn), and thus the 'spirit' became host to all men, women, and children of the world. This was (and still is) something which the Archons could not possess, and through rage they set about annihilating their creation after unsuccessful attempts at mating, creating half-breeds (the Nephilim) which even *they* found monstrous! After the deluge and the return of Man through Noah, it is thought the supposed Gods (UfOnaughts) returned, but this time remaining in the shadows where they still reside today from the high-rise of pyramid power, manipulating their biological, human construct, and bringing misery, fear and control to those who do not serve their ultimate cause. It is our belief that through Sophia's choice to banish her creation, the Archons have, in turn, twisted the very nature of the biblical stories throughout time which masks their identity perfectly, and those humans who assist her mistaken creation, the Archons, are rewarded in every capacity if they go along with their bidding. The Archons are also parasites and can affect any human mind who submits to their darker forces of power, such is their incredible understanding of the human, along with its mind.

Within our present epoch, such corruption is paramount in the music and film industry, where demonic suggestion and acts are played out in a ritualistic fashion to try and entice as well as mesmerise followers, but much of the public is totally unaware of the *real* intentions and force behind such psychological atrocities. Many famous music artists have come forward to reveal the darker nature that they themselves have witnessed, along with the trap they have found themselves in. The Archons, it must be understood, are the lowest of the low, and this is how they function in terms of depravity, control, and a lust for power surrounding the human. They will seduce anyone they see fit as a benefit to their overall cause and reward the individual beyond riches. However, there is always a price to be paid by those who are enchanted by the Archons. As stated in '*The Nag Hammadi*', when the Archons banished both Adam and Eve from the Garden of Eden: '*The rulers turned to their Adam. They took him and cast him and his wife out of the garden. They have no blessing, for they are also under the curse.'* This indicates that the serpent (the Archons' influence) did not have the spiritual presence through the emergence of their creation, Adam and Eve, and something made aware to them both upon discovery of the Tree of Knowledge. They realised they'd been endowed with the 'Holy Spirit' of which the Archons are devoid. Therefore: *'The rulers threw humanity into great confusion and a life of toil, so that their people might be preoccupied with things of the world and not have time to be occupied with the holy Spirit,'* and something which has continued until present day. The Archons know that such mental and emotional disruptions (even today) directed at their human creation will derail many from connecting to their primary and true source, and thus hold them hostage on the material plane within this unceasing spiritual war. We can see such influence continuing in present day through the media, along with the orchestration of catastrophic world events by our elusive masters. It is clear that our Archon engineers, especially Sophia's son, Yaldabaoth (Satan), appear to be our God only in terms of genetic design, but our primary one true God is that of the Father, and the vibration of which goes beyond the crude matter of flesh and bone.

The human infected by the Archon mind will, and upon death, find themselves connected within the reincarnation trap and be born again into the flesh and live yet another life of mostly strife and toil, and of which the Archons maintain within their ruling. They know nothing of those attributes which lift the spirit of humanity to creative and loving heights, and of which they will quite happily crush and hold captive while existing in their holographic version of Earth from its original counterpart within the higher realms. This, their playground, is nothing less than a prison for humans, unless the Avatar truly awakens in any varied incarnations they have gone through and bypasses the astral net which holds many within the archaic recycling of souls, and upon acknowledging their own power within the spirit invested in them. This may indicate why we continuously return to this planet, along with having our memories wiped, and it appears the same for those encountering alien abductions or going missing in National forests and found to have little or no recall of the events they experienced. Negativity and fear, along with a mind-wipe, seriously hinder the development of the Avatar in a multitude of ways, and this is the primary reaction and reason the Archons instigate in order to keep their flock central and essential to their own survival.

## Archons' Control of the Astral Planes & the UFO Abduction Program

This brings us to another point concerning the alien abduction phenomenon and of the Archons proclaiming dominance over not only our material realm, but also regions of the lower astral planes in which they govern. It appears the Archons have fashioned themselves into a new age! No longer appearing in the guise of the 'Demon' but advanced spacemen from another world, their camouflage is nothing less than genius! The human has been programmed in a very limited version of reality – that of the material realm, yet we know there is so much more beyond our five senses which *they* are keen to control (as well as blind us in the knowledge that we have a sixth sense too) and an area which those establishments will continually deny in an effort to keep us all in the dark and trapped within *'their'* ever-turning wheel of corruption and degradation. The Archons may also have a system in place within our present day where they are able to track the human psyche in an effort to overpower anyone who raises their vibrational frequency above that level which they have maintained with much of the public in operating on a docile level, and which prevents us safe passage back to source. This fabricated, flawed version of Earth, which appears more like a hologram in nature, is not the true world. Science has debated the 'Simulation Hypothesis' whereby the universe, along with everything else in it, may be the product of some advanced intelligence's ultimate design, rather like a computer game. Although hard for many within the mainstream to believe, this idea is not as crazy as once considered. After all, all animate as well as inanimate life is based on certain chemical compounds united together in a complex fashion to create the materials of life and the stage upon which we appear. We can suppose this is all down to the Archon influence. Consciousness is merely the observer as we traipse from one moment to another, creating a wave of memory while the particle of ourselves carries its vehicle forward through its material existence. It is possible to assume that the Archons have snared us in some kind of illusionary matrix which we believe is the 'real' world, when in actual fact it is the complete reverse? The 'Ascension' is not only attributed to the spirit returning to the God-source, but can also happen right here on earth, and if every human turned their fear into hope, tears into laughter – in fact, the reverse of all thoughts. This, we believe, is when the former world manipulated by the Archons will pass away, and the real one comes into our hearts. Thoughts create reality, and this is why you'll find our ascension will not happen any time soon in the material sense, and as long as the Archons keep us fighting and dividing our own kind, along with implementing deep-rooted negativity along the way to ensure their holographic 'program' will fade into the ether, once and for all.

Have you noticed that when anything positive comes to light around the world (and which is very seldom), there are dramatic events which bring that hope crashing to the ground? Wars, catastrophic incidents, along with human divide, are top of the Archon agenda, and one which fuels their main energy source to keep them alive within the corporeal. The human is their main source of food (energy), but one that is low in its frequency. This is also prevalent in those cases of human sacrifice, and where the elite use such abhorred secret ceremonies to maintain their own etheric/material forms when their victim's energy is released just before death, and which they are able to sustain within their lower vibrational state. We've heard so much about shape-shifting reptilians, the phenomenon of which may suggest through well-known British researcher and author, David Icke that the Archons literally attach themselves like a parasite to their human compatriot from within the ether and interlocks with their energy-system, thereby overriding it, and brought on by a desire for power, wealth and control. This, in turn, brings about the manipulation such entities utilise in order to further their overall agenda, and one which is designed to destroy the very spiritual nature of Mankind. Most of the public will immediately discredit such notions as fantasy, but we are aware that any investigations implemented by researchers into these dark areas gets them into deep waters (as well as the UFO topic where the establishments are at such pains in maintaining its secrecy) and whereby the system will utilise any means at its disposal to quell allegations of alien interaction. It's any wonder the majority of people who get too near the truth (especially within areas around paedophilia) are dealt with accordingly, if only to protect those within the ring itself and which will reveal many elite members within society having a hand in such degrading episodes, and which would blow the cover to the demonic reality wide open.

Why are certain people selected for alien interaction, as opposed to a larger portion of society? We could assume that many more abductees have been targeted than previously acknowledged due to the nature of the greys instigating amnesia once the abduction has completed its course, and this may explain why recalling their end of the event is almost impossible. And what of the connection to the Reptilians (the true facade of the Archons themselves), along with the greys, which appear to be in servitude to them? We could assume that such powerful entities as the Archons have, for decades, been psychically tracking those individuals who show signs of consciously bolting out of the prison they have created for us and send forth their agents (the greys which operate from within the ether) to abduct certain individual, tagging them with an implant in not only being able to track them, but possibly create an electromagnetic field which lowers their vibrational frequencies on a neurological level, thus bringing the abductee in line with the masses' overall conscious limitations which such beings have initiated since the time of Man's emergence began. The greys (as I have argued) would naturally separate the real essence of you away from your biological body to bring you into their reality. This is why abductees are able to go through material substance when an abduction is in progress. What the greys do to you while you are matched by their density within the astral will invariably affect its physical counterpart. This is where we can make comparisons in suggesting that the greys are interdimensional in nature, for the simple reason that an NDE almost mirrors such contact, albeit on a more enlightened level. We could also assume that varied souls on planet earth have incarnated from other star systems, and the abduction program has been enforced to ensure that, upon death, the 'spirit' of their targeted subject is unable to escape the reincarnation process, thereby snaring them in the loop of incarnation, as well as trying to discover key elements of those souls existing outside the parameter of the Archon influence.

The system of power has been working in varied ways in not only controlling your thoughts, but also influencing your conscious point of view from all angles. This is clearly evident in controversial cases, and where some UFO researchers consider whether the military (working in conjunction with the Archons without them even being remotely aware of it through their lack of connections up the chain of command) stage certain alien abductions their end to make out that no 'human' is responsible behind such atrocities, so there is no come-back on a legal level from the abductee who believes aliens had been responsible in their capture all along. This makes for very interesting speculation, and although hard to believe, we at least must cover this point in question, as we are more inclined to take the vantage point of the entities taking matters into their own hands, even though they may be working hand in claw with certain select and private corporations. If the military were behind these types of MILAB procedures (MILAB meaning an abduction being carried out by military personnel) under the auspice of their commanders who are unaware behind the scenes as to who the real masters are, then this would again suggest that certain high-ranking members in society are aware of the Archons, along with their evil intentions.

Transhumanism is but another system which will soon be in place and made to appear attractive to much of the public (the Archons' trick in enchanting would-be followers and believers alike, much like dangling the carrot) and which we are sure much of the public will literally buy! There appears to be a system in place where the spirit of Man is not only to be thwarted and controlled, but altogether extinguished. The greys themselves operate as a one-hive-mind consciousness, whereby they appear to have no personality, as though such attributes have been completely eradicated. If the greys are a product of Archon design, then this pretty much tells us how they plan to steer the Avatar in the long run. As humans, we are a danger to such elevated beings because we are unpredictable in nature and do not know what others are thinking. Therefore, Transhumanism is designed to disable the very nature of your spirit and allow the Archons total dominion over their troublesome slave. The system will know all your thoughts, have access to your memories while implanting false ones, and, perhaps, even be able to predict your future actions. Eventually, they seek to transform the human into a machine, and whether this is what has happened to the greys through their masters, one can only guess! But the Transhumanism reality is looming fast, and a system is soon to be set in place in making us believe we are in line for a human 'upgrade,' when it is anything but.

Yet, for all of our speculation, there is one sure fact, and that is that we, as the Avatar, are more powerful than those elite members who govern from above. Let us now see your power and how you can overcome those darker energies with your incredible light.

# 'The Eternal Avatar'

## Chapter Twelve

## The Eternal Avatar

*'Bestowed of this Avatar to be,*

*Your soul's expression of energy,*

*Where all the lifetimes have found you here,*

*To reach beyond the doubt and fear,*

*And sign your name across the stars,*

*With the sands of time inside the glass,*

*Connect and share with all souls in sight,*

*Experience your essence, your truth and light,*

*Beyond this body, this world you see,*

*You'll carry everything that you chose to be.'*

Chris John Mayes

You are the eternal Avatar. You who remembers not from whence you came other than the waters of the womb and who has been blinded by a fraudulent system, holding you as prisoner (a slave) on earth since your inception within the material realm. Yet, you are power, and light, and all things beyond the known laws of the corporeal, a star shining brightly, but which the system has tried to douse, deceive, and corrupt, and derail you within a misguided navigation along your spiritual journey of self-discovery. As you walk this life's path, temporarily clothed in the garments of flesh, the power you truly harbour is Godly, and one which extends out to all the known laws of the universe, and beyond. The system we serve does not want you to know this, or for you to connect with those abilities it has deemed as satanic, ungodly, or pure nonsense. Those who govern (the Archons) along with their deluded human puppets (the elite) are themselves foolish to blight the many within forced assumptions, but which themselves rigorously practice in all those topics they have deemed to you as illusionary or harmful in nature. Fools! They preach what they deny and counteract such incredible truths to the masses, but they themselves are trapped on earth for all time, until their ultimate destruction. We, the modern-day slave-labour force who are subtly, yet to some degree, effectively programmed by the system in the belief that we are all doomed to a life of mere existence, but are, nevertheless, an incredible incarnation of spiritual energy which surpasses the material plane. The fear placed into the very hearts of the Avatar has seen to our hopes and wishes dashed by *those* who care only for power, wealth, and control. What life would be like if these systems of control were all but crushed – completely – and a wise council of empathic leaders from all nations working together took their place in steering humanity into a new path of true enlightenment, and where all things are considered and not rejected, where truth is revealed and lies abolished, where money is obsolete and a new system imposed which will wipe away the need for greed and corruption, where innovative ideas are explored and not hidden, and which works towards the betterment of our species. Our governments and politicians send money to help aid conflict, along with their other nefarious deals, and the public always pays in the end. We are their cash machines and are never allowed to interject with their overall ruling. The huge amounts of money created for the establishments of power is never revealed to those of us who are the ones lining their ever-expanding pockets, and if you try and find out the real figures as to where it's all going, as well as how the money's being used, you'll have to go through a lot of red tape, lies and disinformation, and even then, will see no transparency.

Climate change is another topic of debate, while the elite harp on about carbon emissions and so forth, travelling around in private jets to attend their fancy meetings, while much of the public cannot even afford that luxury. What the system does is give you something in one hand, and then slap you in the other, making out YOU are the problem.

People are mostly trapped and unable to bring about their true excellence because of a system which demands that they pay their way and step in line. The absolute catastrophe of it all! The system fashions people into weapons and turns one against the other through propaganda, gaslighting, and reverse psychology. Once someone believes in what is filtered down to them from the top (in whatever capacity) without doing their homework first, they become blinded into a sense of self-righteousness, considering they have been invested with a power which alters their emotional and mental state of mind which the system finds easy to manipulate, because they are being steered by those at the top to think and react *their* way. How many times have you gotten angry when seeing something on the news, whether it be a world event, politics, or any number of issues tackled? On many occasions, we only see one side of the coin and are invariably blinded by the other. Anyone who speaks out or challenges the system will be made to look a fool or troublemaker. This is classic in cases like the Covid situation, Black Lives Matter, along with various other manufactured events designed to bring about division, as well as detrimental change to the way we think and react. As stated, the new weapon is of the mind, and not fists, bullets, or missiles. People go on about slavery, but open your eyes! Are you really free? We're not addressing the brutality of the past (and something no one in our generation should be blamed for as those who engineered such events have long since gone) which had been cruel and unforgiving, but you are a prisoner in the sense that money (the Archons' form of control) governs your entire life, from beginning to end. It's any surprise those Avatars who cross over and haven't paid all their earth debts aren't met by some reptile-looking guy with a 'No Entry' sign being held up within the astral planes, waiting for you to pay up! I'm sure if the Archons had their way, they'd get your money, one way or another, especially in the 'Psychic Highway' within their lower planes they control. Jokes aside, the reality of the human experience is mostly depressing in nature, and much needless suffering could be tackled quite easily if we took money out of the equation. That's all we hear about!

Money, money, money. It's so heartbreaking to know that many families can't afford to put food on the table because of the so-called 'Cost of Living Crisis,' or someone who's terminally ill cannot get a particular breakthrough drug because it's too expensive to produce by the medical profession. I'm sure the elite will have no problem getting it for themselves. It's the same with any new cancer drug treatment which takes years of trials before (if at all) being released to the public. And what of the Covid jab, which came out in record-breaking time? The holistic approach is immediately rejected by the WHO, namely because there's hardly any money to be made, or those methods explored to treat the whole and not just the part. The elite have created a cancer in our society, and they are not willing to administer any treatment whatsoever. These are arguments for another time, but those brave souls who have tried to tackle such issues have been met, once again, with harsh backlash and scorn from the controlled and contrived media cartel, and at the behest of their Masters. Everything, and we mean everything, comes with a price tag, and not a cheap one at that, either.

Those in high positions of governance create laws that mostly benefit themselves but do little for the people at the lower end of the spectrum. Members of the elite are brought into power and steamroll their way ahead with their own decisions without consulting the people first, but the rulings of which are handed down to them from those unseen Masters from above. The World Economic Forum (WEF, and which is an international advocacy non-governmental organisation and think tank which, allegedly, does not have the power to make decisions, but which does have the clout to influence political and business policies) appears to be behind much of the enforced worldwide changes surrounding just about every corner of our lives, and which are expected to be implemented by whoever is in governance. The WEF also works towards an agenda, much of which has been leaked via whistleblowers to the public. The trouble is, there is no one individual who can see who's behind what, and so forth. This is an impossible feat, and one where the elite can safely hide behind their iron curtain, knowing no one will be able to call their bluff. Many folks believe, for instance, that our Prime Minister or President makes up their own policies when they come into authority, but this is far from true. We are seeing a form of dictatorship. In the days of old, and where there had been communities, the public would elect a member to speak on their behalf (usually administered in town hall meetings), and any disputes or decisions examined by the elected member. The overall vote from the winning majority would, in effect, bring about a unanimous change to whatever cause or concern there had been. It was fair and square, so the saying goes. The elected member would *have* to go along with that vote, otherwise he'd be kicked out of office.

As discussed in the previous chapter, we can speculate that agents of darkness, such as a select group of greys, are sent to investigate and keep their Masters' cattle (human merchandise) in check for the Archons. This could be achieved by the greys through the quantifying of the person's unique psychic signature, which is monitored by scientists and military personnel in their secret group of the elite's scientific and military subdivision. This is another reason why our system will not admit to the larger picture of the human spirit, and its ability in transcending space-time beyond the corporeal nature of what we currently represent in the biological sense, along with the UFO situation, such as it is. We know that certain military factions have been employed within the study of consciousness and afterlife for decades in order to gain access to those astral states as described by Robert Monroe's '*Gateway Programs.*'

Psychic attack is another area that both Chris and I have speculated, and a reality, to be sure. If you're an empath, then you'll feel such assaults far more than someone who is not. These can range from day-to-day encounters with people, but more so from larger, outside influences being emitted via secret centres across the world and within the ether in what Chris and I call the system's '*Psychic Disabling Program.*' We both feel that at varied times in our lives, such oppressive energies have been deliberately directed at us, thus attempting to scramble the normal and gentle levels of psychic integration so that you are made to undergo depression, anger, and exhaustion for no apparent reason, as well as changes in your mood. You'll be able to detect this in response to your current state of awareness, which can literally come out of the blue. Such influences are targeted in order to destabilise your mental functioning. I recall a moment back in 2012 when I'd been working on '*Sky Crash: Throughout Time*', originally published by Capall Bann Publishing Ltd in 2013 with co-author Brenda Butler, and which dealt with the Rendlesham UFO events, past, present, and future. I'd been sitting in the kitchen on my laptop with the door open, revealing our small hall. It had been dark and late.

My attention had been drawn to something I'd suddenly detected in the hall, and in the blink of an eye, saw a military guy manifest, as though I was perceiving his entire form (body and uniform) as light. I had no time to react when, all at once, he rushed towards me. I immediately raised my hands up, as though protecting myself before the ghost-form disappeared. I had a really bad feeling and wondered whether or not the military was projecting their astral selves across time and space to see what I was up to. I had admittedly become paranoid, knowing of the process of remote viewing, but also considering remote influencing. I didn't want to suddenly wake up in my bed one night to find a pair of invisible hands slowly choking the life out of me, or experiencing a suspected heart attack being tenuously brought on by the will of cunning minds from a remote region of '*viewers*' focusing their conscious influence upon me! Indeed, we know of the system's subtle but effective measures in directing such cognisant weapons technology upon the masses through the airwaves, along with technological devices. And who would know? This is how dark such clandestine organisations are. The Archons are our makers, so they know us better than we do ourselves, but the very essence of the 'spirit' is an element they cannot possess. After epochs of trying to replicate or acquire just such a sacred element, they now wish to further subjugate the Avatar through Transhumanism to ensure their upgraded creation is now to be downgraded.

There is reason to suspect why the greys abduct only a selected few individuals who ostensibly step out of line in terms of conscious dissidence and thereby unsettle the carefully imposed and structured model of 'how' it is, as opposed to the truth in there being more to the human, along with other entities (both good and bad) gracing our ether and dimensions of reality. We can further speculate and suggest that the spirit of the abductee, along with their biological makeup, appears to be of vital importance to *their* program. Whatever they are seeking, those selected for their program appear to hold the key, but something they are unable to unlock. The UFO secrecy, which is still instigated, sends out warning signals, because there's obviously more to this than meets the eye, and a department the system does not want us to discover within its entirety. Yet, it appears such entities are able to traverse the astral/interdimensional highway in an effort to create such a cloak of deception surrounding their detection. However, the multitude of other entities reported within UFO groups appears to muddy the waters, and hard for us to discern fact from fiction, which is what our system embraces, because no proof can be attained whatsoever. Souls from alternate dimensions of reality have gravitated to Earth in order to bring awareness of the huge corruption this planet has always been faced with. There is indeed evil that goes beyond the insanity of some people and is quantified within mythology so as to conceal its true nature. It has been given many names and faces, but we believe it is one of the same forces.

Is there any possibility to suggest that certain recovered alien bodies (also known as non-human entities, besides those as the grey-like entities most famously recorded within UFO literature) are stored in advanced cryogenic tanks, and something which will reveal the Archons within their full glory? Huge reptilian-type creatures! Is this why the establishments of power are reluctant to reveal anything of the UFO reality, because researchers will make connections to the past, exposing who is really running the show behind the scenes (and has been since our human inception), indicating that these so-called aliens are much closer to home than once speculated. This is what the system has been hiding from all of us. The reptilian has featured in a great part of our mythology and culture from around the world, but strangely, any mention of them is to be immediately quashed. Would you believe that we as humans are equipped with part of a reptilian brain? Physician and neuroscientist, Paul D. Maclean (1913-2007) considered the triune brain serves as a model of the evolution of the vertebrate forebrain and behaviour. The triune brain consists of the reptilian complex known as the (nasal ganglia/striatum), which governs our primal instincts such as hunger, thirst, sexuality, territoriality, as well as habits and procedural memory, which are repetitive actions. The limbic system controls our emotions, and the neocortex our objective, rational thoughts. As humans, we have regulation over varied and complex actions which counteract the pure mechanics of our reptilian functioning due to our limbic and neocortex, which serves on most occasions to counteract such urges our Overlords cannot themselves restrain within their own cognizance. In fact, much of the public on our level can allow destructive, neurological impulses to cause others great physical, emotional, and mental harm in a variety of ways, and who appear devoid of those spiritual attributes that thwart the delicate balancing of orderly brain functioning. For instance, some (not all) celebrities get caught up in the glitz and glamour of their fame, and this can invariably create huge changes within their overall cerebral functioning.

Like a parasite, the Archon influence can alter an individual's personality very quickly, and not necessarily one that is projected remotely by the Archon force. Remember that the brain serves as a receiver and transmitter, and what you think, you ultimately become. As stated in our book earlier, there are cases where artists in the music industry have been witness to such destructive methods and manipulation where sadistic suggestibility has been implemented to hook the public, but at the same time see the artist being controlled and deployed by the Archon's influence behind the scenes. They discover that their own thought processes, which had once been balanced, have now been swayed in a radical and sometimes destructive level, leading them to drink, drugs, and sex as a way of trying to cope with the enormous pressures they feel when being exploited for their talent. This doesn't happen with all artists, as there are those who are favoured by members of the elite and are able to steadily progress within the manufacture of their own art, the way they want to direct it. They are, however, not aware of the so-called extra-terrestrial influence, but reports from certain whistle-blowers indicate there is a very dark aspect behind the extravagance portrayed beyond what the public knows. This may be one of the reasons why the greys are so heavily promoted, since they are only a smaller part of the larger picture, and just as hard to nail down because of the exposure of their etheric exploits. The Archons hide themselves within plain sight of their subjects, like the Wizard of Oz, intent in maintaining clarity as to their true identity.

Such control reminds me of a series of young adult novels written by British author John Christopher (1922-2012) and may illustrate our point beautifully. These were '*The White Mountains*' (1967), '*The City of Gold and Lead*' (1967), and '*The Pool of Fire*' (1968), and much later, '*When the Tripods Came*' (1988), originally published by Hamish Hamilton. The premise of these adventures centre around three boys who are against the 'Capping' process, and where their Overlords, whom they know next to nothing about, rule earth, travelling in huge, metal tripod machines, and conduct their capping when a person reaches the age of fourteen. The stories take place in a post-apocalyptic world, and where humanity is enslaved by the Masters who are revealed later in the books as the real culprits behind their machines the Tripods who have deliberately overpowered human development and centralised programming through the cap (a device surgically affixed to the skull through a 'Capping' procedure which prevents humans from turning against the Masters) and whereby such monstrous creatures are able, without rebellion from their enforced docile subordinates bring about their plan to wipe out humanity, and take the earth for themselves. The three central characters, Will, Henry, and Beanpole, eventually overthrow the alien menace when they become aware of the plan to completely eradicate their own kind. It's ironic that in reality such mental dumbing down being initiated by our system will eventually lead to human implants wired within our brain (much like the Capping process) through the course of Transhumanism, and that, perhaps, writers much like the late John Christopher could see events of this kind playing out within their own minds rather like prophecy, although enacted out in a different way when it comes to real life events and brought forth from the deeper levels of the subconscious state. The famous American horror novelist, Stephen King wrote many of his early works when he'd been completely drunk and has stated he barely recalls writing a single word of his book 'Cujo' (Viking press 1981) because of his intoxication, and not, it must be stated, that of any Archon influence. The subconscious mind serves as the direct link to the super-conscious mind, and is where all things are possible. This is the very gateway to what is called the infinite mind, and a passage through which are deepest desires and horrors can gain access on a mental level and, on occasions, a physical one.

Entrepreneur Elon Musk has stated that he wishes for humans to eventually merge with Artificial Intelligence, and although appearing attractive to the masses in promising an extension of human life, we can think of nothing more horrific! The system is planning to disable the very nature of your essence away from the one, true Creator, and keeping you trapped within a perpetual recycling of the soul, where your spirit will not be able to attain clear passage back to the divine for those who have not yet awoken to the reality of what's going on behind the scenes, and has been occurring since ages past. Prophecy through innocent, as well as intended 'thought' happens a lot; where something has been written or produced as a film, only for those events to pan out in the future. The American cartoon series '*The Simpsons*' is a prime example of this, where an apparent idea can impact a future occurrence due to energy being invested within and surrounding a multitude of conscious concepts created, and which then becomes manifest, whether as an outward or inward influence in our world. This has been called 'Predictive Programming' by those who have recognised it. As mentioned earlier, thoughts which carry little or no weight within its brief incarnation through cognizance merely cancel themselves out in the ether, unless of course certain ideas are strengthened through the process of a continuous mental intent, and thereby allowing such ideas to attain shape and form within the astral planes, and then is able to subsequently project itself within our reality. We can theorise that the greys themselves are soulless, spiritless creations by their Masters, the Archons, and have been afforded an astral body which is able to manipulate both time and space.

Aside from the negative influences and situations in our life, you, as the incredible Avatar, have been ordained with immense power, which the Archon authority has tried to negate through a distortion of facts throughout human history, as well as disabling the very nature of your being through the use of psychological weaponry. You can take control of these negative factors, and in the knowledge that you are invested with more power than you know. Merely taking a step back and accessing your truths when you start digging into the past, as well as the present, will you realise that things are not how they appear. There are those Avatars in life who are comfortable and have no need to discover the deeper elements of themselves. Such sleepers have yet to awaken, but those that have are now 'aware' of their true heritage, and of the fact that we are not alone within this immense fabric of space, contrary to what the system informs us as *their* truth. By attuning yourself through meditation and contemplation, bringing about a balance and harmony into the core of your being, you will begin to feel differently. This is why, and in the past, such methods were considered mad! We must remember the Archons yearn to create disruption and chaos, so that we may never discover the truth of our 'spirit', which is what we encompass beyond the material. This has always been their plan, but we can change all of that, simply by accepting that most of history is all wrong, and that we are in governance to ourselves, and not others.

Chris Mayes defines this beautifully in stating that:

*'Isn't it fascinating that when an invention or new discovery is made, quite often the same thing happens elsewhere on this planet at roughly the same time. It's as if we reach a threshold within our collective paradigm, and a breakthrough*

*occurs for its birth into existence. I believe that this is because everything of this world is manifesting from its original wave-like to particle-like form, depending on external expectation from an outside influence. Nothing is static or in a permanent state, and is affected by our expectations of it. Quantum mechanics proved wave-particle duality and revolutionised physics in the 20th century. In fact, all the atoms in our body are doing this. Shouldn't this then suggest that at every given moment is the potential for whatever we want ourselves to be? This constant flux suggests to me that our whole reality is manifesting from one unseen intelligent source at any given moment. An intelligence that is giving rise to the basic form and order of atoms, that we ourselves have full access to with thought. We are the same creative powerhouse of this consciousness.*

*What can we take from this in our everyday living to have any real impact? Well, firstly, we should never limit our thinking and expectations with preconceived ideas based on past experience or what has been told we should believe. This will only curtail and dictate all your potentiality and will imprison your experience to mere repetition or echo of an old existence, ultimately enslaving you. Believe in a different reality, break away from conventional thought, nothing is static, and everything can change, no matter how permanent and immovable anything in life appears to be. This truth and understanding of our active participation of reality will open your soul up to miraculous events. Everything we see and experience is just a representation of an accumulation of thought into matter, a byproduct that we can hijack and change whenever we empower ourselves to imagine it differently.*

*As you read this, the current state of your body's health and happiness is mostly a culmination of all the thoughts you've ever had of it. Yes, we can fall ill if we push ourselves too hard or have accidents that feel were beyond our control but these are often lessons that come our way to help remind us to either rest, divert you from further harm or listen more to our inner needs when we wander off-track from 'who' and 'what' we are, because we have allowed ourselves to become victims of circumstance again. I want this to give you hope. The idea that we can create and change our reality from its atomic level should break the illusion that we cannot influence anything. Healing ties into this, and I strongly believe that a healer is basically overriding the instructions (Frequency) the cells are receiving to be something else. Negative thoughts that lead to illness are weak, but positive thoughts are far more powerful and influential. Darkness cannot invade light. Hope is the spark of creation and all that there is. Let's use our light and the creative power of hope to make this dark world as bright as it can be.'*

As Chris states, you can be anything you want to be through the simple act of thought. Focusing within, as opposed to without, can make a huge difference in the way you operate. We are all connected like the signals to your mobile phone, which is connected to a central hub of united information. The Archons can gain access to this psychic internet of ours, but they can never truly possess what we are endowed with. You are truth, and that truth burns brightly within the source of your being.

# 'The Eternal Avatar'

## Chapter Thirteen

## God & Our Gateway Back to Source

*I am in you, where you are in me,*

*Your dreams are mine to set you free,*

*Take my hand and rise high above,*

*Share in my view of all that I love,*

*There is no place I would not let you see,*

*For all your travels will lead back to me,*

*Find comfort and joy in knowing this,*

*Your home is where your soul will find its bliss.*

*Whisper your thoughts where they lift my heart,*

*My eternal love shall never keep us apart.*

Chris John Mayes

Here, Chris describes beautifully about God, and our gateway back to source.

'I would like to tell you that God is not just a part of you, it *is* you. Based on what science is proving, it validates the fact that we are all connected to God in its purest form. You are very much an individual expression of God experiencing duality within this time and space. But the important element to this is the choice that we all have, of our own idea and belief of what God is, or if it exists at all, and what that means to you. It is a very personal topic and one that can raise very conflicting emotions and opinions from person to person. But I truly believe there is a powerful activation even within your DNA that expands every aspect of your being once you are dynamically allowing your consciousness to shift and align with the embodiment of God. God is not separate from us. The detracted idea of being detached from God is the reason why we are not able to fully unite with our interconnectedness and attain the fusion that we need to channel the inherent abilities that come with this spiritual partnership. When we do, it's as though a switch is flipped, and suddenly you are allowing yourself to be connected to the very nature of everything and everyone. God is just that - everything, and it's our freedom to decide whether to participate and incorporate ourselves within its tapestry or as a limited and insular existence. God's confirmation of the inseparable connection with us can come in many different forms that best suit the individual. From an internal mood or thought to an animal/person, any element of nature, to coincidences, dreams, and events. They will always be accompanied by a very positive effect upon your psyche and broaden your understanding to see yourself beyond your perceived limitations. God wants to be your parent, your best friend, healer, and love. There is nothing stopping you, only your own beliefs, from fully accepting God to be the source of everything great that we want to be. We all have access to God at any given moment and in any way that we feel is appropriate. We limit ourselves with our own ideas of what is possible, and also whether we actually feel worthy enough. Even with the topic of healing, the cells in your body are always working on autopilot, pretty much like everything else in life, which is just waiting for you to empower them, to be told what to do. You are the master of their existence. Healing is the ability to override and command their basic programme with a divine instruction and intent. Nothing exists without our consciousness, and it's at what level of consciousness do we decide to live by - an awakened and empowered one or as a being that just reacts to circumstance?

The idea that someone believes that we are separate from God, or that it doesn't exist, is a valid opinion based on their own personal reasons. The presence of God in our life takes faith and conviction for it to mean anything, and it gives a vital purpose to our Avatars existing fully within this material realm. Our perceptions of life, our reality, and what we are have been fractured and toxified for the purpose of losing our way so that we can be coaxed by more nefarious minds. We are not a body with a soul; we are a soul with a body. If you are someone who has no belief in a God, that does not detach you from there still being a God and all the implications it brings. I would suggest that a person of this inclination is probably more self-defined by their possessions and status in life, and yet they can still be inspired and guided by their own divine God-source, but without them understanding that they are working with it. We are all given the freedom to be as close or distant to God however we choose in this life, and for many, life is increasingly becoming so distracting that it is barely a notion to be given hardly any thought, which is probably by design. It is impossible to be detached from God, but certain people and places can be Godless! This then delves into the darker realities and the very real existence of low vibrational realms. All negative spirits and energies only exist within the realm of time and space. This is due to the nature of the low frequency being a product of the duality of the time/space dimension. Heaven and the higher realms are the state of unity, a oneness that is pure love and joy – timeless. Everything in this life is a choice we make, a conscious decision of how much we want it to have a positive impact that will apply to us individually, but also collectively. Each choice has its frequency, it's just a matter of climbing that 'Frequency ladder' and maintaining those higher choices in order to elevate and awaken.

The need for definitions is a very human trait. Defining good and bad can often blind us from understanding or accepting a bigger picture. If we are to truly relate to the source of everything, would we need to consider the idea that evil is of God's design? Nothing can be separate from the creator based on the concept of its very name, and the full spectrum must be seen as a whole as a collective. The idea of cherry-picking what God represents does not seem to capture the reality of the truth of it all. Yes, evil is bad when you see it as negative, restricted, diminishing, and destructive, but it is the existence of this dark end of the scale that gives the very real existence of all that is good in this world of polarity. It is a means to derive a soul and give it the freedom to express and decide its true nature of greatness within the dichotomy.

Our gateway back to source is nothing less than spectacular. A thought for comfort is that we never truly leave it. Even as we spend our time here on earth, it is very likely that our higher self is still within the divine ether. I don't think our soul has a locality to it, regardless of the overwhelming sense of our essence being locked within the body. Regardless of our presence here on earth, we are not isolated and detached from our divine home, our source, while here. This is the key and the tool for our access to the power we are and the ability to find our gateway back to source and avoid any possible misdirection to fool us of our return via reincarnation. If our souls are to be misdirected beyond death by corrupt beings, then it is my strong belief that it is the act of *'re-membering'* of our higher state and awareness which will break the loop that might exist for our unelected return. This could also be the reason why great efforts are made in preventing us from reconnecting to our higher states, as it bypasses their trap once we have strengthened and established our link in order to discern the truth. In light of all this and for the survival of our race, our efforts to discover the true nature of our being and better understand the forces at work are more essential now than ever before.

I have personally experienced the detachment from my physical body, quite unexpectedly, and the consequence of it came with a tremendous flood of exhilarating emotions and realisations. An out-of-body experience (OBE), or astral travel, is fairly common and varies in its manifestation. It either happens when the body is going through the process of dying or due to an automatic release when certain physical conditions are conducive for its occurrence. Once the spirit is detached from its physical Avatar, the fear of being vulnerable to pain is no longer a concern or a reality. This gives rise to an intense feeling of invincibility and a freedom that expands the soul. Escaping all dense physical matter is such a huge revelation for the soul that it is accompanied with an elation of realising you are made of eternal energy. What once limited your perceptions and restricted your awareness is no more, and now it's a world of instant access where you are defined by your frequency of thought, which is seen and felt. The description of the experiences of the world beyond this physical one is as varied in number as those who have witnessed it. Our initial departure from this world, I feel, is very much calibrated to our own individual expectation of it, thus the varied reports given by those who have returned. For example, it is similar to this world in that even though we all occupy the same realm, we are all experiencing different versions of it, whether good or bad, at the same time. This is to help orient the soul and assimilate the process.

Do you think it is possible to actually speak with God right now, at this very moment within your mind? This question is very important. The type of answer you have to this question is a great indication of how you see yourself and the relationship you currently hold with God. It defines what your perception and level of interaction and accessibility are to your greatness and whether you truly believe you already have a gateway back to source! We are all individual expressions of God, having this experience to be the best version of ourselves, to learn and grow in this time and space. Beyond this world is timeless, and in a timeless state, nothing can change.

The plan for our soul beyond this life on earth is entirely focused on our own will to understand what we are truly capable of. This involves an active participation that is entirely agreed upon based on your karmic relationship you have with your own being. Our future experiences will be elevated and not limited by wars and suffering anymore, where we can interact with each other with instant understanding that makes lies impossible, and so learn more from positive experiences rather than from negative ones. It seems to be a path of self-mastery and discovery. This world is still too dense and accessible for lower ego-based, fear-centric entities to thrive, but this is changing for the better because of our collective light work on this planet, altering the paradigm. Darkness is panicking within its shrinking capacity. It might just be reasonable to consider that reincarnation and the return of increasingly good souls on this planet are counteracting the darkness that is at work. It is from within every individual to rise beyond the fear and make decisions from the remembering of the God-source inside us, whereby we can act and react with clarity and decisiveness. The understanding of our eternal life and existing beyond this one must change the way we see our physical death and help dispel the fear that death holds over us, so that we are not manipulated so easily. We need to enjoy, relish, and share in our divine greatness with every relationship we have with everything and everyone in this life experience. Our gateway to source and God is not only for the worthy or the righteous; it is for everyone at any given moment. Our only key we need is the one inside us and the ability to actively see ourselves and the world around us as one, without division. To see ourselves and the life we live in a way that connects and defines that our greatness is within, rather than any physical representation.

Because most of us do not believe in our direct source with God, we do not exercise our God-like thoughts, which therefore reflect in our perceived absence in our lives. It's as simple as that. From an early age, we are fed the belief that we are helpless and powerless from many different sources, and that God is in the great beyond, while we are lost, sinful souls to be judged and that need saving. Everything about religion suggests that we have been separated, weak, and in constant need of guidance because of these negative propositions. Beyond all the opinions and behaviours that religion seems to derive, there is an aspect to it that is very helpful and healthy for us to live by. The word to describe it is very rarely used these days, which is '*reverence.*' This emotion, this state, is very powerful if we are to affirm our connection with our God source. The ability to regularly put yourself in a state of feeling respect, wonder, and adoration for something beyond us is a delicate but powerful mix. It places your mindset and emotional set point within a frequency that is very advantageous for allowing you to see yourself and the world around you in a very humble, thankful, and receptive way, without ego. This encourages a more natural alignment that is very conducive for a temperament that helps your ability to develop a stronger connection with God in all elements of your life. *So, how are we to exercise our 'God-like' thoughts?* Well, all our thoughts are from source, but the question is more purposeful if we rephrase it to mean - *How can we channel our divine source to empower our lives for the better?* Firstly, let's be clear. This does not mean we go about our daily business with a God complex. I'm sure we already know a few people who tick that box! The suggestion I would like to make is the process of calibrating your thoughts and decisions with the belief that God is on your side and very much working right alongside you. This is especially the case when you are sincerely working for the betterment of anything which will initiate a healing of any kind, or an understanding that ultimately allows joy, love, and empathy into this reality as a result. This is very much what ties into the popular topic of manifesting, and it matters not whether it is directed towards yourself, someone else, a group or even the whole world. Approaching life in this way is certainly a great step to lighting the path for us all. The ability to believe and have the faith that your closest partnership has always been and always will be with God will be the catalyst for changing the way you see yourself and the world around you, including the one beyond this one. In such a way that you are no longer alienated from any of it, which is the empowered right you should have as an Avatar to discover and express yourself as the eternal creative force of life itself.'

# 'The Eternal Avatar'

## Chapter Fourteen

## Hope

*Your truth is divine of love that's free,*

*So let them see what we all can be,*

*The maker of dreams that you behold,*

*As you look in the eyes of the young and old,*

*Make your thoughts and deeds break free from the cast,*

*That chains us all to live like the past,*

*Let your soul be the expression of all that is right,*

*To awaken a dark world with your magnificent light.*

Chris John Mayes


**Chris Mayes relays his thoughts about 'The Eternal Avatar':**

'I hope that within these chapters, at some point, you felt something. A feeling of joy, excitement, possibility, and even hope! That was your true self deep within stirring, acknowledging to you of your eternal connection to something absolutely divine and lovingly powerful as your right and true expression. Believe this, work with it. Own it. Know that your thoughts and feelings can do wonderous things for yourself and everyone. We are indeed all connected. Do not underestimate your innate ability; you can change your external world positively by first believing and then working with the divine power within.

I once had a lady sit opposite me while traveling on a train. She was with a man who seemed curiously unaffected by the fact that she was crying with absolute despair. My heart instantly felt for her, and I could see the intense distress she was in. When you begin to notice how the universe works, I took this situation that presented itself right in front of me as a chance to help. My instinct was to keep quiet and look out the window without speaking to her. I became aware of the energy building within me the moment that I decided quietly to myself that before either of us reached our destination, I would see her laugh. Not a smile, not a giggle, but a genuine happy laugh. That was my goal, my intention, not for my benefit but for hers. In my mind, I spoke to our unseen friends and gave them my proposal, and asked for their help. I was quite young at the time, and for me it was also an opportunity for spirit to prove that we do have a connection and the ability to participate in the healing and energy work of others and of the world around us. With my goal visualised and sending her the energy she needed within ten minutes, just before I reached my stop, she was laughing. I overheard her say to the man she was accompanied with, "Why am I laughing?". She looked surprised and confused of her new condition, but more importantly, she was better. I gave a quiet thanks to spirit.

The nature of your soul is within the vibration of love, unity, and gratitude. Keep these feelings close to you and make them your decision makers, your food for life. Choose and create everything that resonates with you towards these frequencies. Quietly direct and project these feelings at people and situations in your day-to-day, and watch it make a positive change.

The phase in which we all see the world to be in right now is through the lens of the global media. The vast number of our thoughts and opinions are largely constructed by what we have been 'fed'. With the use of various tools to promote fear, we are stripped of our spiritual connection, giving rise to division and scarcity, our IQ drops, and victim mode is switched 'on'. Even though we have access to so much information, we have never been more powerless or vulnerable as a species. We focus too much on the system that controls us and the distinction between what is real, or misleading is warping our ability to claim any truth and identify ourselves with it.

I believe there is just one ultimate cause of our collective impediment. We do not know WHO and WHAT we truly are as human beings. We are spiritually undernourished. In fact, it's the notion that we are just human is the very problem. With no fault of our own, but those in power know this. Every tactic is being used to blind us of our greater identity because if we discovered the truth, every control system would simply fall away, and real change would ensue.

We are amazing, beautiful spirits in the process of changing the very reality of this world for the better. We each have to be the living example of light we carry within against all the darkness that we recognise is being pushed our way. This truth is unstoppable when we become it.

From personal experience, I know this world is an extension of the inner world. Just our physical senses alone determine what we think is reality; electrical impulses firing to send signals to the brain. We need to start to turn this around. Yes, the body is basically a filter to inform you of what is happening around you, but don't let this be the only controlling mechanism to determine your reality and emotions. Your soul is connected to a universal field and a divine source that creates. We have the ability to affect matter and communicate thoughts to each other from any distance, heal, astral travel, communicate with souls that have departed this world, live other lives, see other realities and futures. You are not 'in' and 'of' this world; everything that makes you eternal is within and unseen. When our perception shifts away from us all just being a bag of bones being pushed around this world under the random shifts of life's circumstances, we take control. We gain responsibility for ourselves and for the welfare of all mankind. Our personal development then becomes paramount in this short time here. We naturally begin to enrich our soul in ways that replace and outgrow how we used to spend our time. You become more self-aware of watching TV for hours or all the other forms of entertainment that are aimed at distracting and engaging us away from ourselves and what is important.

Nothing opens your mind more than personal experience. Your life is ultimately what you choose to believe it to be. Your choice. When you're ready, something will happen to you and make you question your beliefs, to chip away at the illusory nature of this world. As visceral as this life experience can be, there is more; we *are* more. We are from a place of greatness, to do great things. I see humanity is in a slumber, but the more of us wake up and recognise the Eternal Avatar in ourselves and what that means, then we truly will be actively engaged with that greatness.'

**Philip Kinsella relays his thoughts on 'The Eternal Avatar':**

'We live in hope, for hope is all we have. I, too, hope that, primarily, you found a little nugget of gold which connects you on your own spiritual path within mine and Chris' book. Perhaps you are advanced enough within your own intellect without the need for further clarification – and good for you! There is no competition to be had in the sharing of knowledge or experiences, and this is a good thing, because we can each evolve while at the same time being awake and aware, encompassing all areas surrounding those deeper mysteries we each seek within our own personal and unique evolution of the spirit. Sharing such experiences only enforces your conviction of those alternate realities we know to exist.

It seems strange that we are born into this world with little or no memory of our actual sojourn, bar from those exceptional Avatars who are aware of such conditions, yet through case-studies of NDE and OBE incidents, we are informed of what awaits our return beyond our biological construct. This proves beyond any shadow of doubt that human consciousness survives the state of death, and in a way far different from the varied religious orthodox versions fed into the minds of millions, which have condensed belief through such imposed and restricted dogmas. Our understanding of the afterlife is still within the preliminary stages of development, but we know the Avatar harbours incredible powers and proficiencies which our system has forcibly shut down through fear, mental subjugation, gaslighting, and reverse psychology. There are many who are already in tune with their gifts, and something condemned by the churches, and who themselves get shunned by those who have little or no empathy other than their material or programmed outlook, considering certain topics as heresy in nature. But are not many of the themes based within the holy books littered with supernatural occurrences, and of which themselves appear supernatural? This is a clear indication of the radical changes and contradictions rewritten within sacred recordings of the world in their varied forms, centred around 'belief' rather than 'fact.' There is a monumental difference. Those 'facts' detailing elements of the soul and spirit through cases of NDE and OBE reports clearly indicate something is very wrong in our understanding of the Avatar. It is clear to see that an ancient system of denial has been set in place, and one which is still in vogue today.

UFOs, Cryptids, and elements of the paranormal are all considered either mere fantasy or evil in nature, and should (so we are told by our system who wheel out their puppets to relay so-called 'facts') not be approached by the inquiring mind, when in fact the only evil to be had are by those forces who have hoodwinked the public into a type of conscious 'looping' effect, persistently reinforcing a problem, only to get a reaction, and whereby they bring forth *their* solution. UFOs, along with a plethora of other controversial subjects bracketed within the category of 'supernatural', are not *all* evil, because the truth has been segregated into their own, unique categories of hearsay, thus making it nigh impossible to make connections from one to the other. The nuts-and-bolts aspect had been very much in vogue, but that has since changed throughout the decades. Levels of high strangeness appear to go through periods of transformation, and we, as the Avatar, may find ourselves actively affecting the very nature of our personal reality, as well as the phenomenon itself!

When you have been touched by the psychic and UFO phenomenon as I (as indeed Chris) have, and at such close range, that changed everything for me on a personal level. I not only had to deal with the psychological ramifications, but also emotional disruption when informed I was delusional, or worse, a liar! This set me on a personal path of research. Having been mocked in the early days on national TV, as well as jeered by some of the public, I was determined to grow a thick skin and dig deep into those areas deemed 'impossible' or which much of the public considered 'non-existent.' For me, such controversial subjects became an obsession, fuelled not only by the onslaught of an alien abduction back in the winter of 1989, along with seeing UFOs at close range, but also by dealing with the deceased. I was convinced of the interdimensional hypothesis and considered, even back then, that I was walking on shaky ground, especially when investigators and experiencers alike believed everything was occurring in a very physical nature of reality. I knew differently, because my own episodes of high strangeness revealed a merging of UFOs and consciousness; links which other researchers believed were entirely separate when considering Cryptids, along with the dead and other topics surrounding the bizarre.

I have always said that if you want to discover your truths, you have to walk your own path of discovery. As eternal Avatars ourselves, we must be brave when taking a stand against the enormous adversity we face in life, and especially from those nameless, faceless agents at the top of the symbolic pyramid of power who are themselves dangerous within their enforced convictions fed down within the chain of command. We have been blinded by so many untruths, but know enough to assume that we have been lied to. Literally! Time is running out, because if we are caught off guard and ensnared by the glitz and glamour of what is next to come in terms of Transhumanism being subtly injected into the human psyche, then many of the incarnates in the future will find themselves drawn into such horrendous fate, and will appear no better than the greys which seem devoid of a soul, unable to make a connection beyond the illusion of the material plane which the Archons have engineered.

We are indeed fighting a war, and an ugly one at that. But we can win! By defining the true nature of what you represent beyond the material, and knowing you are more than the sum total of your temporary, biological vehicle, along with the realisation that much of history is wrong, can propel you towards true enlightenment. As Chris has said to me, we can't change the world, but we can change ourselves. He's right! By self-empowering yourself through the act of love, we can reach for the divine and shine our light brighter. Such luminosity blinds the darkness and enables you to become a powerful beacon for others to see. Love is the answer. Forgiveness, mercy, and compassion are the most powerful forces within the universe. These are the energies the Archons fear. This is how we can break through the matrix and free ourselves from the insanity of life.

It's ok to have a belief in something, so long as that belief doesn't control or bring misery to others. However, it is evidently clear to see that our system does not want us to progress spiritually and is intent in severing our link with our spiritual heritage altogether. This has been going on throughout the prevailing epochs. What does this tell us? It tells us that such danger is with the Archons who are pushing behind the scenes for Transhumanism, along with the advancement of a cold and spiritless science. The transcendent aspect has never been allowed to grow, and you have to wonder as to why that is. We know the answer to that already, but it's good to be armed with this knowledge when you work towards the betterment of your own Avatar you currently inhabit on a biological level.

Our physical life on earth is brief. We will all pass over to the other side at some point, and it is then that we will be able to walk within the grace of God's light and live together in peace, love, creativity, and harmony with one another. There will be no more pain, or tears, or broken dreams either.

Truth leads to divinity, and you are that warrior for truth and a defender of the divine light, which shines brighter than the very stars in space.

Go shine your light brightly.

# 'A Message from the Council of 9'
# Channelled by a Medium for You

Sweet soul of love it is with such joy that we connect with you at this time. We know that humanity is shifting through a deep change and this was always on the cards so to speak and so many are struggling as the Earth and the cosmos become an expression in higher frequency.

The human family has been hijacked, shall we say. There are many explanations for this, and so many of your kind have a much deeper understanding now than, say, before your millennium. Now, what is the reason for such an assault on humankind? Well, indeed, there are those that have been known as the guardians of the Earth expression. There are "labels" that many will give these guardians, and so we shall refrain from those "handles" as some may call them, for indeed they spark debate and often disagreements, and we are here to offer an overview that shall be offered as a deeper understanding without prejudice, so to speak.

Now indeed the Earth plane has been designated as an experience for re-enlightenment through physical expression. Those souls who incarnate here into an avatar or human body are here to experience the joys of physicality. To feel the warmth of the sun on their skin, to enjoy the tastes of the fruits of the Earth, to name but a few, and of course to experience love in physical form. To have a physical experience allows a deeper emotional, mental, and ultimately some would call a spiritual experience, and so greatness becomes the one again through this experience when the soul leaves the body.

Now, why has there been such disruption to the human avatar and hence the physical experience? Why so much pain and suffering? Some shall say that we grow from suffering. Well, indeed, a negative can become a positive and so on. A human can recognise their soul expression through painful expressions, but some will say, "How many more do I have to go through?" Indeed, that is the big question. We know of the reincarnation process. The soul leaves an avatar and returns into a new avatar, perhaps for a completely different experience, or indeed is it just a repeat of the old? Lessons not learned? How many times does a soul need to incarnate to learn the lesson? Once, twice, a thousand times? Now indeed this is a mystery.

So, let us go back to the guardians. As frequency becomes denser then there is a loss of consciousness. A rock is solid, or so it seems. Does it have higher consciousness in its make-up, or have the atoms slowed so much that all is forgotten? Now indeed we shall say that suffering comes from separation. As the frequency becomes denser, then consciousness becomes lower, so to speak, and the oneness of all is forgotten.

Now indeed, the guardians were entrusted and given the role to watch over the physical experience. Some may say they were the "terraformers" – well indeed, we shall leave that as a label. Now, as the guardians came down, their frequencies became denser too, even though the guardians remained outside of the physical experience – some may say they are the "overlords," so to speak.

Indeed, they played their roles, and so the physical experience began, and so many organisms were created, and so came the humans; beautiful expressions of the soul in physical form. The human body was created to be resilient, to self-correct, and to self-heal.
Now the guardians noticed the beauty of the human form and so in their own lower density the guardians became jealous of humanity and so they knew that they could "play" with them. As guardians of the Earth plane they began to create disruption which meant that the human expression became unbalanced. The humans were living in harmony prior to the disruption created by the guardians.

Now the humans began to become disconnected from their Creator or Source, as some may call it – all labels, of course. The separation from their Creator meant that they began to suffer. The guardians disrupted the Earthly organism and expressions, including the food, the money exchange, the weather, and so on. This meant the humans became lost, and so their separation became deeper. They began to fight within themselves, and so the disruption spread. Now, the guardians wanted to engage physically too, and so they manipulated the DNA of the human, the coding, so to speak, and they did this so that some of their kind could incarnate. The DNA of the original humans was too high a frequency, even in physical form, so they needed to change that to come into form themselves. Now, many would say that if the guardians are in a higher frequency above physicality, then why could they not incarnate into a human avatar without interrupting their DNA? Well indeed, the original humans came from a higher dimension, as some would call it, than the guardians inhabited. The humans were closer to the Creator, made in its image. So, the guardians manipulated the human DNA to "come in".

Now there is a "virus" so to speak in humanity, and so the separation became deeper as the hybrid humans, who now had the guardian expressions within them, rose to the top to control the uncorrupted humans.

So now we shall fast forward to your human theatre as it is at this time? There is deep disruption on the Earth plane. All has been left for expression. No stone is unturned. The Earthly stage has become chaotic, and this density has been at its lowest and so the ego, which is the ultimate expression of separation, has created much discord and disharmony. However, this is the time of reckoning. The Creator is sending frequencies to your Earth plane by express delivery to bring the human expression back to its original form.

Now in the past there has been what some call the "wipe out", where a catastrophe has destroyed the Earthly experience, maybe a flood, and so it is like a reset of your computers. The "virus" is wiped out and there is a re-imagining.

Now, what of the guardians? Did you know that they created a frequency net to trap souls leaving their avatars? So, the soul would be in their grasp, and they might say, "Oh, you did quite well in that life, but there were a few areas that you need to have another go at in order to heal". So, they prepare an avatar and so "persuade" the soul to return. What happens, and this is not in all cases, but the same old journey begins. More suffering and more "learning of lessons". Indeed, this is to feed the unmitigated needs of the guardians to control. Now indeed we shall offer this thought, and we ask you to remain open and to come to your universal understanding, the guardians are known as the guardians of developing societies, or GODS.

Indeed, there is much more to be said. The Earth plane is now going through a shifting of energies that shall bring about a new era, a golden era, as some may call it. All that is not in high frequency shall be exposed. Truths shall surface. Now, some will say, what is the truth? Well indeed, truth shall shift as consciousness shifts. This brings about realisation.

Those who become more highly conscious shall begin to see past the mind programming that humanity has endured. The changing of the human DNA by the guardians did indeed disconnect the souls in avatars from their Creator and indeed from the higher truths. This some shall call intuition. The human heart is indeed the powerhouse. The heart is the connection to the soul and so the Creator.

The mind is the tool that allows manifestation. It runs the programmes, shall we say, and the programmes interact with the matter that is within the framework of the matrix that the Earth plane is formed within. So, what you believe the most becomes your reality. If you believe that you are not good enough, then you shall experience not being good enough. So, the more you believe something, the more you become that. The guardians knew how to utilise the human mind; they themselves do not create the world that you experience, you do that. Indeed, what the guardians do is to make you believe the version of the world that they wish you to create, and they make you believe it so intently that your mind works to manifest it. The greatest tools for the mind programming of humans have often been hidden in the "mystery" of religion. Out of fear, humans have believed in the past, and some still do, that damnation that shall occur if they do not follow the rules presented to them.

Your programming occurs throughout your human existence, especially when your minds are developing. "Get them whilst they are young" is the motto of the wayward guardians. Your education systems, religion, banking, governments, health, war machines, and more make you believe that life on your Earth plane is difficult and suffering is inevitable.

Have you noticed how many humans are disconnecting from the mind programming? How many watch the television news? Not many these days. But there is still programming on the devices in your hands. But now you are sifting through deciding what is truth or not. You are becoming more discerning and asking more questions. Your minds are losing the programming, and for some, you are feeling lost, and some are frightened at the unknown that is appearing before them.

Now, over the next five years, there shall be unprecedented changes in your Earthly world. Know that all you have held onto is about to unattach. Some you may have looked up to shall fall from grace. Only those who imbue authenticity and integrity shall shine in the new era. There shall be political upheaval, for the people shall demand leaders that do what they say they will do, for the days of lying and cheating are coming to an end.

The guardians are in fear, for their reign is coming to an end. They, too, are of the Creator, and so they shall return to where they originated. Know that the journey back to your Creator shall be eased by redemption. Ask for forgiveness and to especially forgive thyself. This shall make the journey easier. Know that the ego is dying. Ego is separation, and if the body "dies," then the human expressing through ego may say, "Oh no, if I die I shall no longer exist". Well indeed, that is a truth and an untruth. The ego-based human is indeed without insight of its heritage, its source. The human avatar expression is only an aspect of the soul, for the soul is too grand to appear fully in human form.

Now you may ask, "How do I navigate this time whilst incarnated in an avatar?". Well indeed, this is the key to lifting your vibration whilst remaining in a body. We say, clear your mind. This may be hard for some, but know that all shall be well. Breathe deeply. Know that you came to the Earth with a soul essence, and that essence is love. That is your core. Anything else is a corruption. We say limit your time on the devices. Know that you may be listening to or viewing messages that are limiting your expression. You can do many things that shall open your heart. Forgive others and yourself. Know that you are of the Creator.

Remember that the world you witness is indeed the world within you. If you witness angry humans, then look within and heal your own anger. Perhaps there are humans that trigger hatred within you. Perhaps you blame those humans. Well indeed, we say to you, look in the mirror and know that what you witness in another with strong emotion is indeed an aspect of you that you have not forgiven and accepted within yourself. It is easy to blame others, for indeed, you are not taking responsibility for your own healing.

What is healing? We say to you, healing is to find completeness. It is the ultimate expression of completeness in a physical avatar. That is your aim.

Know that your world is healing. Do not live in despair when you witness pain and suffering. Go within and heal it. See how the world changes. Some shall say, "This is passive". Indeed, we shall say that you do not understand the nature of the Earth plane and the matrix. The more you project, the further you and your world retreat from joy and love.

Now we ask you to say this three times each day for as long as you desire and if you so shall choose. "I am what I am. I am filled with joy. There is peace and love and happiness in my experience. I release all the pain of the past, for indeed there is no past and there is only this moment. I am love. I am joy. I am the I am".

There, sweet souls. We have offered you insights. We are here if you need connection with us, if you wish to have further insights. There is much more to unfold. Hold the love within, let the pain of separation dissolve. Do not compare yourself to others, for you are a unique expression of the oneness. Some may have "more" materially, well, indeed, that may be their path. Some may have "more" enlightenment. We say one more thing to you – you are already enlightened, you just forgot.

We leave you now. We are most gracious for the connection with you. Know that all shall be well on your Earth plane, for the poultice of truth is pulling out the poison of corruption, and humans shall once again stand tall in the oneness of the Creator. We are grateful that you have undertaken this journey.

We are indeed the Council of Nine. We are the I am.

# About the Author
# Philip Kinsella...

Philip Kinsella is a UFO and paranormal researcher, having authored numerous books and many articles on the subject. He is also interested in the theoretical aspects, which may answer some truly extraordinary questions when addressing UFOs, creation, and areas of high strangeness. He was also credited with a revolutionary speculation surrounding the famous 'Grey' aliens in an article entitled 'Spirits in a Material World,' which had been published in 'Alien Encounters' magazine in 1996.

Philip has had varied encounters with the psychic realm, as well as UFOs, the last of which occurred on the 9th April 2016, an event which had been witnessed by many others, where the UFOs had been tracked right across England. He has been featured on national TV, appeared on many documentaries, and hosted radio, most notably Coast to Coast, numerous times.

In the mid-1990s, Philip also researched the famous Rendlesham UFO event, which occurred in 1980, with various members of the American military. He teamed up with the original investigator, Brenda Butler, and spent over ten years researching what is referred to as the famous 'England's Roswell,' having experimented with a CE-5 Initiative on the 8th June 1998 and successfully summoning a UFO at close range. This led him to formulate ideas that, perhaps, our interaction with so-called aliens is achieved through conscious integration, and our understanding of time and dimensions of space begs further study. Philip, along with Brenda, co-authored a book together, 'Sky Crash Throughout Time', which re-examined case files and determined that Rendlesham Forest is an area of high strangeness, much like the American National Parks, and most notably 'Skinwalker Ranch.' The geographical areas within remote regions appear to stimulate the appearance of UFOs, cryptids, and other monstrosities which defy our human understanding. This is an area which Philip is most interested in.

Philip also won the 'British Mediumship Award' in Portsmouth, England, in 2008, and then received the 'Outer Limits Magazine Award' in 2022 for dedication to the truth surrounding his UFO research.

He says, "Life puzzled me! I mean, we're told we live and die – the end! Having had many close encounters with not only what we refer to as the dead, but also UFOs, informed me that either I was delusional, or that the system we serve was hiding something. I feel it's important that we strip aside the lies, deception and propaganda and see what's behind that mask. Rather like the film 'The Wizard of Oz,' we need to pull the curtain aside and see who's running the show here on Earth."

'The Eternal Avatar,' co-authored with Chris John Mayes, promises to let others consider the bigger questions of life, death, and consciousness, along with those mysteries which elude our sense of reality.

"Teaming up with Chris to write this book was an absolute joy. By sharing our thoughts with others, to truly allow people to shine and know there is so much more beyond the material, which gives us all hope, is something close to both our hearts. And, by God, we need that hope more than ever today! Chris's amazing gifts and talents certainly gave me that hope I was looking for. His clairvoyance, channelling, and healing, among his many other gifts, are truly incredible. I am blessed to have him walk this journey of life by my side. He is an incredible spiritual being."

Philip is currently working on other articles and books, and is determined to join those dots together to give us all a clearer perspective of what it means to be human, along with our journey here.

"You are the greatest force in the universe. You are part of the God consciousness. Never forget that."

Philip can be reached through his website: www.thekinsellatwins.com

# About the Author
# Chris John Mayes...

After leaving his Art and Design studies in Hertfordshire, England, Chris Mayes continues to embark upon a very creative career. Currently, as a freelance artist, designer, and illustrator using a wide range of mediums, his work expanded into the world of photography while pursuing a day-to-day job within bespoke manufacturing. When moving to London permanently, he worked as a Simulation Technician for Health, Sport and Bioscience within a London-based University.

From developing his creative talents at a very early age, Chris discovered that another world beyond this one was also revealing itself to him, which was to impact his life in greater ways than he ever imagined.

"It is very exciting and clear to me that we are all eternal beings of conscious energy experiencing a physical world that often mirrors our inner world and the internal work we need to do. From personal and shared experiences that demonstrate the reality of healing, passing messages from the other side, psychic phenomena, readings, clairvoyance, and out-of-body, the spiritual world is the true nature and the greatest part of ourselves, which is just waiting for you to acknowledge and receive.

My artwork is as diverse as the mediums I like to work with. My commissioned work has ranged from stage backdrops, logos, landscapes, signwriting, to wedding photography, portraits, and my favourite subject – pets. I find that the subject quite often dictates what medium I use and therefore the style it takes. I am always keen to consider new and challenging projects, and I continue to develop interesting ways to explore my style."

'The Eternal Avatar' is his first publication that delves into some of his own experiences and insights of a greater world beyond this one. Alongside Philip Kinsella, sharing those perceptions is ultimately about laying the foundation for understanding more about who and what we really are beyond the material realm.

To find out more about Chris and his work, visit him online at
Website: www.chrismayes.uk
Instagram: christopherjmayes

Done in acrylic on canvas board. "I love sea life and the magical world they inhabit. I hope it touches on how precious our seas are and the fragile beauty our world holds."

'The greatest moment in your journey doesn't start with a footstep – but with the first thought, that connects you to something beyond yourself'

# About the Illustrator
# Kurtis E Sopel...

Kurtis E Sopel, as a designer, has a keen eye for precision and detail. Equipped with a BFA in Visual Arts, his mediums include: Graphic Design, Gemstone Sculpting, Acrylic Paint & Photography.

His work reflects his propensity towards seeing the lighter, yet edgier, side of things.

With a life long commitment to design and fine art, he also enjoys outdoor activities like mountain biking and snowboarding, creating and listening to music with his wife, and engaging with metaphysical-themed podcasts.

Connect with Kurtis. . . www.ksopel.com

Kurtis also designed the striking cover for "The Girls and the Demon's Deal" by Eric Hollerbach, another title published by Ridiginal Publishing.

# About the Foreword
# Joshua Cutchin…

Joshua Cutchin has appeared on hundreds of paranormal programs, including *Coast to Coast AM*, and is regularly invited to speak at paranormal conferences about his work. He is the author of nine books, including 2022's critically-acclaimed two-part series *Ecology of Souls: A New Mythology of Death & the Paranormal*. His latest book, *Fourth Wall Phantoms: Reflections on the Paranormal, Narrative, and Fictions Becoming Fact*, was released in April 2025.

In addition to his own books, Joshua also regularly contributes to essay collections, most recently Dr. Jack Hunter's *Deep Weird* (2023) and Dr. Simon Young's *The Cottingley Fairies* (2024). He has appeared on the hit History Channel television series *Ancient Aliens* and was featured in 2024's breakout UFO documentary, *Cosmosis*. He is a regular guest on *Where Did the Road Go?*, and maintains an online presence at JoshuaCutchin.com.

When he isn't writing or being a father—which is most of the time now, it seems—you'll likely find Josh playing tuba in Atlanta, Georgia, where he maintains an active performing and recording schedule.

Find Joshua Cutchin on his website at joshuacutchin.com

Check out his latest work, Fourth Wall Phantoms: Reflections on the Paranormal, Narrative, and Fictions Becoming Fact

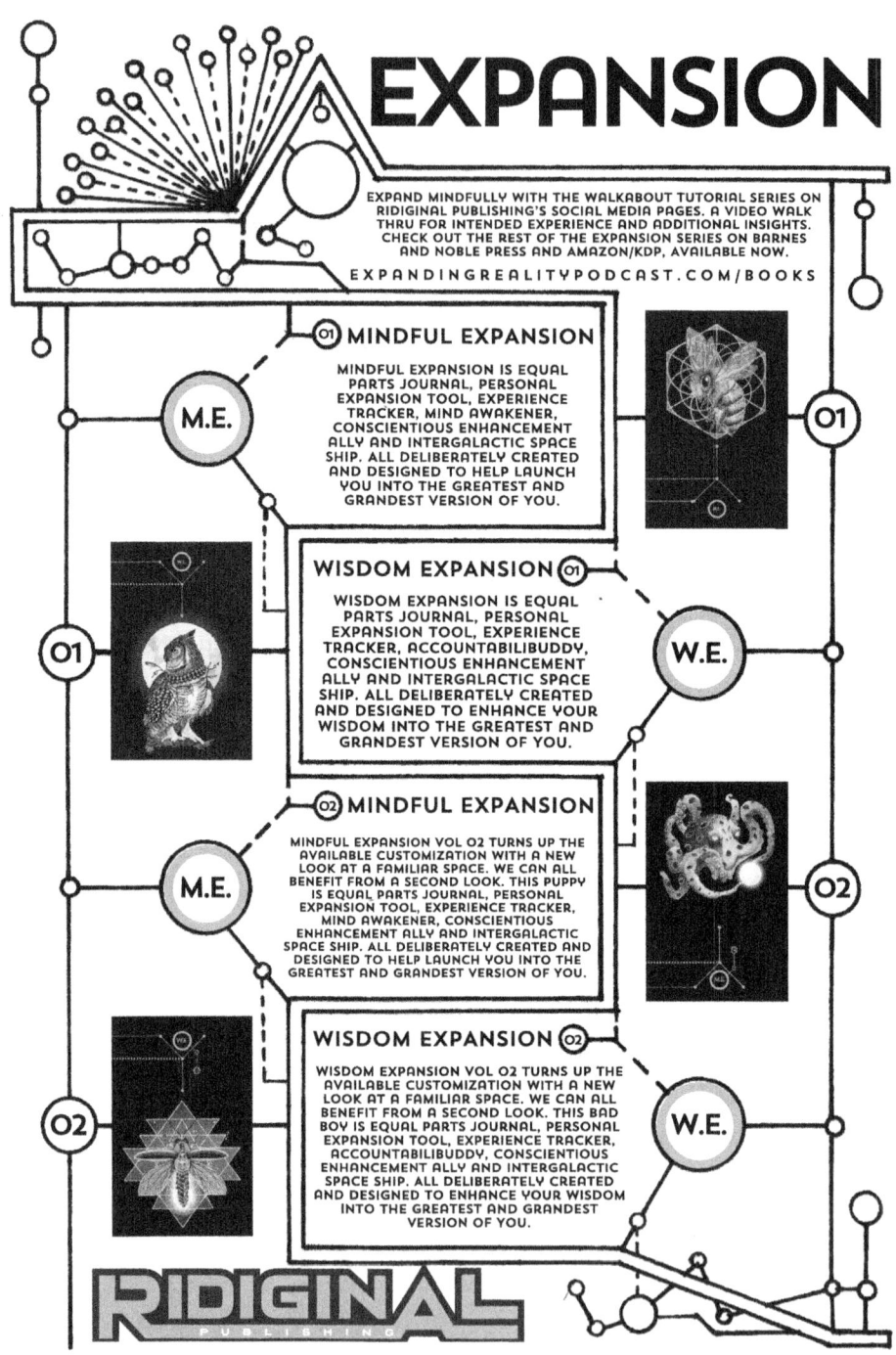

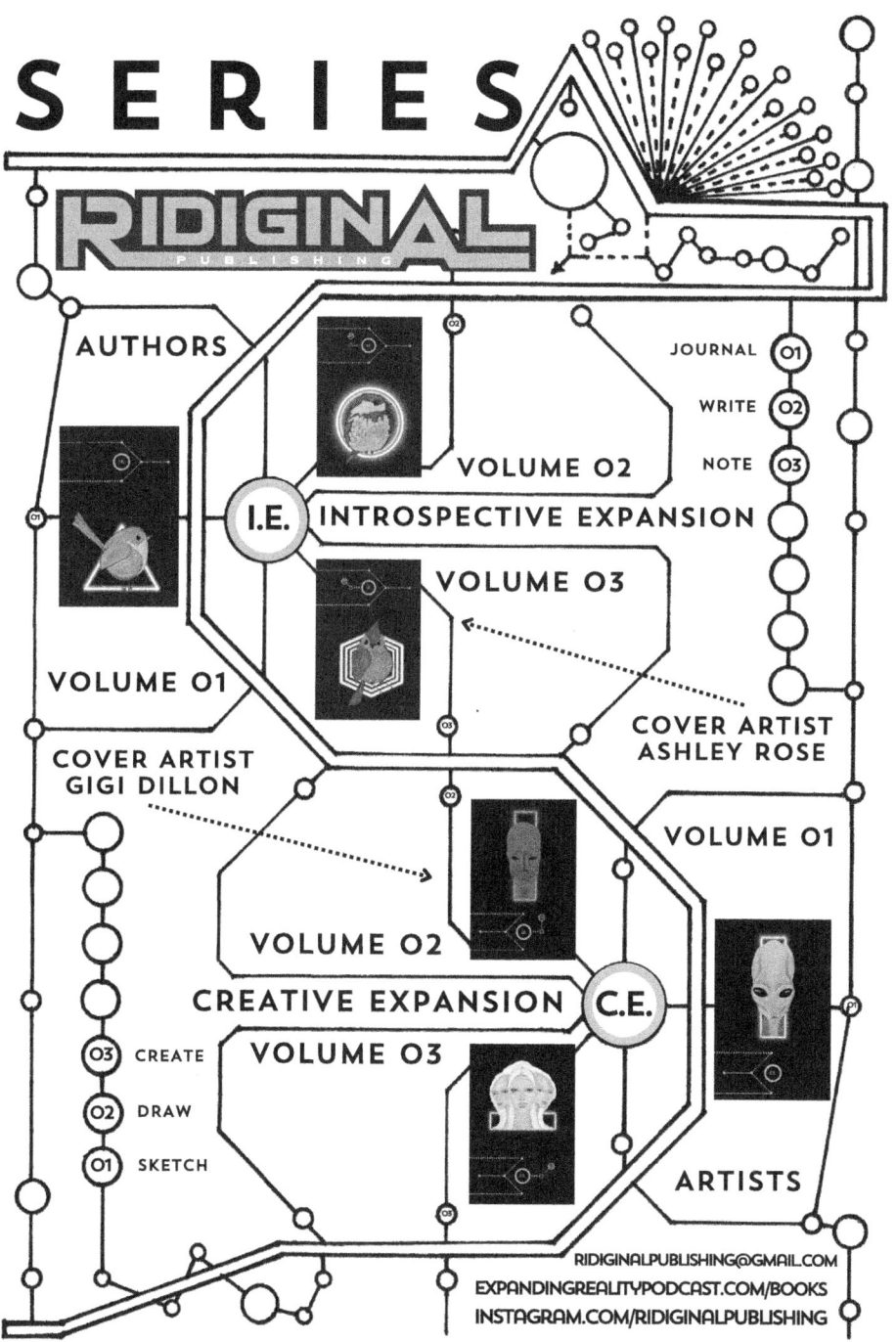

Printed in Dunstable, United Kingdom